DAILY COMPASS for *Living*

DAILY COMPASS for Living

DAILY READINGS AND REFLECTIONS FOR A YEAR

DR. SETH ASARE

PARTRIDGE

Copyright © 2016 by Seth Asare.

ISBN: Softcover 978-1-4828-6313-0
       eBook   978-1-4828-6312-3

All rights reserved. No part of this book may be used or reproduced by any means, graphic, electronic, or mechanical, including photocopying, recording, taping or by any information storage retrieval system without the written permission of the author except in the case of brief quotations embodied in critical articles and reviews.

Scripture quotations marked NIV are taken from the *Holy Bible, New International Version*®. *NIV*®. Copyright © 1973, 1978, 1984 by International Bible Society. Used by permission of Zondervan. All rights reserved. [Biblica]

Because of the dynamic nature of the Internet, any web addresses or links contained in this book may have changed since publication and may no longer be valid. The views expressed in this work are solely those of the author and do not necessarily reflect the views of the publisher, and the publisher hereby disclaims any responsibility for them.

Toll Free 0800 990 914 (South Africa)
+44 20 3014 3997 (outside South Africa)

www.partridgepublishing.com/africa

Introduction

Some of my friends, students and parishioners have asked me why I stopped sending out "the word for the day" in 2011. That was the year I retired from active service. Upon popular request, I have decided to compile some of my daily blogs into a devotional that could be used alongside other resources. They are now called the "Daily Compass".

These are reflections and thoughts on Bible verses for each day. There is no attempt to do an exegesis of passages or provide information for a Bible study. So feel free to disagree with me, but I pray that a sentence or two may challenge and uplift your spirit during the day.

The goals of these reflections are to inspire, challenge, encourage and help individuals find a bearing as they navigate their way through each day. The ways in which God has used people in the Bible are lifted up as our guide and compass for living.

My prayer is that the Holy Spirit will breathe life into these words for someone who is struggling with the challenge of being a Christian in our modern society. Be blessed as you read along.

Acknowledgements

I wish to thank my dear wife Rev. Dorothy Asare for her support and encouragement in getting this project completed.

Preface to Daily Compass for Living

The Compass has been used in different ways by explorers and navigators to find their way around. Sometimes when there is nothing left to guide people the proper use of a compass will be the difference between life and death.

A Spiritual compass can serve the same purpose except that the terms of usage might not be the same. More so when the destinations are not so defined as geographical north and south. Sometimes people have to step out in faith based on a very limited amount of knowledge. I define faith as knowing enough to act upon.

A suggestion on how to use the daily compass for living would be setting a few minutes aside each day for meditation on the word. You may bring along your Bible or just use the scriptures provided in the book. Begin with as short prayer or a time of silence for centering. Then read the scripture provided a couple of times. Pause before reading the reflection. Then you may make a note or two on what the compass is saying to you. Close with a prayer or a brief moment of silence.

In the Bible, we encounter people who have acted on the limited knowledge of Yahweh or God and have not been disappointed. In this preface, I encourage you to go through sample readings of people using this daily compass and then decide if this book will be of help to you.

Sample Day 1

³¹ Terah took his son Abram, his grandson Lot son of Haran, and his daughter-in-law Sarai, the wife of his son Abram, and together they set out from Ur of the Chaldeans to go to Canaan. But when they came to Harran, they settled there. Genesis 11:31

Abraham is a name that rings a bell for many people. But few people have heard of Terah, who was the father of Abraham. I like this character called Terah because he was one of the people who can see what no one else has a clue about. He made a decision to go to Canaan at a time when this location was not attractive and was not in the news. This was not only a bold decision, but it anticipated all that was to be known as a land flowing with milk and honey.

Terah took his son Abram, his grandson Lot (who had lost his father), and the wife of Abram and set off for Canaan. We are not told much about this bold move and what prompted it, except that we know of the death of his son Haran. Did that death precipitate a crisis for Terah? The question is: why did he leave his other son Nahor and his family behind? Is it at all possible that God had something to do with the decision? There is however no suggestion that the latter was the case.

It seems Nahor and his family did not buy into this huge move from the land of the Chaldeans to Canaan. But Abram and Sarai were ready to go along with the plan or were conscripted. There are decisions that we all make that have life changing consequences. The person we hitch ourselves to can make all the difference in the plan that God has for our future. Terah and Abram felt responsible for Lot and decided to take him along with them.

The vision to go to Canaan was cut short by the attractiveness of Harran. The original plan was not to settle in Harran but there was something about that place that caused Terah, Abram, Lot and Sarai to settle there. Have you felt like settling in a place or with a decision because that is the comfortable thing to do? It seems that at least some of the reasons for going to Canaan were fulfilled at Harran. So humanly speaking, there was no reason to push forward with the original plan.

Is there a 'Harran' that is distracting the original vision that the Lord has given you? Settling for anything less than God's vision should not be an option. It is true that the decision to go to Canaan was not presented as a vision from God to Terah. If it is not of God, then we will labor in vain.

Let us stick to God's original plan for us.

Sample Day 2

¹ The LORD had said to Abram, "Go from your country, your people and your father's household to the land I will show you. ² "I will make you into a great nation, and I will bless you; I will make your name great, and you will be a blessing." Genesis 12: 1-2

Haran was a good place for Terah and his family to settle. There was no necessity to move and so the vision of reaching Canaan was aborted. We do not know how many years the family spent in Haran but it must have been a considerable amount of time. Now, the Lord intervenes and speaks to Abram: "Go from your country your people, and your father's household to the land I will show you." The Lord called Abram to abandon the comfortable conditions that he had known since he and his family came to Haran.

Abram was invited to take a step of faith. He was invited to move from the known to the unknown. There comes a time when all of us will have to hear God and do the unthinkable. We will have to move away from the comfort of Haran not necessarily to a more comfortable place, but to a place of God's choosing. What made this leap of faith from Haran so interesting were the invitation to the unknown and the invitation to a life of trusting God.

Have you ever been invited by God to move beyond your comfort zone? It is never easy to abandon the familiarity of home cooking and the comfort of family and friends. But we may have to do what we believe God is calling us to.

All that Abram had was the word of the Lord. There was no way for Abram to double-check what he was hearing. All he knew was that God had appeared to him. He had no doubts about that. He also did not question the clarity of the words he was hearing. God promised to bless Abram and to bless all those who bless Abram. The options that Abram had were either to obey or to refuse to obey. Sometimes the problem people have is not that they have not heard about the promises of God. Rather, the problem is to believe that God will take care of them no matter what happens.

Trust and obey where the compass is pointing.

SAMPLE DAY 3

⁴ So Abram went, as the LORD had told him; and Lot went with him. Abram was seventy-five years old when he set out from Harran. ⁵ He took his wife Sarai, his nephew Lot, all the possessions they had accumulated and the people they had acquired in Harran, and they set out for the land of Canaan, and they arrived there. Genesis 12:4-5

"So Abram went as the Lord had told him". That is really a good definition of faith: "Going because the Lord has told you". There was no argument, and there was no need to clarify the summons. Why would Abram do such a thing? It was because of what he saw and heard when the Lord appeared to him. What he saw and heard were enough to convince Abram to take the step of faith. That is a definition of faith: "knowing enough about God to act upon God's words." The truth is that we will not know all that we need to know about God to be convinced about what God is saying to us. The real issue is whether we know enough to take God at his word

Abram did know enough about God and decided at the age of seventy-five years to set out from Harran. He was going to a land that God had promised him. He took his wife and his nephew and stepped out in faith. It seemed that Abram and Sarai had accumulated quite a bit of material possession in Harran. They took everything they could on this journey of faith. Can you imagine the discussion on the road as Lot asks: "Where are we going? Are we there yet? Steadily, they walked along and arrived in Canaan.

One of the things that stand out for me is that Abram and his company arrived in Canaan. When God is leading us, we can be sure that we can leave Harran behind and arrive at Canaan. That does not mean that there were no distractions and temptations on the journey. But we are sure to arrive at the destination when God is leading the way.

Where He leads me I will follow! Follow the leading of the Lord to the destination.

Thanks for taking the time to sample the daily compass for living.

January Day 1

Peter remembered and said to Jesus, "Rabbi, look! The fig tree you cursed has withered!" [22] "Have faith in God," Jesus answered. [23] "Truly I tell you, if anyone says to this mountain, 'Go, throw yourself into the sea,' and does not doubt in their heart but believes that what they say will happen, it will be done for them. [24] Therefore I tell you, whatever you ask for in prayer, believe that you have received it, and it will be yours. Mark 11:21 -24

What does it mean to have faith in God today? What is happening in your world today that makes you hear this verse differently? What situation calls for a walk of faith today?

In the context of this passage, something happened which surprised the disciples. What was unexpected became reality in front of their very eyes. A tree responded to the command of Jesus. The withering of the fig tree was 'a first' for the disciples.

Jesus spoke to a tree in a casual conversation without any fanfare; the fact that the tree responded to the words of Jesus was beyond human comprehension. Now, the disciples were confronted with a new reality, and that is the words from the mouth of Jesus had power over all living things including trees. Have you come to that realization?

Have faith in God! There is no situation in our world that is beyond the reach of this savior of the world. He is still speaking and making a difference in the lives of people. How do you know that it might not be your turn today to receive the word of faith spoken in your situation? Receive the word of faith today!

Dr. Seth Asare

JANUARY DAY 2 HEBREWS 1

God has always been speaking to people. That is what the book of Hebrews tells us. We are told that God spoke to people of old in different ways. Some people heard God speak through the Prophets, but others heard God in visions and dreams. But in these last days God has spoken to us through Jesus Christ.

Why is it so important that we should hear God speak? Part of the nature of God is to reveal or disclose things to the created order. We serve the God who is more eager to make things known to us. That is because one cannot have a meaningful relation with another if they do not know each other very well. So God has been making every effort since the beginning of time to reveal what we need to know as humans.

In Jesus Christ we encounter the supreme revelation of God. This a revelation rooted in God's love for humanity. This type of love speaks louder to all of us because it is sacrificial even unto death. We cannot run away from someone who loves us with an everlasting love. Indeed, God so loved that He gave us His Son that whoever believes in Him should not perish but have everlasting life.

That is how God speaks to us in these last days. But it seems many people are still oblivious to the voice of God. There are many who still say: "if I really heard the voice of God then I will believe" I wish I could shout from the mountain top and say God has spoken and God is still speaking in the Bible if we will care to listen. The words are simple: "I Love You"

January Day 3

Someone has prayed for you and is praying for you.

No one can be called a solitary Christian, because Christianity involves a whole community. From creation, God affirmed that it was not good for the man to be alone. God makes sure that we all have prayer partners to share fellowship with. Jesus had disciples to walk with him and he prayed for them. Paul did the same as he traveled on his missionary journeys.

In Ephesians 3, Paul indicates his prayer for the church in Ephesus and probably for all the churches. Carefully pay attention to what he prays for. First, he prays for inner strength for the believers. He knew that there were going to be times when they would have to dig deep for the strength which only Christ can give. We all need that inner strength and I pray that God will give you that Holy Spirit strength today.

Then he prays that they may comprehend God's love. He knew that there will be times when people will feel unloved or think that God has forgotten them. But remember this love is so wide and high and deep. It is the love that will not permit us to go our own way because we have entered into a relationship with Jesus. God is saying to you today: "I love you"

Thirdly, Paul prays that we may all be filled with the fullness of God. All that God has promised to be yours should be given to you today. Sometimes we are not ready to be filled with all that God has for us. My prayer is that you will be filled with enough manna to carry you through today. That is all that you can gather from God today!

I am praying for you today and I trust you are doing the same for me.

JANUARY DAY 4

What does it mean to be more than a conqueror in Christ Jesus? This does not make us super human beings; neither does it make us better than other people. What our position in Christ does is to make us aware that we have the presence of Christ with us daily. Paul, in this passage is dealing with the reality that faces Christians each day. He is concerned with the forces within and without that are seeking to tear Christians apart from their relationship with Jesus Christ.

These forces may be overt and sometimes subtle but they are real. They may hit us in the form of trials, illness, financial problems, work problems and conflicts. Whatever these forces may be, their goal is to make us shift our relationship with God. Being a conqueror under these circumstances will mean knowing the faithfulness of God. And therefore trusting God no matter what happens.

There is something about this God that we will not fully understand, but there are many things that we can be certain of. I am talking about God's love for us and God's presence with us. That is what makes us conquerors. We know that this God who will not spare the sacrifice of his own Son for us, will carry us through any struggle we may have today.

God desires that we be more than conquerors. Thank you Lord for giving us what it takes to be overcomers!

January Day 5

"We believe and know that you are the Christ"

These are the words of one who has abandoned himself on the Lord Jesus. Peter and the other disciples were confronted with a question from Jesus. This question is a soul searching one. "Will you also go away?" What is it that made Jesus put this question to his disciples?

Jesus was observing some of his disciples abandon him because of the words he was saying and his teaching. I cannot imagine what it will feel like when close friends of Jesus become deserters. Jesus was talking about eating his flesh and drinking his blood. He was claiming to be the bread of life.

People left Jesus because their expectations were not met in the words he was saying. At this point, Jesus was willing to allow the twelve disciples to join those who were leaving. Why was Jesus so confident to the point of risking the departure of the twelve disciples also? Probably Jesus knew something that we all have to learn. The work of the kingdom does not depend on any particular group of people. God will do God's work even if the twelve disciples decide to leave.

Peter's answer is one that we can all learn from. "Lord to whom shall we go?" What Peter is saying here is that he has weighed the alternatives and he cannot find anything comparable to the teaching of Jesus. But more importantly is the next statement that Peter makes. "You have the words of eternal life, and we believe and know that you are the Holy one from God." That is a bold and insightful statement.

God's desire is that we will all come to the point where we can boldly say: "We believe and know that you are the Christ" That is the place to be and when we are there, we can also ask: "Lord, to whom shall we go?"

JANUARY DAY 6

"I know the plans I have for you"

God promised that a time was coming, when God will make a New Covenant with God's people. God has a plan when it comes to making New Covenants. Jeremiah was well assured that the new covenant was far superior to anything that was known at that time. But how will the people of Jeremiah's day know and trust that there was something better in store for them?

The same question can be asked today. How can we know that God has better things prepared for us? The people had to place their trust in the word of God. The same thing is true for all of us. When the covenant making God speaks, we will do well to listen. What is God saying in God's word to us today?

We live in a time when it is easy to ignore the Word that is given to us. But the prophet sees a time when the word will be put in our minds and written on our hearts.

Oh, that the word of God may be put in the minds and hearts of all.

January Day 7

Pray, Pray, without ceasing! I have always wondered why Paul will give this admonition. I am sure Paul will concede some bathroom "time out" and some time for food and probably a lot of time to get some work in. This will of course will include sermon preparation and travel time to prayer meetings.

Yes, I am sure Paul will make allowances for all that, however the emphasis here is an attitude of prayer. We can never say we have prayed enough. There is always room to send some prayers "upstairs" on behalf of others and when you do not have anyone to pray for, please pray for me and for Christ's church. Remember, prayer is not just petition, give me! Give me! Praise, thanksgiving and meditation all qualify as prayer. So you see we can pray without ceasing.

Paul specifically says: "Give thanks in all circumstances; for this is the will of God in Christ Jesus for you." God wants us to learn to say "Thank you God" in all circumstances. Did he really mean ALL circumstances? I guess so. It means the circumstances that we find ourselves in today, tomorrow and every day. We may not want to say: "thank you God" but we are told that is the will of God for us in Christ Jesus.

Several people have indicated to me that if they truly knew the will of God for their lives they will do it. Well, I have news for you today! The will of God is that we give thanks in all circumstances. So let us begin with our circumstance today. We give thanks for everything that is happening. Even for the ones we do not fully understand.

Give thanks with a grateful heart for the gift of our savior Jesus Christ

Stay blessed.

Bro. Seth

January Day 8

Where do we fix our eyes? Where we fix our eyes is very important because it helps to determine our destiny. There are many temporary things and issues that are capturing the attention of many. Very often these issues seem to loom larger than life and we are made to believe that we cannot survive in this world without them. It is not surprising that the broad way has become attractive to those who live and walk by sight.

Paul is suggesting the road that is less traveled to Christians. It is a road on which we fix our eyes on eternal values rather that what is temporary. I know that we are people who believe that a bird in hand is better than a thousand in the bush. That certainly may be true for material things. But when it comes to things of the Spirit this type of logic does not hold. Why not?

It is because in the eternal scheme of things, one is not dealing with instant gratification. Simply put, there is more than meets the eye than what can be seen now. The final chapter of your life is not written yet!

We are not focusing on just flesh and blood. We focus on things that can make a difference by bringing about transformation. Yes, we are concerned with the welfare of generations to come as well as our own destiny. It is for that reason that Christ invites us to walk by faith and not by sight. This is an invitation to live a life that factors into it a relationship with God. Those who believe that the things we see now will soon be gone, make their aim to press towards eternal values.

Let us fix our eyes on our Lord Jesus Christ, the one who is, who was, and who will come again.

January Day 9

Today is a day to give thanks. Those who have jobs have to give thanks and those who are challenged in their jobs and in finding jobs should give thanks. Thanksgiving is an attitude. We can always find something to give thanks for. Just look around, see what could have been and what is now and say thank you Lord.

We give thanks to the Lord because we are convinced of the reality of God. Some of us can say "where will we be without the Lord?" We are aware that life has not been easy, marriage life has not been easy, raising a family has not been easy, and making a living has not been easy. But God has brought us this far by faith.

How have we experienced God's faithful love? Yes, we may not be at the place where we want to be in our spiritual walk. But one thing we can say is that God has been faithful every step of the way. I went with a group of 28 people to Africa on a mission trip. This was the first trip after our automobile accident in Africa. We were all grateful for the faithfulness of the Lord. All those who were injured in the accident in the previous year went back and carried out God's mission. Before we left for Africa, several people asked us: "why are you going back?"

The simple answer is: "God is good!" God has given us the strength and health to serve others. We can all count on the goodness of God all the time.

JANUARY DAY 10

What does it mean when one says God will deliver? What does it mean when one expects God to be exalted in their body? Most often we understand these to mean that things are going to turn out the way we anticipate. What happens when the cancer does not go away, what happens when the pain is still there, what happens when the prison chains are not removed and there is no miraculous intervention.

Paul turns things around and reminds us that there are many reasons to rejoice in the prayer of the saints and the presence of the Spirit of Jesus Christ. In verse 20 of Philippians 1, the author notes that Christ will be exalted in my body whether by life or by death.

In Hebrews 2:14 we are told that: "Since the children have flesh and blood, Jesus shared in their humanity so that by his death he might destroy him who holds the power of death. And free all those who all their lives were held in slavery by their fear of death" This is a pivotal scripture that should be lifted up more in our day. The fear of death seems to be crippling many a Christian. We have become tentative in all that we do because we want to live as long as possible. There is nothing wrong with that, but we should have the desire to be in the will of God.

That is what Paul lifts up when he says: "for me to live is Christ and to die is gain." Paul had the assurance that going to be with the Lord was far better. However, if there was an unfinished business, then he would rather hang around and accomplish that task.

We are invited to live with the assurance that God has broken the fear of death with the death and resurrection of Jesus. Real victory comes when we affirm that nothing can separate us from the love of God in Christ Jesus.

January Day 11

"For it has been granted to you on behalf of Christ not only to believe on him, but also to suffer for him." Philippians 1:29

In our youthful culture in which suffering and pain are supposed to be excluded from life, the Christian message is not a popular one. The Christian life is a "not only believing, but also suffering proposal". Most of the time what we hear emphasized is the blessings of walking by faith. The other aspect of the Christian life is reserved for the end of the passion week.

The church in Philippi was well aware of the imprisonment of Paul and Silas. They certainly could recall what happened when the apostle had his feet bound by chains. This church can well appreciate the emotions that Paul was going through as he writes to them from another prison cell. I will not be surprised if some were asking why this new faith in Jesus Christ attracts so much hostility?

This church was going through its own internal struggles and individuals were suffering for bearing the name of Christ. These Christians are being encouraged to receive faith and suffering, as gifts that are inevitable. To walk with Christ is to believe in Him and to suffer for Him. The call to Christian discipleship involves taking on the yoke of Christ and learning of Him.

The assurance is that the same presence of God that walks with us as we trust in the Lord Jesus will be with us in whatever struggle that we are going through. Lift up your head and behold the promise of the ages coming to you.

I pray that our hearts will be open to all that God has for us. Not our will but your will be done.

January Day 12

"If you have any encouragement from being united with Christ, if any comfort from his love, if any fellowship with the Spirit, if any tenderness and compassion, then make my joy complete." Philippians 2:1

Have you received anything from following Christ; if the love of Christ has made any difference in your life then the joy of Paul is complete. The author believed that "uniting with Christ" has some benefits. It is the basis of salvation. Without a union with Christ one cannot claim salvation as the Christian gospel teaches.

From this relationship with the savior one should expect the fruits of the Spirit. Jesus had reminded his disciples earlier of the mystical union that exits between him and those who come to him. Jesus said it plainly with these words: "apart from me you can do nothing". Abiding in Christ is another terminology Jesus used to describe the relationship the tree and the branches.

The choice of words by our Lord and by Paul is deliberate. They are meant to emphasize the permanency of the relationship. Being united with Christ does not give one the option to walk out of the relationship. It is a long-term relationship. To be precise, one can say the union is meant to be eternal. Yes, you and I have been united to Christ. I do not know about you but for me this alone is a reason to shout Hallelujah.

Out of this relationship should come some fruit of the Spirit. One of these fruits is encouragement. We should be encouraged by the fact that we are not alone in our joys and our struggles. God is in us and we are in Christ. Be encouraged today because the battle is the Lord's.

Also the love of God should comfort us every day. During the days when you are tempted to say "not again" Remember you are united with the fountain of love. I pray that the comforting Spirit of the Lord will flood your heart today.

May the tenderness and the compassion of the Lord be your portion today. You are a daughter of the King and you are a son of the Lord of Lords.

JANUARY DAY 13

"Make my joy complete by agreeing with each other, loving each other, being one in Spirit and purpose" Philippians 2:2

What will Christian unity look like? What will it look like if all the people in your church agreed with each other? Oh, let us say most of the people loved each other? That is the ideal that the apostle Paul was pushing the church in Philippi to consider. I like the tenderness in the tone of the request. He says: "Make my joy complete by doing these things".

For starters, how do we work on Christian unity? Probably we can start from the things that unite us instead of always emphasizing our differences. Christians have a lot of things in common. That is confirmed each time one travels to another culture and participates in their Christian worship. The centrality of the life, death, and resurrection of Jesus can be experienced in word, song, images, paintings, and the preaching of the gospel message. Yes, sometimes one may not fully understand what is being preached or said but we can still make connections that affirm our faith.

We can at least make an effort to love one another because Christ has first loved us. Love is a language all of us can understand and can respond to. It often requires someone to extend the loving hand. It takes the grace of God to extend that hand instead of dwelling on the past and what happened some time ago. It may be your turn today or my turn to break down the dividing wall because of Christ.

Just think about this! If the same Holy Spirit abides in all Christians, then how come we cannot be of one Spirit? It is partly because we have not yielded our human spirits to the full control of the Holy Spirit. God wants to have all of us. When that happens we will be asking ourselves all the time: What will the Spirit have me or us do? Those who are led by the Spirit, they are the children of God.

One Spirit and One purpose is our goal. Lord, do it in us!

January Day 14

"What do I get from this?" What is in it for me? Do we benefit from going to church? These are the questions that we are being conditioned to ask in our modern society. If there is no reward, then the answer is simple! "It is not worth it!" Selfishness is an enemy to the building of a Christian community everywhere in the world. Whenever the ego or the "I" takes a prominent place in whatever we do, then we have a problem. When selfish ambition takes over, it seems that people put on blinders and keep forging ahead thinking only about themselves. The attitude of getting to the top at every cost and by any means does not come from Christ.

Christian communities are built on the foundation of Christ. All others become living stones in the structure of the community according to Peter. The lesson we learn from Christ is to count others better than ourselves. In so doing we help to bring out the best in the other. We all need each other; our goal is to build a community of faith in which each person's gift is valued and appreciated. This attitude is possible when we truly believe that God is in control and God will provide everything that each member of the community needs.

The words of the apostle Paul challenge us to widen our circle of what we call Christian community. The Christian community extends beyond our shores to people in Sudan. So we have brothers and sisters all over the world who may be going through their own struggles. There are some in North Korea who are praying for the day when they can be united with their brothers in other parts of the world. When our world is limited to those around us and who look like us we are not heeding the call to put the self on the back bench and work for the unity of the family of God.

What does it mean to be conceited? This is the mind-set of the person who thinks the world revolves around them. They wish to be the center of everything. But we know that it is not about any of us. It is about Christ and what God is doing in the Christian community.

Let us pray that Christ will be exalted and all of us will decrease.

January Day 15

Someone told me the other day that God did not make us to be doormats. I did not fully grasp what this brother was saying. But that is not important because the challenge to me is how to consider others better than myself. That sentence is not in isolation. The full sentence should add the first half of verse 3. "Do nothing out of selfish ambition or vain conceit, but in humility consider others better than you." The context sheds light on what it means to count others better than self.

The author is not suggesting that Christians should have low self-esteem. The admonition is a remedy for selfish ambition and vain conceit. When people are full of themselves they fail to appreciate the value of the other person. We are all created in the image of God. And we know that whatever God created was good and God pronounced it so. This means that each time we consider another person to be better than ourselves we are affirming the goodness of God's creation. Hopefully, the other person can also affirm the image of God in us. This type of mutual benediction is what builds a strong Christian community.

When we have a right attitude towards ourselves we become liberated to see what the Lord is doing in another person. Moreover, Christ's love constrains us to serve one another. We are always free to insist on our rights but that will not be the example that was set for us by our Lord. In Romans 12:10 we are told: "Be devoted to one another in love, Honor one another above yourselves." There is no doubt that what is being asked of Christians in these passages is not the normal human love. It takes a mind renewed by the Holy Spirit to be able to love this way.

Thanks to God who is transforming each one of us into the image of Christ. Christ understood humility in a way that none of us will be experience. Just imagine the glory that was laid down by Christ so that he can be one of us, and by so doing save us from the power of death.

O Lord, grant us the mind of Christ!

January Day 16

"Who, being in very nature God, did not consider equality with God something to be grasped," Philippians 2:6

"You also have rights!" "You deserve better!" "Assert yourself and get what is rightfully yours!" Yes, yes, yes, but sometimes we may choose to walk on the road which is less traveled. We do that not because we do not have other options. We do what we do because we want to have the attitude of Christ. Christ cannot be described as a loser the way we are looked at by some people in the world. That was a question somebody posed to me one day. He asked me: "why do you hang around with these losers?" In this person's mind, I seemed like a good person and I could do better than hanging around these Christians.

Just think about this! Someone who was in the very nature God, decided to give up everything for my sake and the sake of all the sinners in the world. Jesus did not insist on his rights in heaven and he did not do that on earth either. He decided to go the way of the cross. That is what we call "the attitude of Christ". It is the attitude that is willing to do anything for the salvation of one sinner. This is the attitude that did not insist on his rights as God in the flesh.

It is the attitude of obedience, Obedience to the Father and to God's plan for the whole of humanity. The willingness to subject our own comfort for the greater good of others is a revolutionary message. Often people will say many people are doing it and even some Christians are walking the broad road. The attitude of Christ has never been a popular way to go and it will never be. The attitude of Christ delays instant gratification so that the will of God will be done.

"Each of you should look not only to your own interests, but also to the interests of others."

January Day 17

Each time one reads a scripture passage that begins with "therefore", it is important to stop and read what comes before the verse. In this particular case what we are paying attention to is "He humbled himself and became obedient to death" Humility and obedience are a powerful combination all the time. Christ set the example for all of us by living out that combination.

We are told that He humbled himself to death on the cross. Christ in his humility suffered the unthinkable. But thanks be to God that there is more to the story. I am grateful that the story did not end there. God begins when the human mind has come to its end. God's work starts when human possibilities are exhausted. "Therefore God exalted Jesus" and God will exalt all who follow the example of Jesus. Yes, the combination of humility and obedience to God works for all people in all places and all the time.

In the case of Jesus, He was exalted to the highest place. I often remind people the position of savior is already taken. Thanks to God! Jesus was lifted to place that was rightfully his in the first place. God will also exalt all who follow in the steps of Jesus to their rightful places.

Jesus was also given a name that is above every name. It is the only name that has been given to Christians as the way to salvation. There may be names that are revered in many cultures and societies. But the Bible does not make apologies when it talks about the name of Jesus as the name above all names. We are told that at the name of Jesus every knee should bow. That is an interesting statement because the Bible insists that we are to bow only to God. For Christians who accept the deity of Christ, the statement does not present any problems.

The one who humbled himself and became obedient is the one to whom we bow.

January Day 18

Peterson's translation of this passage Phil. 2 12 reads: "keep on doing what you have been doing from the beginning." It emphasizes the confidence the author has in the church at Philippi. There are many people I will shudder to encourage "to keep doing what they are doing now". I am aware that for many the charge will rather be "keep adjusting your bearings in Christ as you go along". Probably Paul is saying something similar based on his knowledge of the house church in this city.

Paul was with this Church right from the beginning. He was there at the conversion of Lydia and her household and also the conversion of the Philippian jailor and his household. Paul knew that these Christians have had a solid foundation. He remembers the solid instruction in the Christian faith that he provided at the inception of the Church. He wants them to continue doing what they did when they were initiated into the Christian faith. The foundation of Christ is the best that can be laid anywhere in the world any time. All other foundations are not able to stand the test of time.

To work out one's salvation begins with a foundation. How does one work out their salvation if salvation does not depend on works? What is implied in this passage is living out what God has started in each Christian. If anyone is in Christ they are a new creation, the old has passed away and the new has come. When the new comes, it has to be shown in our actions. We cannot claim to be in Christ and still live the old life.

Working out of our salvation is something that is done with the power of the Holy Spirit. We are not able to live out the Christian life without help from the Holy Spirit. All that is asked of us is to learn to co-operate with the power of the Spirit that is at work in us. Learning to recognize and respond to the promptings of the Holy Spirit is basic to working out our salvation. We do this with fear and trembling because we know that it does not depend on us.

May the Lord give us grace to live out our salvation to God's glory!

January Day 19

"Working out your salvation" is not something that humans do; neither does depend on human ability. God works in people and the end product is salvation. How often do we take credit for what God is doing in us? If we will be honest to ourselves, it is all a matter of God's grace. All the accomplishments, every victory should be truly credited to one who is at work in us.

God can work without us but the truth is that God chooses to work through clay vessels like us. That is the mystery of salvation. It pleases the infinite God to work with finite humans to achieve the purposes of God. Why did God set his love upon you and me? We cannot explain it. All we can say is that it is grace! Infinite grace!

The passage in Philippians 2:13 says: "For it is God who is at work in you both to will and to act according to God's good purpose". The reference here is to the intention which leads to faith and the obedience which is the result of faith are all attributed to God. The indwelling Holy Spirit is not only the prompter but aids the Christian in their actions. Paul says in Romans 8 that those who are led by the Holy Spirit are the children of God. God is ready and willing to lead us. The question is, are we ready and willing to follow the leading of the Holy Spirit?

God has a purpose for our lives and we may not know what God has in mind for us, but we can be sure that whatever God is doing is good. God is good all the time!

January Day 20

There is a member of my church who responds to my inquiries about her health with the words "no complains". She may once a while add to those words: "who will listen anyway if you complain". I gathered up courage to ask why she will not complain occasionally if she had to. Her response was that "people do not like to be around those who complain a lot" That was an interesting comment.

The context of Philippians 2:14 is slightly different. In this instance the call is to Christians working out their salvation with fear and trembling. Why would Christians live a life that is "complain free"? I will like to suggest that the first reason is that they are appreciative of the love that has been extended to them. To live out the Christian life is an honor for anyone who knows that they do not deserve such a gift.

Secondly, we complain when we believe that we have been unfairly treated or our rights have been infringed upon. But these scenarios do not apply when we are talking about serving the Lord who walks with us daily. Instead of complaining we just talk to the Lord. We have an avenue to let out our frustrations; and that is the prayer language. Indeed, what a friend we have in Jesus all our grief and sins to bear.

What is the point in arguing? When our arguments have not won a single person to the Lord Jesus. The challenge for Christians is to live out their faith in all circumstances of life. That is where the authenticity of the faith they profess becomes evident.

I need no other argument or plea, it is enough that Jesus died on the cross and that he died for me!

January Day 21

"Do everything without complaining or arguing so that you may become..."

There is a reason for living the way a Christian should. There is a goal to which Goal is calling all of us. The goal is to become what God has purposed for each one. Another way to put it is: "Obedience leads to transformation into the likeness of Christ". To become a child of God is not a static situation. Rather, it is a dynamic goal to which God is calling all those who are in relationship with Christ. The thought of being pure and blameless can be scary for a number of us. But we know that it is God who is at work in us to will and to act for God's purpose.

Paul indicates that Christians are surrounded by a society which is crooked and depraved. I do not think things have changed much from what persisted in the days of Paul. If anything things have gone worse. It is interesting that God chooses to work in such an environment. God does not put Christians in a glass bubble where they are shielded from all dangers. We are placed in a society with all the failings of humanity. But God is in this particular environment with Christians. He has said: "I will never leave you nor forsake you".

What God asks of Christians is a wholehearted devotion that seeks to do the will of Christ. Another way of saying that is a propensity to co-operate with the indwelling Holy Spirit. Yes, we cannot do it by ourselves but with God's help Christians are able to shine as stars. We are called to be the light of the world. So let us get out and let the light of Christ shine through us.

January Day 22

Christian joy is mutual. Our joy affects others and that is one more reason to rejoice in the Lord always. Just imagine what happens when we put a smile on the face of someone who has been looking for a reason to rejoice. Paul was inviting Christians in Philippi to share in his joy. He knew how some of these Christians were struggling hard to accept his imprisonment. Now as these brothers and sisters read about the joy expressed in this letter they are encouraged.

The joy being recommended here is not based on external circumstances. It is based on the fact that the Christians are holding out the word of life. The result is that the word of God is spreading to many more people. Just imagine what will happen if fifty percent of Christians were actively holding out the word of life to their communities and friends. I know that we will not have room for the influx of people. There are people who are waiting to see the joy of the Lord in us.

Paul mentions that it is possible that his life would be poured out like a drink offering. What is being referred to here is a possible martyrdom. But that does not seem to take away the joy of this servant of the Lord. Needless to say how that puts most of us to shame. We cringe and start to complain when things do not go the way we expect. But that cannot be compared to what Paul is talking about here.

You may say to me, "but I am not Paul" and my response is this "but you are a Christian". The same Christ who walked with Paul is walking with each one of us. We can do all things through Christ who gives us strength.

Rejoice in the Lord always.

JANUARY DAY 23 PHILIPPIANS 2:19

These words of testimony are given about Timothy who had gone to Rome to check on the welfare of Paul and also bring report to Paul of how the new churches were doing in the region of Macedonia. The words of Paul here reveal what he thought about his traveling companion.

There were others who were ministering alongside Paul. But Timothy stood out when it came to caring for the Church in Philippi. A distinction is made between having interest and having genuine interest. I want to believe that Paul was deliberate with the choice of words here. There are so many people who seem to show interest about the gospel or about the work of God. But those who show genuine interest go beyond the superficial or ordinary concern to the type of concern that Christ had for the Church,

The words of Paul in Philippians 2:4 reads: "Each of you should look not only to your own interests, but also to the interest of others". It seems that Timothy fits what is being talked about here. The challenge is that this should not be a description of just one individual, but a description of all those who have the attitude of Christ.

What does it mean to have genuine interest in the welfare of others? Seeking the well-being of another person begins with a solid relation with Christ Jesus. When that foundation has been established then all other aspects of physical, material, and social needs can be built on that foundation. Any interest in another that does not respond to the material needs is short sighted. We are called to be stewards of the whole person and the whole creation.

Genuine interest in the welfare of others is our goal.

Dr. Seth Asare

JANUARY DAY 24 PHILIPPIANS 2:16

Paul has his eyes fixed on the "prize". Not so much on the reward to be received or the crown to be worn, but the realization that his work is producing everlasting fruit. He calls the end "the day of Christ". He encourages his disciples to hold out the word of life with all earnestness.

The challenge in our day of short attention span and entertainment culture is how to hold out the word of life. There are many things being held out there. Some of these are religious and others are secular. How we package our product is essential but more importantly is how we allow the Holy Spirit to breathe through the word that is being held out to the thirsty and hungry.

Paul is expecting a response to the word of God that is being put out there. It has been said that: "aim at nothing and you will hit nothing" Those who "hold out the word of God" to our world should be confident in the Lord to bring about the desired results, because the whole power of heaven is standing behind the word that is being proclaimed. That is the basis for Christian confidence.

The message that we proclaim is sharper than a two edged sword. It has power to convict and reveal the intentions in people hearts to them. That is why the writer can boast in the finished work of Christ. The reason for boasting is what God has done through Paul. The same reason holds true for each one of us as we live out our faith and hold out the word of life.

My sister and brother, your labor is not in vain in all that you are trying to accomplish in the name of Christ. Hold out the word of life in your corner. I am doing the same and may all the glory be to God.

January Day 25

There is a difference between learning about Christ, and knowing Christ. The first case, accumulates facts that can become a teaching tool. In the other case one experiences the life changing power of the living Christ. There is more to knowing Christ because a change takes place that can be costly. One cannot know Christ and remain the same. A part of us dies and new life replaces the old nature. Most of the time the change is not overnight, because we grow in our knowledge of God.

Part of this spiritual growth is the thirst placed in our hearts for more of God. It seems we are always saying: "I want to know more of Christ". Because as we get to know Christ, we are also surprised by how little we know of his ways. There is always more to learn and to know of Christ. We never want to get to a place when we believe that we have known all that there is to know. The Holy Spirit is continually revealing new things about Christ.

Knowing the power of his resurrection is something that we cannot wrap our minds around. Just think about this. The same power that raised Jesus from the dead is available in Jesus Christ for those who wish to walk with the Lord. I am talking about the immeasurable greatness of his power in those of us who believe. I pray that I will come to appreciate in some measure that God has placed this power at my disposal.

This is not power over other people. On the other hand, it is power to be used to serve others and enhance the well-being of others for the sake of the kingdom. To keep us from dwelling only on the power that is available, we are reminded of the fellowship of sharing in the sufferings of Christ. The two seem inseparable. We cannot talk about power in Christ outside the suffering of Christ. The power is released in his suffering. Those who do not want to share in his suffering, know very little of the power in Christ.

I invite you to know all that is in Christ, his power and the fellowship of sharing in His sufferings.

January Day 26

We are all called into the service of the gospel. Sometimes it takes some people longer to discern that calling. You do not have to be a preacher to be in the service of the gospel. And we do not have to earn any title in the church or otherwise to be in the service of Christ.

Timothy served as a son to Paul in a number of his travels. The former was well aware that he was serving in the extension of the gospel long before he had the opportunity to oversee a church. In Acts, we read of the deacons who were full of the Holy Spirit and were called to serve tables. Each one of them including Stephen were convinced of their service in extending the good news before they got the opportunity to serve tables.

Where is God calling you to serve Christ? Is it in your home, your church, or your work place? Wherever the Lord has placed you, I believe that God is going to use you as you serve others. Timothy in this context was serving as a messenger between Paul who was in jail and the churches of Jesus Christ. The challenge is for me to prove myself as an ambassador for Jesus Christ to the people under my sphere of influence.

Remember the words of Jesus Christ "as you did it to one of the least of these you did it for me". Who are the forgotten and the least of these around us that God is calling us to bring the Love and the grace of Jesus Christ each day? That is how we are going serve Christ.

JANUARY DAY 27

Nothing can replace a trusted brother or sister in the Lord who is willing to serve the Lord in whatever capacity that they are needed. There are many who want to take the leading roles and there are few who are willing to lay themselves and their gifts at the feet of the Lord with an unusual tag that reads: "ready to be used as needed and when needed".

Epaphroditus was one of these individuals in the church at Philippi. He was sent to Rome with a gift for Paul and to take care of the needs of Paul. He was willing to put his own life and agenda on hold for this mission for God. Making such a long trip in those days were not as easy as we have it today when you can just get up and go. Epaphroditus was ready and willing to take on this mission on behalf of the church, Paul and Christ. Some of us would have had many reasons why someone should or should not go to Rome. But this fellow soldier for Christ saw an opportunity to serve Christ and he decided to do what Christ will do.

The missions of God sometimes have unexpected twists and turns. Epaphroditus became ill on the trip and almost died. Listen to way Paul puts what happened: "But God had mercy on him, but not on him only but also on me, to spare me sorrow upon sorrow". Someone will ask why should someone who has given up so much in the service of the Lord go through such a difficult time. All I can say is that, there are no easy answers especially when one considers that suffering is part and parcel of serving Christ.

Paul wanted this brother to be given a big welcome in the Lord. And he recommends: "Honor people like him". There are many brothers and sisters who are laying it all on the line in the service of Jesus Christ and I pray that we do not forget them.

January Day 28

It is a blessing to minister to the needs of the saints who are serving in the trenches of the faith. There are missionaries who have returned home and found that there is something missing in the fellowship of believers. Paul realized that this missionary who had been away for many months might find it difficult to readjust to a new situation in Philippi.

Epaphroditus was returning to a church that he had been away from for several months. What type of welcome awaits Epaphroditus when he returns? He may not have anticipated that but his father in the faith who was seeking the welfare of this ambassador was a step ahead. Paul calls on the church to welcome the young man in the Lord and with great joy. This is one of those occasions when it is appropriate to celebrate with a lot of fanfare. I can just imagine the tears welling down the cheeks of Epaphroditus as he senses the love of the brothers and sisters.

How do we welcome one another with great joy? Why should we be happy to see one another after some time of separation? We do that because we know that each day is a gift from the Lord. We also know that so many things could have happened in the time we were apart from each other. The time for taking things for granted is over. We are now grateful for the gift of brothers and sisters who help us to build the body of Christ.

I thank God for each of you and the many ways you have been used to enrich my life and the Lord's work. To God be the glory! No matter what happens, Jesus will be Lord in your situation and in mine.

January Day 29 Philippians 3:8

What is it that the author considered a loss? He included confidence in the flesh, and legalistic righteousness. He believed that he had the type of pedigree that will put him in the "in crowd". He also believed that he did what was expected in his day to make anyone righteous. Paul had come to a place in his relationship with God that enabled him to call all these human achievements a loss. He acknowledged that this was not always the case. In-fact some may even see these human achievements as profit. But now he could consider everything as loss.

There is a reason for coming to this conclusion. The reason was that a transformation had taken place and he was now in possession of something far greater. Paul was not just considering everything as loss. But everything compared to the surpassing worth of knowing Christ Jesus as Lord. Compared to Christ, our best trophies do not match up.

What I find interesting is that this statement cannot be taught. It also cannot be handed down from generation to generation. Rather the statement of Paul is an experience that people testify to. Yes, I mean people all over the world who have experienced the surpassing greatness of knowing Christ Jesus as their savior. They may not have the elaborate and flowery language of Paul to express what they feel but it nevertheless is as authentic as any other testimony.

This is not a borrowed faith neither is it grandma's. Each one of us should be able to talk about knowing Christ Jesus our Lord.

I thank God for those who came to Africa to share the good news of Jesus Christ so that I can also say my Lord and my God!

Lord give us grace to count everything as loss.

January Day 30

There is a reason for counting everything as loss. Some people ask why do you do what you do? Others say they will find it difficult to lay everything aside for the sake of Christ. Paul had a reason, what about you and I? Thank God that we can also say that it is worth counting everything as loss, not because somebody says so but we have also tasted and seen the goodness of the Lord.

To gain Christ, there are some things that have to fall by the way side. Many a Christian has tried to hold on to the old habits and the old ways of life. But ultimately they come to the conclusion that light and darkness cannot dwell together. One of them gets the upper hand. The question we all have to ask is "what are we going to count as loss in order to gain Christ?"

The other reason is that we want to be found in Christ, not having a righteousness of our own that comes from human achievement. We need that daily fellowship with Christ that springs from abiding in Christ. We are not talking about past experience or what happened sometime in the past. Rather, we are talking about the Christ who talks with us and walks with us today. Yes, it is possible by grace. The grace and power of God that make us count everything as loss.

This right relationship comes through faith in Jesus Christ. God may be speaking to you today to let something go. You have to count it as loss. Most of the things we are counting as loss are things that have been dear to us sometime in the past. We do not count anything as loss if it has no value to us. It takes sacrifice to say I count it as loss because of Christ.

January Day 31

All that one has to do is to take an honest and hard look at themselves and they will come to the conclusion that there is much more to be done to reach the goal to which God is leading Christians. God has not finished with us yet and we know that there is a long road ahead of us. At the same time, we are also confident of the fact that we are on the path to Christian perfection.

There shouldn't be any illusion that we have arrived because we have entered into a relation with Jesus Christ. We should not also use the gifts that God has given us as merit badges to signify to others that we have achieved the goal. There should always be the attitude that we have not reached perfection yet. It is an attitude that allows us to have a teachable spirit. There is more to learn from Christ and other Christian pilgrims along the road.

This is an ongoing process in which the more we know of Christ we rather come to the conclusion that there is so much more to be experienced. That is why our prayer should be "more and more of Christ and of his power". It also means attaining the resurrection of the dead. This is one of the aspects of our salvation that will continue to be in the future for all of us. We press forward to attain what is our inheritance in Christ.

"We press forward to take hold of that for which Christ Jesus took hold of us." There is something in store for each one of us. Christ had a reason for taking hold of us and he is not going to give up on us until he has accomplished that for which he called us. The road may be dreary, we may feel discouraged at times, but we know that God will finish the work in us as we press forward.

The situations around us may suggest that we have not made much progress but I encourage you to press forward in Christ Jesus. Press on! Press on!

February Day 1

James, a servant of God and of the Lord Jesus Christ, to the twelve tribes scattered among the nations: Greetings. Consider it pure joy, my brothers, whenever you face trials of many kinds, James 1:1-2

We will try in the next few weeks to walk through the book of James. It is generally accepted that the author of this book is probably James the brother of Jesus and the leader of the Jerusalem Council (Acts 15). He called himself a servant of God and of the Lord Jesus.

One does not often find Christians calling themselves servants of one another. The resurrection appearance of Jesus to James to James made a lasting impression on brother James (1 Corinthians 15:7). He became one of the pillars of the early Christian Church in Jerusalem.

He wrote to Jewish Christians who had scattered through the known world after the persecution that arose with the death of Stephen. These Christians who were mostly hiding from people like Saul of Tarsus, needed encouragement in their faith. These believers understood what it meant to be uprooted from their surroundings because of beliefs that they held dear.

James addresses the believers as brothers. Oh, that all believers would realize that we are brothers and sisters in the Lord. This realization should transform how we see each other and think about one another. The world is waiting to see the living out of Christ's love in truth. There should be more than talk in the Christian community. There are still far too many barriers between Christians.

"Consider it pure joy, when you face trials of many kinds." James is writing from personal experience as a leader of the church in Jerusalem. That is the only way we can talk about trials and temptations. Those who have not experienced difficulties can only lecture on the theory aspect. But it makes a difference when one can say: "I have been there!

FEBRUARY DAY 2

¹If any of you lacks wisdom, he should ask God, who gives generously to all without finding fault, and it will be given to him. James 1:5

How many of us will be honest enough to say that we lack wisdom? It is not normal to find people admitting to any kind of need that could be described as weakness. This is all because the society that we find ourselves in has conditioned us to appear tough. This should not be so among the children of God. We know that we owe everything that we have to God and that being the case there is no shame in admitting that we do not have it all together.

Those who admit to lacking wisdom are in good company. Solomon admitted to lacking wisdom and therefore went ahead to ask for wisdom to be able to discern and to lead the people of God. He had the opportunity to ask for riches and many other things but Solomon decided to ask for wisdom. He was however surprised by what happened to this humble request.

Admitting that we lack wisdom is another way of saying that we humble ourselves before the Lord. By saying that we do not know it all and we do not have it all together we make ourselves vulnerable to God and to other people. God has a habit of exulting all those who dare to humble themselves to a point of total dependency. That is the challenge for all of us.

Let us go ahead and ask God who gives generously without finding fault. Yes, we do not deserve what we are asking and God is not going to tell us about our faults, rather God will look at our hearts and our desire to seek his guidance. Let us go head and ask God today for wisdom to handle the situation that looks like a mountain in front of us.

I assure you that God will give the wisdom needed to stand still and behold the salvation of God.

FEBRUARY DAY 3

But when he asks, he must believe and not doubt, because he who doubts is like a wave of the sea, blown and tossed by the wind. James 1:6

Folks, it is not enough to say I need wisdom. There is more to this prayer of faith. What we are saying is that we acknowledge God to be the source of wisdom. This not a haphazard hit and miss approach to asking. It is asking that is based on a relationship that has been tried and proven. Those who know this God to be one who gives freely without finding fault are encouraged to boldly bring their request.

The person asking must believe and not doubt. This is another way of saying that the petitioner must have faith. This is the ability to open oneself to the mighty power of God. It is not how much faith the person has but placing our faith in a big God who can do more than we are able to ask or think. Yes, this is the faith that is able to act on the little that they know about God.

The one who promised has been faithful to people down the centuries and the one who did not spare his only son but gave him up for our salvation is able to handle your situation. There is no reason to doubt the ability of God to provide wisdom that is needed at this particular time.

Those who doubt are not able to receive from the Lord. This is because their lack of faith indicates that they do not have confidence in the ability of God to intervene in their particular situation. Those who act like waves tossed to and fro have not settled the question of God's abilities in their minds. On some days they are high on God and at other times they are not sure of all this God business.

We are invited to be people who are fully relying on God no matter what happens.

February Day 4

That man should not think he would receive anything from the Lord; [8] *he is a double-minded man, unstable in all he does. James 1:7-8*

We are talking about the type of doubt that prevents us from boldly approaching the mercy throne of God. It is a doubt that paralyzes people and prevents them from placing full confidence in God. How else can anyone seek to approach God when they are not even certain that God exists? Under those circumstances we are delving into the realm of chance.

James instructs us that those who approach God in that manner should not think that they would receive anything from God. This means that we are the ones who place limitations on God. When we are tossed to and fro like the waves, we are only affirming our inability to make up our minds concerning the possibilities of God.

James calls that state of affairs double mindedness. Some would describe that as taking an "insurance policy" just in case God does not come through or our own plans do not pan out. Unfortunately, all it does is to reveal our lack of trust and confidence in God. That type of instability is not able to receive anything from God.

Let us approach God with a single-minded devotion and ask for wisdom from above for today.

FEBRUARY DAY 5

The brother in humble circumstances ought to take pride in his high position. [10] But the one who is rich should take pride in his low position, because he will pass away like a wild flower. [11] For the sun rises with scorching heat and withers the plant; its blossom falls and its beauty is destroyed. In the same way, the rich man will fade away even while he goes about his business. James 1:9-11

These verses remind us to always put things in perspective. The conditions that we find ourselves in life presently should not be seen as permanent. Those who fail to understand the temporaries of life fail to appreciate the eternal values in life.

Those who find themselves in humble circumstances at present have to remember that this is not a permanent condition in life and that God will lift them up in due time. The suggestion is that those in humble circumstance should take pride in the high position that is reserved for them. That is a challenge to walk by faith and not by sight. The ability to greet things that are far off before they become reality is the true definition of walking by faith.

The encouragement is that we should go ahead and speak the word of faith so that things that appear to be impossibilities to the people of the world could be embraced even now. That is how those in lowly circumstances can take pride in their high positions.

Those who are rich on the other hand have to take pride in their low positions. They are challenged to look at their situations as something that will pass away like the grass that is here today and gone tomorrow. The rich person will fade away like everything else. The only enduring thing is the word of God.

February Day 6

[12] Blessed is the man who perseveres under trial, because when he has stood the test, he will receive the crown of life that God has promised to those who love him. James 1:12

Have you ever considered what it means to be called blessed by God? Those blessed by God have received a special favor from God. Some will say God has smiled on them and given them a special standing in God's reckoning.

If that is the case, then we should pay particular attention when James says that God blesses the person who perseveres under trial. Note that there is no promise that Christians will not go into trial. There is also no assurance that God is going to deliver so quickly that we might not experience the pain and the weight of the trial. On the other hand, Christians are admonished to persevere through their trials in order to receive the blessings that are promised.

The emphasis is placed on "standing the test". These are the very words we do not want to hear when we are praying for deliverance from what we are going through. I am talking about the days when we are tempted to say: "Why me?" and "how long O Lord?" Remember that the blessings come after when we have gone through the test.

But there is more! The faithful God promises to walk with us through every inch of the test that we are going through. Oh No! God has not forsaken you. He promised to be with you even when you are in the midst of the waters. In the midst of tears and questions. I pray that you can join me in saying that "My God reigns!"

There is a crown awaiting all those who have loved the Lord enough to go through their period of testing with faith.

February Day 7

^{13} When tempted, no one should say, "God is tempting me." For God cannot be tempted by evil, nor does he tempt anyone; but each one is tempted when, by his own evil desire, he is dragged away and enticed. ^{15} Then, after desire has conceived, it gives birth to sin; and sin, when it is full-grown, gives birth to death. James 1:13-15

We are advised not to blame God for the temptations that come our way. The reason is that God is good and it is against God's nature to be associated with evil. God cannot be tempted with evil and God does not tempt anyone. The author points out that temptation has to do evil and the end result of not overcoming temptation is sin.

Why would God who cannot entertain sin lead people into sin? That being the case we have to look for the root cause of temptation somewhere else other than our Holy God. James begins by causing us to look inward at the human heart for the source of temptation.

The suggestion is that there are human desires that are evil, that lurk within the human heart. Each person is tempted when his or her own evil desire gets the upper hand of the individual. The problem is not just desire because a distinction is made between good desires and evil desires. The latter has a way of dragging and enticing us to seek the very things that are not good for us and separate us from God.

"After desire has conceived it gives birth to sin". This is another way of saying the cumulating effect of desire results in something that was not planned initially but it is the logical consequence. Sin on the other hand leads to death ultimately. The reference here is to spiritual death. A desire that might look innocent is able to have eternal consequences. It is for that reason that temptations have to be taken seriously and dealt with before they destroy God's image in us.

February Day 8

^{16} Don't be deceived, my dear brothers. ^{17} Every good and perfect gift is from above, coming down from the Father of the heavenly lights, who does not change like shifting shadows. James 1:16- 17

God is good! All the time! That is what James is trying to communicate to us. We should not confuse the good God with all the evil that surrounds us. Every good and perfect gift is from above. This means that we have to lift up our eyes to the one who desires to give us what is for our good.

James has caused many of us to begin to search for the source of temptation. We know that Jesus was tempted by the devil or the evil one. We also pray that the Lord would not lead us into temptation. That means that there is another force at work in the human being besides our own desires. That force is not God the giver of every good and perfect gift.

Some people have the notion that God is a joy killer who takes away every form of happiness and joy from those who surrender to him. In an attempt to move away from what God offers, people have turned to self and listened to the devil who promises instant gratification. The result is that people are enticed and dragged into areas that are far away from the good that God has promised to all humanity.

Those who have settled on the source of all good and perfect gifts know that there is nothing in the world that can be exchanged with what God offers. James tells us that this God is unchangeable. Everything around us is shifting like sand. But we are offered something that is good and permanent.

FEBRUARY DAY 9

¹⁸ He chose to give us birth through the word of truth that we might be a kind of first fruits of all he created. James 1:18

"God chose to give us birth". What is this birth that the author is talking about? It definitely means more than the fact that God created us. The author is talking about new birth that God gives to those who put their trust in the Lord Jesus Christ as their Lord and savior. The reference here is being born of the Holy Spirit. This is something that only God can accomplish in the human heart. When Nicodemus wanted to know more about this new birth he was told that the Spirit blows where it wills and so is anyone who is born of the Spirit.

God is the initiator of this new birth. No one dares to question God about how this is done. But the results become evident in the human life. All that we know is that the word of truth has something to do with it. This word is both the spoken word and the incarnate word of truth. The spoken word has a way of convicting humans of sin and revealing the need for salvation. The incarnate Word takes residence in the human heart and transforms the individual to be alive to the truth of God revealed in scripture.

James states that those who experience this new birth become the first fruits of what God is seeking to do in the world. God is making all things new and it starts with created humanity. We become the first fruits of the purposes of God.

If anyone is in Christ she or he is a new creation. The old has passed away and the new has come 2 Corinthians 5:17. Thank God for choosing to make us new to his praise and glory.

FEBRUARY DAY 10

¹⁹ My dear brothers, take note of this: Everyone should be quick to listen, slow to speak and slow to become angry. James 1:19

If we are going to walk on this path laid down for us by Christ, then there are a few things we would have to take note of. James places an emphasis on what every Christian has to observe in an attempt to live out the new creation that God has so graciously purchased for us.

First, we ought to be quick to listen. The place to begin is listening to the word of God. This comes to us through the written word and the living word. The Bible is the daily companion of the Christian. Listening and meditating on the word daily are the disciplines that would help us discern the voice of God from the many voices that are clamoring for attention. The emphasis is on "quick" to listen. It does not help us when we are always playing "catch up". That is what happens when we are slow to listen to the word of God. The other word that we have to listen to is the indwelling Christ in the form of the Holy Spirit. The convicting and prompting work of the Spirit continues in the life of the Christian if they would listen.

The second thing for those who are new creation in Christ to pay attention to is: "slow to speak". Sometimes we are too eager to open our mouths and in so doing say many regrettable things. If we would pause and say a word of prayer first, we would find the wisdom that James is talking about. The temptation to respond would always be there. But remember to be slow to speak.

The third is to be slow to be angry. That is related to the second. The enemy of our faith is always seeking to put us off balance to get us to be angry. But the word is that we should exercise patience. Remember that the Lord is in control.

FEBRUARY DAY 11

Everyone should be quick to listen, slow to speak and slow to become anger, [20] *for man's anger does not bring about the righteous life that God desires. James 1:20*

"Everyone should be slow to become angry". Why do we allow anger to destroy so many things in our world? There have been world wars and ethnic wars because the anger of men and women. The inability of people to control their temper is the root cause of much destruction in our world. On the micro level, families are being torn apart because husbands and wives are not able to keep their anger under check. Individuals are suffering from heart diseases because they are angry most of the time.

When people are angry, they tend to think that the world revolves around them. They believe that they have been aggrieved to a degree that they are justified in their actions. Inappropriate responses to situations are the result of people having "knee jerk" reactions to stimuli.

The author of the Book of James directs our attention to things that lead to righteousness. There is a righteous life that God desires for all. We are all admonished to seek first the kingdom of God and its righteousness. Human anger has never been a candidate for those who a seeking God's righteousness. It is for that reason that all are being told to be slow in becoming angry.

What I find interesting is the emphasis on being "slow" to become angry. The fact that people are prone to anger is not disputed. We are told in scripture to be angry but not to allow the anger to lead to sin. That is in line with the admonishment to be slow to become angry. When people have had time to think through a particular situation, they tend to react appropriately instead of allowing their anger to have an upper hand.

Remember that the destination is the righteous life that God desires.

FEBRUARY DAY 12

²¹ Therefore, get rid of all moral filth and the evil that is so prevalent and humbly accept the word planted in you, which can save you. James 1:21

There is something that is prevalent in the world today. You see it everywhere you turn. It has become the best way to sell goods and it is also on the lips of our youth and adults. The only words that could be used to describe what I am talking about are moral filth. It is unfortunate that this filth has encroached into the church and the people of faith.

The advice of James is that we should get rid of all moral filth and evil that is so prevalent. If James calls the situation in his day prevalent then I do not know how we will describe the evil all around us. We might call it co-habitation with evil. We are supposed to get rid of all of it and not just some. A radical surgery of evil is the prescription. This surgery will require help from above.

James is pointing us to the word of God that is planted in the human heart as the starting point for this radical work. Christians have to accept the word that is within and allow it to bring about the desired change. The symbolism is allowing the Holy Spirit within to effect change. The convicting work of the Spirit is in progress. But we have to co-operate with what the Lord is seeking to do. That is the path of salvation. God has started something that has to continue until the victory is won.

FEBRUARY DAY 13

[22] Do not merely listen to the word, and so deceive yourselves. Do what it says. [23] Anyone who listens to the word but does not do what it says is like a man who looks at his face in a mirror and, after looking at himself, goes away and immediately forgets what he looks like. James 1:22-24

It is so easy to keep listening to the word of God and not do anything about what we hear. If all the people who hear the word at worship and other settings were to take the word to heart and do something with it, our world would be a different place. Jesus put it best with these words: "Not everyone who says Lord, Lord will enter the kingdom of God." James called that way of responding to God "deception". It is the knowledge that we are not putting into practice what the Lord is saying to us in the word.

That attitude is likened to people who look at themselves in a mirror and walk away without attending to the defects they see. The whole point of having a mirror or looking at ourselves in the mirror is to correct the defects that we see. God is always honest with us as we approach the word of God. The word acts as a mirror in our lives. It would convict and direct us to what needs to be done. It will be left to us to decide to obey or reject what the word is saying.

Let us be diligent in doing what we know the word of God is telling us. That is the only way to grow in our knowledge of our Lord

Trust and obey for there is no other way to be happy in Jesus.

FEBRUARY DAY 14

25 But the man who looks intently into the perfect law that gives freedom, and continues to do this, not forgetting what he has heard, but doing it—he will be blessed in what he does. James 1:25

There is a law that gives freedom. It is the law of Christ. Those who respond to the invitation to bring their burdens to Jesus Christ have embarked on a journey of looking into the perfect law. There is only one person who is perfect and that is the Lord Jesus Christ. The law that he gives is sometimes called the law of the Spirit. It is a law that is written on the hearts and consciences of those who wish to be followers of Christ.

All that is asked of those who would be disciples is that they look fully into the wonderful face of Christ. That intent look into the perfect law gives freedom. Indeed, if the son shall make you free you shall be free for all time. The challenge presented in this verse is the ability to continue to gaze into the face of our Lord without forgetting what he has told us. That is another way of saying that we have to do what the Lord is telling us.

Most of the time all we need to do is to meditate on the Lord and His word and then be spurred on to action. The compassionate, loving, and encouraging face of Jesus is enough to cause us to get up and do what he tells us. When we are able to do that we reap blessings untold. Blessings that are pressed down, shaken together and overflowing are reserved for those who would dare to gaze into the perfect law that Jesus Christ gives.

FEBRUARY DAY 15

[26] *If anyone considers himself religious and yet does not keep a tight rein on his tongue, he deceives himself and his religion is worthless. James 1:26*

"If anyone considers himself religious" What is the author referring to in this phrase? He is calling attention to a relation with God. It is not pointing to religiosity as knowing more about religion or God. There is more to what James is asking us to consider. When one claims to be a child of God or is walking with God there has to be something that shows that the claim is not just lip service. That individual must keep a tight rein on his tongue.

What does it mean to keep a tight rein on the tongue? It means the person has submitted all his members to the Lordship of Jesus Christ. Submission and surrender to God cannot be partial events. It has to be a total surrender that allows the Lord to take full control of the tongue. The truth is that we cannot in our own power keep a tight rein over our tongues. What we can do is to surrender our tongues and all our members to God and allow God to sanctify them.

The Christian who is still operating in his or her own might will soon find out that he has been deceiving himself all along. This is because Christians cannot trust in the power of the flesh. Our tongues will betray us. We will be tempted to speak when we have to keep quiet. Our desire to revenge will make us use our tongues inappropriately. The ability to yield ourselves completely to God leads us to the point where we say: "What will the Lord have me say and do at this time?"

The faith that is worth anything is the one that has mastered what it means to have all our members under the control of God.

February Day 16

²⁷ Religion that God our Father accepts as pure and faultless is this: to look after orphans and widows in their distress and to keep oneself from being polluted by the world. James 1:27

Those who are led by the Holy Spirit are able to call God "Abba". It is a word of endearment and conveys a relationship that is active. Those who call God "Abba" also know that they are expected to listen to what the Holy Spirit witnesses in their hearts. Those whispers of the Spirit come to us through the written word of God among other things.

James reminds us of the type of religion that Abba accepts as pure and faultless. It is the type of religion that puts faith into action. It does not just talk about what acts of compassion that could be done, it is moved by the Holy Spirit to put into practice what others talk about.

Who is not aware of the fact that there are orphans and widows in distress in our community? And what is the Lord saying to us when we become aware of those who are in distress? We are told to do something about such situations. When it is in our power to do something about those in distress. It helps to listen to the Holy Spirit and do it for the Lord Jesus. That is the religion that was passed down to us by our Lord and savior. It is the religion that "Abba" accepts.

The religion that is recommended as pure and faultless also has another component. It keeps itself unstained by the world. The world is seeking to force Christians into its mold. The challenge for all of us is to resist the pressure to conform to the patterns of this world. There is no doubt that we are going to need all the help from above to live out this "Abba given faith".

The world is seeking to pollute our faith. God on the other hand is seeking to sanctify us so that we can conform to the image of Christ.

FEBRUARY DAY 17

My brothers, as believers in our glorious Lord Jesus Christ, don't show favoritism.
James 2:1

James is making a special appeal to all those who call themselves believers in the Lord Jesus Christ. He recognized a situation that was common in society. We refer to this as favoritism. Unfortunately, this situation has become a norm in most churches. One would have expected things to be different in Christian churches. But no! That is not the case we still judge people based on their race, class, gender, and social standing.

James begins by identifying his audience and reminding them of who they are and whose they are. They are first and foremost his brothers and sisters. They have a common address when it comes to their faith in the Lord Jesus. It makes a lot of difference when we come to understand that we share a common address with somebody irrespective of the race and social standing of the person. That is what it means to belong to the household of faith.

I know that there are some who would do everything in their power to prevent sharing a common address with me. So people are fighting great battles to prevent others moving into their neighborhoods or their children attending the same school with other children. But those who belong to the household of God have covenanted to share the same address.

It is one thing knowing that we are one in Christ and another accepting each other in Christ. There is no need trying to qualify what this means or using "Buts" and "ifs". All that the word says is that we have one address in our glorious Lord and savior Jesus Christ. So there is no room for favoritism.

FEBRUARY DAY 18

Suppose a man comes into your meeting wearing a gold ring and fine clothes, and a poor man in shabby clothes also comes in. If you show special attention to the man wearing fine clothes and say, "Here's a good seat for you," but say to the poor man, "You stand there" or "Sit on the floor by my feet," have you not discriminated among yourselves and become judges with evil thoughts? James 2:2-4

Oh! Yes, I can literally hear someone screaming! What are you talking about? Our church is different we treat everyone the same. We have few people of other races and social standings in our congregation and they are all treated fairly. Well, pray about that! James was speaking from experience in the first century church. If James was bold enough to admit what pertained then, then we should be honest enough to say that we have made some progress but we are still culpable.

The practical example given by James is one that we can all identify with. It is a case that vividly described how those in different classes are treated not only in society but also within the church. Gold rings and fine clothing are contrasted with wearing shabby clothes. We could bring these down into our contemporary society by talking about baggy clothes, tattoos and earrings in all sorts of places on the body. Is it possible that these could be a basis for discrimination in our churches? Is it important who sits on the stage or reads the scripture?

As believers in our glorious Lord and savior we are challenged to think and act differently. God shows no partiality and we cannot do otherwise.

FEBRUARY DAY 19

⁵ Listen, my dear brothers and sisters: Has not God chosen those who are poor in the eyes of the world to be rich in faith and to inherit the kingdom he promised those who love him? ⁶ But you have dishonored the poor. Is it not the rich who are exploiting you? Are they not the ones who are dragging you into court? ⁷ Are they not the ones who are blaspheming the noble name of him to whom you belong? James 2:5-7

There are some issues that require our attention. When we fail to pay close attention, we could find ourselves going off on a tangent with ideas that God did not intend. It is easy to read this passage and conclude that a group of people has been chosen and others have been rejected based on their material wealth. That certainly is very far from the truth. The love of God and the invitation of God are extended to all people.

It just happens that, most of the time; those who are materially comfortable find little use for spiritual things. The converse happens to be true not all the time but most of the time. The real determinant is not the wealth of individuals but how rich are people in the faith? What allow people to inherit the kingdom of God are their investments in God. For indeed where our treasure is there would our hearts be also. The real virtue is where people place their total confidence.

The kingdom of God was promised to those who love the Lord. Those who love the Lord have placed their faith and hope completely in the Lord Jesus. A half-hearted commitment will not do because there are so many things tugging at our hearts and inviting us to follow a different agenda.

Those who have settled for the treasures of this world have no regard for those who are rich in the faith. It is not uncommon to hear the name of our Lord being blasphemed. Neither is it far-fetched to encounter Christians suffering for their faith and their stand for the Lord

FEBRUARY DAY 20

⁸ If you really keep the royal law found in Scripture, "Love your neighbor as yourself," you are doing right. ⁹ But if you show favoritism, you sin and are convicted by the law as lawbreakers. James 2:8-9

James invites his audience to pay attention to scripture. There are numerous records of how people have allowed scripture to shape their lives for the better. It has been suggested that scripture informed the basis of the legal codes in several societies. Those who have learned the secret of hiding the word of God in their hearts have also found how that leads to victorious living.

The suggestion by the author is that scripture is something to be taken seriously as a way of life. James identified for us what he termed the royal law found in scripture. What makes this law unique is the inherent truth that it conveys. One does not have to argue for it or against it. Love is a universal language that we can all understand and speak.

The standard for loving our neighbor is how we love our self. In other words, we will not do to the other what we do not wish others would do to us. Note that the neighbor is not identified or defined here in this royal law. It is understood only in relation to self. And that is all we need to know and understand in every situation.

Adherence to the royal law is a path to righteousness. The other half of the royal law is "Love for God". One does not fully understand love until they appreciate how God has loved them. In other words, when the love of self is incomplete, the love for neighbor would suffer the same fate.

We love because God first loved us.

FEBRUARY DAY 21

[10] But the rich should take pride in their humiliation—since they will pass away like a wild flower. [11] For the sun rises with scorching heat and withers the plant; its blossom falls and its beauty is destroyed. In the same way, the rich will fade away even while they go about their business. James 2:10

Learning to walk humbly with God is one of the things that God requires of all of us. The prophet Micah did ask that question: "What does the Lord require of you? The answer given included doing justice, loving mercy and also walking humbly with God. The way of humbleness is a road less traveled. In a society where everyone wants to be number one, it takes character to seek the humble road.

James gives an advice to the rich that can serve all of us very well whether we are rich or poor or somewhere in between. He calls on us to put the whole of life in God's perspective. In that view we see finite human beings living like the rest of creation. The plant is used as an example but that could be any one of us. We are here today and run our courses and then we exit the stage in God's timing. The ability to reflect on life as God sees it allows us to appreciate how vulnerable we are in spite of all human advancement.

All that we can achieve or accumulate in this life would not profit us if we miss out on God's eternal goals for humanity. We dare not make the temporal situations we find ourselves in the most important things. "These too shall pass". There is certainly more to life than this revolving stage with its many actors. When we learn to walk humbly with God we begin to value life and others in the bigger scheme of things.

Walk humbly with your God

Dr. Seth Asare

February Day 22

¹⁰ For whoever keeps the whole law and yet stumbles at just one point is guilty of breaking all of it. ¹¹ For he who said, "You shall not commit adultery," also said, "You shall not murder." If you do not commit adultery but do commit murder, you have become a lawbreaker. James 2:10-11

Have you ever heard someone say: "I try to keep the whole law"? Some people think that all they have to do is to keep the law and they would be fine. James reminds us that keeping the law has become a selective enterprise for some people. They rate some aspects of the law as more important than others. In so doing they convince themselves that so long as they do not kill or do something outrageous they must be doing fine before God.

James says "not so fast folks!" It is not a matter of keeping some major laws and forgetting about some minor points in the law. Breaking any law, however tiny, makes people guilty of the whole law. What that means is that none of us can pride ourselves as being guiltless before the Lord. Stealing and stretching the truth can therefore be put at par with murder and adultery. Because the same God who said you should not kill also said you shall not bear false witness against your neighbor.

That gives us a new understanding of who could be described as a lawbreaker. We all have sinned and fallen short of the standard of God. That is how we all stand before the Lord. But for the grace of God where will all of us be?

February Day 23

[12] Speak and act as those who are going to be judged by the law that gives freedom, [13] because judgment without mercy will be shown to anyone who has not been merciful. Mercy triumphs over judgment. James 2:12-13

I pray that we act and speak like people who are under the law that gives freedom. What do I mean by that? Whenever we fail to forgive one another or hold grudges against our sisters and brothers, we are behaving like ungrateful children. Just think about this! Where would any one of us be without the grace of our Lord Jesus Christ? If God were to judge every sin that we have committed, none of us would be able to hold our heads high before the Lord.

Sometimes we speak like those who are under grace but our actions betray us when we fail to show mercy to our sisters and brothers who are caught in a struggle of their own. We are saved by grace; this is not our own doing. When I think about the words of our Lord to Peter: "Satan demanded to sift you like wheat but I have prayed for you". I am humbled by the fact that had it not been for the prayers of our Lord and the saints I would be in a deplorable condition.

We are challenged to show mercy in the way we pass judgment on one another. For that is precisely what the Lord has done for us. The truth is that mercy will always triumph over judgment in the books of our God. Remember that was the whole reason for sending Jesus Christ. Those who remember this do not think too highly of themselves. They rather attribute any righteous acts or goodness in them to the grace of God.

February Day 24

[14] What good is it, my brothers and sisters, if someone claims to have faith but has no deeds? Can such faith save them? James 2:14

Sometimes we hear people talk about faith in abstract terms. What do I mean by that? It is easy to make faith the end all and be all in a way that makes it difficult to grasp. Faith has to be directed at something. We can have faith in God or faith in people or even faith in ourselves. When we place our faith in an object we are willing to perform some actions that demonstrate the faith we have placed in the object. We do not sit on chairs with broken legs because we know those chairs are not able to support us.

When we have faith in the ability of a chair to support us we go the next step by sitting on the chair. Faith leads to action or deeds. The same is true when someone claims to have faith in the Lord Jesus Christ. That faith leads to action that results in deeds. If anyone is in Christ they become a new creation, the old has passed away and the new has come. Faith in God leads to transformation of the individual into the likeness of Christ.

God is love and those who have faith in God will find themselves loving like God. That is the message of James to us today. We cannot claim to have faith in God and continue living in our old ways. There ought to be actions and deeds that show that we have walked with Jesus Christ. It may be time to start sitting on the chair if we have faith in the ability of the chair to support us. The same is true for having faith in Christ.

FEBRUARY DAY 25

[15] Suppose a brother or a sister is without clothes and daily food. [16] If one of you says to them, "Go in peace; keep warm and well fed," but does nothing about their physical needs, what good is it? [17] In the same way, faith by itself, if it is not accompanied by action, is dead. James 2:15-17

James gives a practical example of the type of faith that he is referring to. Saving faith is the one that leads to action and deeds. The question is how do people recognize this type of faith in daily life? He gave an example that his audience could relate to in their society. The need for clothing and food was common in the community. Not only that, there were Christian brothers and sisters who were experiencing these hardships.

What should be the faith response to these practical needs in the body of Christ and in our world? Note that James was calling on Christians not to wait for these brethren to come knocking on their doors asking for help before they did something about their plight. The other response is that we could use lofty words to console them without attending to their physical needs. We have all heard the usual jargon: "We will pray for you". Often the prayer is forgotten when the person turns around.

James is calling for that faith response that will act and clothe the needy in the name of the Lord. When Christians experience the prompting of the Holy Spirit concerning a need there is no need to wait for others to join in before acting. Learning to live by faith is a matter of responding to the leading of the Holy Spirit through our actions.

If faith is not accompanied by actions that type of faith is not good to anybody. James calls it dead faith. Since we serve a living God, our faith should be alive at all times through what we do in the name of Jesus.

Faith should never be separated from our actions.

February Day 26

[18] *But someone will say, "You have faith; I have deeds. "Show me your faith without deeds, and I will show you my faith by my deeds.* [19] *You believe that there is one God. Good! Even the demons believe that—and shudder. James 2:18-19*

We are confronted with absurd situations where people would like to separate faith from deeds. One claims to have faith and the other claims to have deeds. The question that is posed is this: Is this dichotomy possible and should it be encouraged? Of course not! It is not a tenable proposition.

It is not possible to demonstrate faith in the absence of actions or deeds. On the other hand, it is possible to demonstrate our faith through our actions and deeds. We are encouraged to live in a manner that people will come to appreciate our faith through our deeds.

Faith has to be made practical and removed from the realm of ideas and mere talk. There is so much talk about faith in the church but little action to support it. This is the condition that James is seeking to address. It is much easier for people to claim that they believe in God. What is expected is that belief would be translated into deeds.

We are told that even the demons believe that there is one God. But that does not impact on their deeds. In other words, it is not enough to profess belief in God. That should ultimately lead to transformation that is evidenced by actions.

February Day 27

[20] *You foolish person, do you want evidence that faith without deeds is useless* [21] *Was not our father Abraham considered righteous for what he did when he offered his son Isaac on the altar?* [22] *You see that his faith and his actions were working together, and his faith was made complete by what he did James 2:20-22*

Now the author gives us a scriptural example of what he was talking about. He used Abraham as the perfect example of what it meant to combine faith with works. Abraham was considered by many to be the father of faith. So whom else do we turn to if we want to understand the relation between faith and works?

God pronounced Abraham righteous. The question is this: What was the basis of this pronouncement? James says that it was because he put his faith into action by making up his mind to sacrifice his son Isaac to God. He believed that God who had given him Isaac in the first place was trustworthy and was able to replace his son. Abraham did not question the demand of God. He was ready and willing to offer his only son in obedience to the directive from God. This is a difficult demand and concept for us to fathom today.

The author reminded his audience that the faith of Abraham was working together with his actions. That is precisely the point. The two have to work together for either to be credible. The faith that allows God to call us "righteous" is the one that is never separated from actions. The temptation to make faith a form of belief system that can be learned and known will always be with us. The challenge is how to put that faith into action in our daily dealings with people around us.

Our faith is made complete in what we do!

FEBRUARY DAY 28

²³ And the scripture was fulfilled that says, "Abraham believed God, and it was credited to him as righteousness," and he was called God's friend. ²⁴ You see that a person is considered righteous by what they do and not by faith alone. James 2:23-24

"And the scripture was fulfilled"! What scripture is this? And what does this mean for us? The scripture related to how God declares or accepts an individual as righteous. One may even go a step further to ask what does it mean to be righteous before God?

Righteousness has to do with right relationship between people and God and between one another. The holy God is the only one who can declare any of us righteous. All our good works and human effort will fall short of the righteousness that God expects of us. It is because of the latter that the statement: "Abraham believed God and it was credited to him as righteous" becomes very significant.

Righteousness is something that God credits to people. We do not earn it but God declares and credits to people as he did to Abraham. Anytime one person is credited with righteousness that amounts to the fulfillment of scripture. I pray that God would give insight as you ponder over that statement. It has always been the desire of God to see the fulfillment of scripture in each of our very lives and in our churches. It happens when people are credited or made righteous in the sight of God.

Abraham became a friend of God and we all could become friends of God through faith. We know that his is the faith the puts into action what God says to us. That is precisely what Abraham did. So when we cry Abba we are doing so on credit. God in God's mercy has credited us with righteousness because of the action of Jesus Christ. We in turn ought to put our faith into action.

"You see that a person is considered righteous by what they do and not by faith alone".

February Day 29

[25] *In the same way, was not even Rahab the prostitute considered righteous for what she did when she gave lodging to the spies and sent them off in a different direction?* [26] *As the body without the spirit is dead, so faith without deeds is dead. James 2:25-26*

Abraham was not the only person who demonstrated faith in action. We are given another example in scripture. This time it is a woman called Rahab. Her profession did not make her a likely candidate for faith in action. She was a prostitute besides being a foreigner. In spite of all that she believed that the hand of God was with the people of Israel. She also believed that God was with Joshua and the Israelite army.

Rahab did put that faith to work by risking her life and giving lodging to the spies from the camp of Israel. Joshua had sent these spies to go out and scout out the land and bring a report back to him. The action of Rahab saved the lives of the spies. She hid the spies when their lives were in danger and sent them back in safety. Her life was of course spared when the city was captured. She became an icon of faith that allows an individual to abandon all that they have known and turn to God and the people of God.

We are all called upon to demonstrate the type of belief that makes us turn from all that we have known to a point and turn to our Lord and savior Jesus Christ. This is a risky business but it is something worth doing.

"As the body without the Spirit is dead, so faith without deeds is dead". A dead faith is of no use to anyone.

Extra Day 30

[1] Not many of you should become teachers, my fellow believers, because you know that we who teach will be judged more strictly. [2] We all stumble in many ways. Anyone who is never at fault in what they say is perfect, able to keep their whole body in check.
James 3:1-2

To become a teacher is to take on a great responsibility of trying to shape the lives of other people. The weight becomes ever so greater in the spiritual realm or in the Christian community. James is quick to point this out to all those who hear his words. James appeals to his fellow Christians on this subject. He does not say that no one should become a teacher, as some would have us believe. Rather he emphasized the fact that "not many should become teachers".

The church will always need teachers and leaders. But people should not be in hurry to aspire to teaching positions as believers. The reason given by the author is short and straight to the point. Teachers would be judged more strictly. Why should that be the case? Those who teach are expected to know better. Those who have been given the gift of teaching should be sensitive to the leading of the Holy Spirit when it comes to putting into practice what the Spirit is leading them to teach.

The Spirit who leads and guides would also be our judge. James makes the point that we are all prone to stumble as humans. But that should not be an excuse for those who have been trained to be sensitive to the Holy Spirit. That is the only way to keep the whole body in check. On our own, it is impossible to claim perfection. The more we depend on the Lord, the smoother it is to walk, as the Lord would have us.

Extra Day 31

[3] *When we put bits into the mouths of horses to make them obey us, we can turn the whole animal.* [4] *Or take ships as an example. Although they are so large and are driven by strong winds, they are steered by a very small rudder wherever the pilot wants to go. James 3:3-4*

Human beings are experts in controlling things around them. It seems like one of the greatest achievements of society is how to subject our environment under our control. That may be a survival instinct that is innate in humans. We continue to look for answers to how to bring plants, animals, and even harsh environments under control.

James is driving at something when he talks about the way horses have been tamed by humans. Bits are put into the mouths of horses to make them obey. The horses respond to pain and as a result we are able to guide them to where we wish them to go. The principle is simple. Punishment and reward form the basis for guiding the animals. Same principle has been used to tame several animals. We can make animals who are much bigger than us respond to our bidding.

The author uses another example for how humans are able to control much larger objects. The example is how ships are controlled. These large cruise ships, which are the size of several stadiums, are moved around by small rudders. These instruments use the forces of the natural environment to respond to the pilot's command. When one thinks about the way these large objects are controlled one is amazed at what humans can do.

The question is how do we bring our own bodies under control?

We continue our daily compass for March through the book of James. The use of the tongue dominates the earlier part of the readings. Then we move to practical living in the community and in the world. Read on!

March Day 1

⁴ Or take ships as an example. Although they are so large and are driven by strong winds, they are steered by a very small rudder wherever the pilot wants to go. ⁵ Likewise, the tongue is a small part of the body, but it makes great boasts. Consider what a great forest is set on fire by a small spark. ⁶ The tongue also is a fire, a world of evil among the parts of the body. It corrupts the whole body, sets the whole course of one's life on fire, and is itself set on fire by hell. James 3:4-6

Now the author drives home the point he has been trying to make when he talked about the taming of horses and the steering of ships. He was getting at the human tongue and the words we use the tongue to say. When one considers the size of the tongue relative to the whole human body, it is very small. James admits that this small instrument has the capability to do more than its fair share of boasting and harm.

Rulers and kings throughout the ages have made bold claims with their tongues and some have even claimed to be gods. Things have not changed in our time where we believe that our scientific achievements have made God irrelevant. Wars have been fought because of the tongue. People have also been destroyed by what others have said about them. It takes only a small spark by the tongue to set nations on fire.

James is asking all of us to be mindful of the tongue and what we say because the tongue is capable of much greater devastation than any of us will want. What is whispered in secret could be the dagger that is being pushed into a sister or a brother.

March Day 2

⁷All kinds of animals, birds, reptiles and sea creatures are being tamed and have been tamed by mankind, ⁸ but no human being can tame the tongue. It is a restless evil, full of deadly poison. James 3:7-8

Now, James widens the imagery of what humans have been able to tame. The examples cover a wide spectrum of animals. The indication is that these creatures have been tamed or are being tamed. This statement reveals that people have been in the business of taming wild animals for quite a while.

This is sharply contrasted with the inability of humans to tame the tongue. Why is this the case? We do not get a lot of clues except the indication that the tongue is a restless evil, full of deadly poison. That is a particular harsh statement when heard for the first time. But when one considers what we do with our tongues, it becomes clear that the author is right.

People are unable to allow their tongues to keep silent for any length of time. It seems we are afraid of silence and we have to keep the tongue going all the time. Unfortunately, what the tongue keeps babbling is full of gossip, backbiting, tearing people down and puffing the self with pride. No wonder James describes the tongue as full of deadly poison.

How do we get rid of this deadly poison in the community of faith? We first have to understand what we are doing with our tongues as Christians before attempting to address the problem. Then we have to appreciate the purpose for this wonderful human organ in the body. We may be moved to gradually yield this member of the body to God who gave us the tongue.

All the gifts of God are good when used as intended.

MARCH DAY 3

⁹ With the tongue we praise our Lord and Father, and with it we curse human beings, who have been made in God's likeness. ¹⁰ Out of the same mouth come praise and cursing. My brothers and sisters, this should not be. James 3:9-10

What is the purpose of the tongue in the first place? We are told that we praise our Lord and Father with the tongue. That statement suggests that recipients of this letter acknowledge God as creator and "father". Love for God is not complete unless it is linked with love for neighbor. So we can say that the tongue should also be used to praise our neighbors who are part of God's creation.

But instead of using the tongue to praise God and neighbor, the author indicates what we do in practice. With the same tongue we curse human beings, who have been made in the likeness of God. That is unfortunate description of a reality that pertains even in the community of faith. This has become a disturbing situation that should not be allowed to go unchecked.

Anytime a person who is created in the image of God is cursed with a tongue, then God is being cursed. Everything created by God is good and who are we to use the gift of God to curse the Creator. The point has to be brought home to all of us so forcefully that we would hold our tongues anytime we are tempted to fire outbursts with our tongues.

Should praises and cursing come out of the same mouth? That is something left for us to ponder and reflect upon as Christians. The Author however comes up with what he thinks should be the case in the community of faith.

"My brothers and sisters, this should not be!" The tongue should be for praising God and blessing our neighbors.

March Day 4

[11] Can both fresh water and salt water flow from the same spring? [12] My brothers and sisters, can a fig tree bear olives, or a grapevine bear figs? Neither can a salt spring produce fresh water. James 3:11-12

We have a rhetorical question here. The answer is obvious but the question had to be asked to heighten the absurdity. We know that when fresh water is mixed with salt water we no longer have drinkable water. The spring ceases to pour out fresh spring water under those circumstances.

The point of the questions put forth in these verses is that we cannot use the same tongue to praise God and turn around to curse our neighbors. James is hinting at the transformation that has to take place when anyone is in Christ. The Holy Spirit has a way of changing the tongue in the Christian if one is willing to yield and co-operate.

The transformation may not happen overnight but there sure should be a steady progress. We are all being changed from one degree of glory into another. The goal is the likeness of Christ. Then the fruit of the Spirit that is borne by us would be consistent with what Christ would have. God has better things for us.

A grape tree cannot bear figs, in a similar way the Holy Spirit in us is bound to bear fruits of the Spirit.

MARCH DAY 5

¹³ Who is wise and understanding among you? Let them show it by their good life, by deeds done in the humility that comes from wisdom. James 3:13

There is a shift from discussing the tongue and what it can do in a community of faith to what it means to be wise. Certainly, there were several in the audience of the writer who would claim to be wise. James is not just seeking out only wise folks. He talks about those who are wise and understanding.

Could it be that he was driving at something? There are many who would be called wise by all standards but lack the ability to empathize and relate to plight of others. To be "understanding" is the ability to put oneself in the shoes of others. To know that but for the grace of God, the suffering of another person could have been yours. This way of thinking and relating to others could change attitudes and world-views.

The author knows that being wise and understanding shows itself in practical ways. This is more than talk or appearance. It is revealed through good deeds. The wise and understanding are able to discern what the right action to take is in a particular situation. Not only that, but what they do are carried out in humility with a full understanding that it is the grace of the Lord that makes all things possible. They do not call attention to themselves but rather point to God.

That is wisdom indeed!

March Day 6

[14] But if you harbor bitter envy and selfish ambition in your hearts, do not boast about it or deny the truth. [15] Such "wisdom" does not come down from heaven but is earthly, unspiritual, demonic. James 3:14-15

The converse of being wise and understanding is given in these verses. It is shown in harboring bitterness in the heart against one another. Those who harbor bitterness are never free to actualize their full potential. There is always something that holds them back from knowing the fullness of the freedom that Christ offers.

Envy is another vice that chokes the life of liberty. So long as one is not satisfied with what the Lord has given them they would always see the grass as being green on the other side. The desire to be like others or to want what others have has led many people down a slippery path of no return.

Then there is that ambition that is focused only on self. It is the type of ambition that makes people ask what do I get from this? Every move is calculated for the selfish gain of the individual. This is a cancer that is destroying the secular world and unfortunately has crept into the church. People are looking after their own interests and not that of the Lord Jesus Christ.

We are told that such "wisdom" or way of thinking and acting does not have its origins in God. So it cannot be deemed spiritual because it is self-serving. James would describe this type of wisdom as demonic.

We are challenged to be wise and understanding.

MARCH DAY 7

[16] For where you have envy and selfish ambition, there you find disorder and every evil practice. James 3:16

The earthly, unspiritual, and demonic wisdom is gradually taking over in our world. This is the way of doing things from a competitive perspective. People are always trying to outdo each other in all respects. There is no attempt to work together and help each other. The question that is often asked is who has the biggest house, the best car, and most money in the bank.

That way of thinking leads to envy and covetousness. There are people who make it their goal to forcibly take what does not belong to them because they believe that those who are ahead have cheated them. Personal responsibility has been thrown out of the window and everyone is fending for what they see fit. This can only be described as selfish ambition.

James sees all that as leading to disorder. Some of the disintegration that we observe in society has its roots in the selfish ambition and greed that is now accepted without question. In an attempt to reject the wisdom from above people have succumbed to practices that are unspiritual.

It is time to root out all the unspiritual practices that bring us down and create chaos.

March Day 8

[17] But the wisdom that comes from heaven is first of all pure; then peace loving, considerate, submissive, full of mercy and good fruit, impartial and sincere. [18] Peacemakers who sow in peace reap a harvest of righteousness. James 3:17-18

Considerable attention has been given to the wisdom that is unspiritual. It is time to take a look at what Godly wisdom looks like. This type of wisdom is described as the wisdom that comes from heaven. The origin of the wisdom is not man made and it cannot be contrived by human ingenuity.

It is first of all pure. This is a perfect description of the source of this wisdom. God who is the giver of wisdom is pure and no shadows are found in him. The holiness of God is implied here. All those who seek to approach God or be in relation with God cannot overlook the holiness of God. The question that is often asked is this: How can mortals who are prone to sin draw near a holy God? The answer screams out at us: "It is by grace and because of mercy".

The wisdom that this Holy God gives is also peace loving, considerate, submissive and full of mercy. The list of qualities associated with the wisdom from above read like the fruit of the Holy Spirit. That is not surprising since the source is the triune God. Moreover, the Holy Spirit plays an integral part in the manifestation of the wisdom from above.

We are reminded that peacemakers who sow in peace reap a harvest of righteousness. May the Lord give us more peacemakers!

March Day 9

¹ What causes fights and quarrels among you? Don't they come from your desires that battle within you? ² You desire but do not have, so you kill. You covet but you cannot get what you want, so you quarrel and fight. James 4:1-2

Fights and quarrels among people are as ancient as the creation of humans on earth. There have always been quarrels since the time of Adam and Eve. Fights among siblings are as old as Cain and Abel. There is indeed nothing new under the sun. The question posed and answered here is this: What causes fights and quarrels in communities and in our world?

We are informed that at the root of most fights and quarrels is human desire. What does this mean? It means that the desire to have our own way; the desire to dominate others, the desire to be in control; and the desire to win at all cost are what cause fights and quarrels in our world. It may look so simplistic but when you come right down to it, it is so true.

When people desire something rightfully or wrongfully and they do not have, then they will move every mountain to accomplish their goal. Some will even kill to achieve their ambitions. The converse is also true. The way that people respond to those who are trying hard to fulfill their desires could lead to fights, misunderstanding and quarreling.

What if we did not allow these desires to have the upper hand and carried them all to the Lord in prayer? One could be assured that most of the fights and quarrels would be abated.

March Day 10

You do not have because you do not ask God. ³ When you ask, you do not receive; because you ask with wrong motives, that you may spend what you get on your pleasures. James 4:3

Those who have confidence in God know that God is their provider. But sometimes Christians forget what they have learned and begin to trust themselves and other things. James reminds us that we do not have because we do not ask God. The problem is not just asking but who they ask. Asking God is something people do because they have placed all their confidence God. Trying to do it ourselves by looking at other sources suggests that we have no need of God.

It is easier to turn to other sources in our times of need. But the ability to turn to God all the time does not come easily. It comes with practice and a few disappointments. It takes faith and trust to keep asking God and trusting God for our needs.

Sometimes we ask and do not receive. What happens under those circumstances? We are told that we ask with wrong motives. What would be described as a wrong motive? When the asking becomes selfish that is wrong motive. When we ask so that we can fulfill our desires and pleasures we have missed the point. We are not including God in the equation under those circumstances. By so doing we should not be surprised that we do not receive what we ask for.

God has the bigger picture in view. Whether we receive answers or not should not really be the issue. We should be more concerned with being in the will of the Lord all the time. What may be called a desired end may not be the answer that God has in mind.

Wait for God's answer.

MARCH DAY 11

[4] You adulterous people, don't you know that friendship with the world means enmity against God? Therefore, anyone who chooses to be a friend of the world becomes an enemy of God. [5] Or do you think Scripture says without reason that he jealously longs for the spirit he has caused to dwell in us? James 4:4-5

James seemed to have taken the gloves off and was ready for a fight with the people of God. He invoked an Old Testament image that the prophets were fond of using. This is the image of harlotry and adultery. The community of faith was accused of harlotry or adultery each time they forsook the God of Israel and went after other gods or idols. James considers friendship with the world to be the same as forsaking God.

He asked a question that should jolt the people of God back to their senses. "Don't you know that friendship with the world means enmity with God?" He is in effect saying that you cannot serve God and mammon. This idea of "eating your cake and having it" does not work. The command of God is that we love with all our being. It is unfortunate that some have chosen to use God as an insurance policy just in case the word of God is true.

James says no! It ought not be that way. When we decide to be friends with God we allow the world and its pleasures to go in the other direction. Our wills and desires are transformed to conform to the workings of the Holy Spirit. So whatever we ask of the Lord should be in line with what God would have us do. The Spirit that God has caused to dwell in us is always leading us in the directions that God would have us go.

MARCH DAY 12

⁵ Or do you think Scripture says without reason that he jealously longs for the spirit he has caused to dwell in us? ⁶ But he gives us more grace. That is why Scripture says: "God opposes the proud but shows favor to the humble." James 4:5-6

The Holy Spirit who comes to dwell in believers is part of the presence of God in the life of a Christian. The Spirit is the guarantee that we belong to God and God has taken residence in our lives. We are therefore encouraged to make every effort to guard the power of God in us so that we do not grieve the Holy Spirit. James goes as far as saying that God jealously guards the Holy Spirit in the believer.

We do guard anything that we deem precious to us. Sometime we would insure them or place them in a secure place. God does the same thing with the Holy Spirit that has been placed in a Christian. The word jealous is used in a positive sense in this verse. It denotes the desire of God to prevent anything from tarnishing the Holy Spirit invested in us.

God gives more grace to those who recognize their need for God. Those who think that they can do it by themselves are left to their own proud devices. It always takes a humble heart to receive more of the grace that God has in store for people. Let us approach the mercy seat of God with all the humility that God inspires in us.

MARCH DAY 13

⁷ Submit yourselves, then, to God. Resist the devil, and he will flee from you. James 4:7

Submission to God is one of the virtues of the Christian faith. Submitting oneself requires a self-understanding that one cannot achieve much without humility. This is especially important when it comes to humbling ones-self before God. Those who are proud in their own eyes fail to see the full picture of what God is doing in our world

Any world-view that does not submit to God becomes myopic. It fails to see that there is more to the world that what we can see, feel and touch. Moreover, an attitude that does not submit to God gets puffed up. It makes people think that they are at the center of the world and everything should revolve around them.

The truth is that those who are unable to submit to God find it difficult to submit to other persons. Just think about that. If one cannot submit to God how can we expect such people to listen to the points of view of others? We begin to see the world differently when we learn to submit to God and to our fellow human beings.

When Christians learn to submit to God they are able to see clearly the forces of evil that they must resist. The many hurdles that are placed in the paths of Christians become clear and obvious. A prideful attitude would prevent us from seeing clearly what we are up against. To be able to resist the devil we will need all the help from God. Those who have faced the devil on their own abilities have learned the hard way that they are not able.

With all the armor of God we are able to resist the devil to the point that the enemy of our faith flees. So resist the devil with the whole armor of God and he will flee from you.

March Day 14

[8] *Come near to God and he will come near to you. Wash your hands, you sinners, and purify your hearts, you double-minded.* [9] *Grieve, mourn and wail. Change your laughter to mourning and your joy to gloom.* [10] *Humble yourselves before the Lord, and he will lift you up. James 4:8-10*

The invitation to draw near to God is one that is as old as life itself. Since creation, God has been seeking a relationship with people. As part of that search there is a standing invitation for all to draw near to God. The writer indicates God's eagerness to draw near to all who come. The truth is that God has already made the first move by issuing the invitation.

But drawing near to God requires that we know that we are dealing with a holy God who cannot entertain sin. How else can sinful persons draw near to God? They must first deal with what separates them from God. That means repentance and confession of sins are in the offering. We are told to wash our hands and purify our hearts. We dare not approach God with a double-minded attitude.

There should be clarity on what this drawing near to God is about. Those who do not see the dire circumstances that humans have plunged themselves in would find no need to draw to God. The repentance that is called for would involve mourning and wailing instead of laughter. Mourning for our sins is more than just saying I am sorry. It would require us to cast ourselves on the mercy of God by falling at His feet. We trust that in due time the Lord in his infinite mercy would lift us up.

MARCH DAY 15

11 Brothers and sisters, do not slander one another. Anyone who speaks against a brother or sister or judges them speaks against the law and judges it. When you judge the law, you are not keeping it, but sitting in judgment on it. James 4:11

Now the writer turns to the Christian community and addresses them with endearing words. He calls them Brothers and sisters. These are inclusive words to make sure that no one is left out. It is an admonition for all Christians in the community. The fact that he calls them brothers and sisters shows that the author is not speaking to outsiders but to members of the household of faith.

The message given is powerful and shocking: "Do not slander one another". Slandering is a vice that one would not expect to be associated with people who are addressed as "brothers and sisters in the faith". But here it is, because it does happen that Christians slander one another and as someone has said they sometimes "shoot their wounded". Speaking evil or malicious lies about another should not be heard among Christians but unfortunately, it does happen.

Who are we to judge and condemn another brother or sister for whom Christ died? There is only one judge and it is the same one who gave the law. God is the only one who has the ability to judge all things without prejudice. We will do better if we deferred all judgment to God concerning the actions of brothers and sisters.

All those who are created in the image of God should be seen as people of sacred worth and treated as such. Only God has the ability to weigh all sides of the issue and judge correctly.

March Day 16

[12] *There is only one Lawgiver and Judge, the one who is able to save and destroy. But you—who are you to judge your neighbor? James 4:12*

Some have tried to behave as if they are above the law. Others think that the law does not apply to them. Yet still, there are those who would like others to believe that they are the law. James emphatically states that there is only one Lawgiver and Judge. Note that the words Lawgiver and Judge begin with capital letters.

The author wanted to set God apart from all those who pretend to be something that they are not. The ultimate Lawgiver is the only one who has the ability to judge all people justly. When people forget that fact they become presumptuous. Who are we to even think that we have the right to place ourselves in a position to judge others? We only see dimly and in part. The one who is both Lawgiver and Judge is able to search the human heart to a degree that none of us can imagine.

We are talking about God who has the ability and capacity to create life and give life to humans. This same God is able to save and destroy life. No one questions the potter about what has been created and what is refashioned for another vessel. The sovereignty of God is what we are talking about.

In the presence of this God all our achievements and what we think we know amount to filthy rags. They are not worth anything. Who are we then, to think about judging another person? "Lord have mercy on us!"

March Day 17

¹³ Now listen, you who say, "Today or tomorrow we will go to this or that city, spend a year there, carry on business and make money." ¹⁴ Why, you do not even know what will happen tomorrow. What is your life? You are a mist that appears for a little while and then vanishes. James 4:13-14

For people to be at peace with themselves and with the world, it is important that things in life have to be put in perspective. It is important that we come to terms with the fact that we are finite beings who know very little of what God is about. As some say: "we should hang loose and be ready for a change in plans all the time."

How do you feel when you hear someone say: "Today or tomorrow we will go to this or that city, spend a year there, carry on business and make money?" The immediate thought is that this individual has all plans made for the next year. But we also know that these are only plans that are subject to change.

James is calling us to be mindful of this type of attitude that makes us feel that we are in control or we can plan everything to perfection. We do not even have full control of today let alone to talk about tomorrow or a year from now. There are more variables in life than we would want to care for.

We are on this earth for a brief period and we move on. The only one who is permanent is God. When we begin to put things in perspective we appreciate how miniscule humans are in the bigger scheme of things.

It is important that we do not think too highly of humans and their capabilities.

March Day 18

15 Instead, you ought to say, "If it is the Lord's will, we will live and do this or that." 16 As it is, you boast in your arrogant schemes. All such boasting is evil. 17 If anyone, then, knows the good they ought to do and doesn't do it, it is sin for them. James 4:15-17

The author is now giving us what he deems as the right perspective to take in life. We are advised to say: *"If it is the Lord's will, we will live and do this or that."* What is suggested in this verse is the understanding that God is in control and holds the whole universe together. To admit that humans are subject to the will of God is not something that people accept easily. By so doing we admit that we are subject to the influence of God.

These verses have caused some of us to rethink our responses to situations in life. We now add "God willing!" to all our plans and anything we are asked to do. That way we are reminded that our plans are subject to God whether "the creek rises or not".

To live or die is not something that is in the human power. If that is true as our scriptures say, then we have to be cautious of the statements we make and how we live our lives. Our boasting is baseless because we are subject to the power of God. All our arrogant schemes are thrown out of the window.

If anyone knows what is good to do, then they should go ahead and do just that. The issue is how do we act on all the good stuff we have acquired through our knowledge of God. It is not enough to study the Bible if we do not put what we learn into practice.

Those who fail to do what they know to be right fail God and others in the process.

March Day 19

¹ Now listen, you rich people, weep and wail because of the misery that is coming on you. ² Your wealth has rotted, and moths have eaten your clothes. ³ Your gold and silver are corroded. Their corrosion will testify against you and eat your flesh like fire. You have hoarded wealth in the last days. James 5:1-3

Now, a strong warning is given to those who use their riches to oppress the poor. In reality the stern rebuke is addressed to people who put all their confidence in riches or wealth. For these people, all they care about is how to make more money and forget that there is God who is interested in the plight of the poor.

The warning is about a reversal of fortunes that was about to take place. Those who are wealthy are going to find themselves in an uncomfortable situation. They will be weeping and wailing because of the loss of their wealth. What they thought was a permanent condition was going to change. They are going to realize to their surprise that the only thing that is permanent is God.

We are told the wealth of the rich people would be corroded and moths will feast on the rich linen that they have prided themselves in. The indication is that all material things are temporary and subject to decay. What has been hoarded and accumulated will disappear so quickly that people would be wondering what happened. Even precious metals like gold and silver will corrode and be found to be worthless in time of need.

The only place to put our confidence is in the one who is eternal and would not change with time.

March Day 20

⁴ Look! The wages you failed to pay the workers who mowed your fields are crying out against you. The cries of the harvesters have reached the ears of the Lord Almighty. ⁵ You have lived on earth in luxury and self-indulgence. You have fattened yourselves in the day of slaughter. ⁶ You have condemned and murdered the innocent one, who was not opposing you. James 5:4-6

The wealthy have taken for granted that the money will continue to flow as they have in the past. They have depended on cheating and taking advantage of their workers and the poor. Now, the writer appeals to the consciences of the wealthy. Listen to these words: "The wages you failed to pay the workers who mowed your fields are crying out against you."

That is a dramatic way of making the point. The author moves his description a notch higher by stating that: "The cries of the harvesters have reached the ears of the Lord Almighty." That changes the whole equation. It is no longer about how others are affected but God knows exactly what has happened because the cries of the poor have reached the throne of God.

The wealthy have lived in a state self-indulgence without thinking of the plight of others. In an attempt to get what they want, innocent people have died because the rich wanted to have their way. But it is always important to remember that God has something to say about all that. That should cause all of us to stop and ponder.

MARCH DAY 21

[7] Be patient, then, brothers and sisters, until the Lord's coming. See how the farmer waits for the land to yield its valuable crop, patiently waiting for the autumn and spring rains. [8] You too, be patient and stand firm, because the Lord's coming is near. James 5:7-8

It has been brought to my attention, that in yesterday's message, I came across as saying that all wealthy people were bad. I am sorry if that was the way I interpreted the passage. Wealth and prosperity are gifts and blessings from God. However, God expects these blessings to be used to help others.

Our passage today says: "Be patient". This virtue or fruit of the Holy Spirit is often talked about but ignored because of what it takes to practice it and let the fruit be evident. The people who are in a hurry to see results do miss out on patience. To be able to bear this fruit one has to endure a life that is not attractive to many contemporary Christians.

The ability to wait for God's time to break unto the scene is easier said than done. This is because there are no guarantees except the knowledge that God is there no matter what happens. The early church understood that they had to wait in patience for the Lord's coming. At that - time they expected the reversal of their fortunes. In the mean-time all that they could do was to wait in patience.

The example of a farmer waiting patiently for a crop that has been planted to reach maturity was one that James' audience could relate to. They understood that after all the hard work had been done there was nothing left but to wait patiently.

There is a valuable crop to be harvested sooner or later. In the mean-time patient endurance that focuses on the one who called us is recommended.

"Lord teach us how to wait patiently!"

MARCH DAY 22

⁹ Don't grumble against one another, brothers and sisters, or you will be judged. The Judge is standing at the door! James 5:9

What causes grumbling? When people are dissatisfied with the course of events they do grumble. The dissatisfaction may stem from the perception that they have been treated unfairly or they have not received a just reward. Whatever the cause for grumbling may be, one party is angry because in their judgment someone has been less than fair.

When people grumble against one another a tension is created that affects the harmony that previously existed between the parties. This becomes serious within the body of Christ or in the community of faith. When grumbling begins within the community, things are never the same. People view each other with suspicion and they begin to second-guess the motives of the other.

So Christians are admonished not to grumble against each other because in so doing they quickly jump to conclusions and judge each other. It is important that we go to the sister or brother and attempt to talk things over so that every cloud of doubt is removed.

We have one judge who understands each one of us to the core. There is nothing that can be hidden from God. God's judgment is different from that of humans. It is always perfect.

MARCH DAY 23

[10] *Brothers and sisters, as an example of patience in the face of suffering, take the prophets who spoke in the name of the Lord.* [11] *As you know, we count as blessed those who have persevered. You have heard of Job's perseverance and have seen what the Lord finally brought about. The Lord is full of compassion and mercy. James 5:10-11*

There is no way of talking about patience without putting it in the context of suffering. When we are faced with challenges in life, we are placed in crucibles where we can either learn patience or resort to grumbling against one another and against God. The prophets of old were great examples of how to learn patience in the face of challenging circumstances.

Any-one who speaks in the name of the Lord has to learn patience. This is because God's ways are not our ways. So everything has to be understood in God's time. In a society where we want to see things happen quickly, this attitude of waiting for the Lord to act is not embraced easily. Those who have persevered in the face of all odds are counted as blessed. The prophets in the Old Testament are shining examples of patience.

We are able to read the last chapters in the lives of these prophets and observe how their patience paid off. Job stands out as an example of patience. In all that he suffered he did not curse God. I do not know if I could exhibit that type of patience. One thing is clear. It takes the grace of God to bear this fruit of the Spirit.

Let us be patient with one another because God is still working on each one of us.

March Day 24

[12] *Above all, my brothers and sisters do not swear—not by heaven or by earth or by anything else. All you need to say is a simple "Yes" or "No." Otherwise you will be condemned. James 5:12*

Why do people swear in the first place? That question could be turned around and asked differently. Why are people made to swear? The intention of swearing is to get at the truth. The assumption in society is that when people swear by something they respect or worship they would not tell a lie. They would fear incurring the wrath of the person or the "god" by whom they swear. But experience has proven that assumption to be false. People would go ahead and give false witness or tell lies after swearing.

It is in that context that James cautions people in his community to refrain from swearing. His argument was that: the fact that the people in the world were not able to keep to their word should not mean that Christians could not keep their word. The Christians honor should be above reproach. The Christians were admonished to let their "yes be yes and their no be no." By so doing no one would have the opportunity to second-guess the honor of the people of God.

The standards for Christians should be different from that of the people of the world. Indeed, we are the light of the world.

MARCH DAY 25

¹³ Is anyone among you in trouble? Let them pray. Is anyone happy? Let them sing songs of praise. James 5:13

As the writer brings the chapter to a close, he addressed some practical ways to keep the community of faith alive and healthy. In my ministry, I have turned to these words to challenge myself as to how I can be proactive in addressing the needs all around us.

James asked a question that hits at the core of life in the community of faith. "Is anyone among you in trouble?" That is not a rhetorical question rather it is existential one. There will always be someone in trouble within the community of faith. Trouble comes in varying degrees to different people. The first step to healing is to admit that we are in trouble. So when the author asks the question he is already preparing the ground for a holistic healing.

Those who admit that they are in trouble are directed to a spiritual resource. That is prayer. In other words, they are encouraged to look beyond themselves and turn to God for healing and help. There is no point praying if one does not believe in the one they are praying to. When we resort to prayer we have accepted that the God who made the whole universe has the power to do something about our particular situation.

The enormity of the trouble is inconsequential because we are dealing with a compassionate God and the all-powerful one. The same goes for the times that we are happy. We do not pray only when things are not going well. We praise the Lord in the happy times.

That is a balance in life that God would want us to have. It may be time to sing a song of praise.

MARCH DAY 26

^{14} Is anyone among you sick? Let them call the elders of the church to pray over them. James 5:14a

The writer narrows down the discussion on Christians in trouble and addresses a theme that is dear to the heart of all. James asks: "Is anyone among you sick?" That questions points to the fact that sickness is a universal human condition that does not know any boundaries. Sickness has been with humans as long as people have been on this planet. There have been all sorts of medicinal and spiritual approaches to sickness. That situation has not changed very much in our day.

The suggestion of James in this passage does not limit the Christian approach to dealing with sickness. It rather recognizes the power of prayer in dealing with all manner of issues that confront individuals. James believed that prayer to God was the first place to begin when confronted with any problem.

Secondly James made a theological statement when he suggested that the elders of the church should be invited to play a role in the healing prayers. The author was saying that God has invested in the Church and the elders the power to heal. This power to heal is represented by the Holy Spirit that has been given to the Church. Unfortunately, several churches have abandoned this birthright of the Church that was given on the day of Pentecost. Fear has crippled many churches from freely and boldly exercising the power that is in the name of Jesus.

The elders and leaders of the Church should be taught and encouraged to exercise the gift that God has invested in his church.

MARCH DAY 27

14b Let them call the elders of the church to pray over them and anoint them with oil in the name of the Lord. 15 And the prayer offered in faith will make the sick person well; the Lord will raise them up. James 5:14b-15a

Those who are sick are challenged to call the elders of the church to pray over them. I am praying for the day when people in faith will be calling their elders and reminding them of this scriptural injunction. I know it will make people take the position of being an elder of a church more seriously. Elders are to be spiritually ready to discharge their duties anywhere and anytime. There would be no "time out" to get ready for the challenge ahead. We should be prepared to do the work of the Lord anytime that the Lord would need us.

Note that the prayer of faith begins when the sick person takes a step of faith and calls for an elder. We all have a role to pray in taking the steps of faith. Both the elder and the sick person are challenged to exercise their faith in God. I am not suggesting that without one party playing their part God would not step in and work. Rather I am saying that God calls all to participate in their healing.

Now pay attention to what the elders are asked to do under such circumstances. They are to anoint them with oil in the name of the Lord Jesus Christ. Then finally they are to offer a prayer of faith. Folks we are not talking about a mechanical going through the motions here. Neither are we talking about a magical procedure with special incantations using oil. At the heart of praying for the sick is the dependence on the power of the Holy Spirit. That is symbolized by the use of oil. Then there is the faith in the name of Jesus Christ.

Why would anyone attempt to pray for someone in the name of Jesus if they did not believe that Jesus Christ had the ability to heal? Note that the whole emphasis is shifted from the elder, and the sick person to the Lord. It is the Lord who heals.

March Day 28

^{15} And the prayer offered in faith will make the sick person well; the Lord will raise them up. If they have sinned, they will be forgiven. James 5:15

What does it mean to offer a prayer in faith? This is an attempt to prevent the whole idea of praying for the sick from becoming a formality that can be copied and used by anyone who knows what to say or do. The person praying must have faith in the Lord and what he or she is doing. It is not how big one's faith is rather it depends on the one in whom the faith is placed.

When we believe that God will honor God's word. We step out in faith in the ability of God to intervene and do what God has always done. It is important to keep the focus on the Lord who is the healer. The glory would go to God no matter what happens. It is God who will make the sick person well. This means that how and when the person gets well is not a matter for us to contemplate. We act as faithful servants of the Lord who are only doing their duty. Remember it is the Lord who raises the sick.

Then the author talks about forgiveness of sin as a gift of God and something God does. If there is any sin that is implicated in the sickness of the person being prayed for, it is the Lord that deals with that. The power of the Holy Spirit is able to convict, expose, as well as forgive sin. There is so much about praying for the sick that depends on the ability of God. All we can do is to step out in faith and let God do the rest.

We are not asked to play God. All we are asked to do is to pray the prayer of faith.

March Day 29

¹⁶ Therefore confess your sins to each other and pray for each other so that you may be healed. The prayer of a righteous person is powerful and effective. James 5:16

What does it mean to confess our sins to one another? Some have been brought up to believe that the only person we confess our sins to is God. So this admonition to confess our sins to one another seems strange to the Christian who has been brought up in a tradition where confession is something between the individual and God.

There are those who have had unpleasant experiences when it comes to confession. They have confessed things to people they trusted and loved only to find out that the confidence had been betrayed. Confidentiality has become a big issue whenever we talk about confession. In some societies it has become necessary to protect confidentiality that is confessional in nature. Even there, it has become necessary to qualify what could be considered as confessional in nature by introducing mandatory reporting.

The Bible is on to something that we are only beginning to scratch the surface. That is the therapeutic effects of confession. When people are able to talk about the sin and guilt that separate them from one another and from God, some healing takes place. We have tried to institutionalize that recommendation here with counseling and therapeutic centers. However, the injunction still stands that we should confess our sins to one another so that we may be healed.

The writer relates confession with prayer. The Christian's understand of confession is always tied with prayer because when it comes to this issue, it is God who does the healing. The confession is certainly part of the healing process but eventually it is God who will finish the healing.

March Day 30

17 Elijah was a human being, even as we are. He prayed earnestly that it would not rain, and it did not rain on the land for three and a half years. James 5:17

When we hear about the matriarchs and patriarchs of the faith, we are tempted to think of them as super humans who are far above mortals like us. James debunks that notion by reminding us that Elijah was an ordinary person like any one of us. So one would ask the obvious question; "What made these heroes stand so tall on the stage of life?"

We are reminded of the confidence that people like Elijah placed in the big God who is able to do all things. At one level we all believe that there is nothing too hard for God. We know that the God of our Lord Jesus Christ has the power to bring into being things that are not.

Then on the other level we are always second-guessing whether this God would act in our particular circumstance. What separates the people of faith from most people is that, the former do not place any limitations on God. They wholehearted believe that God would bring to pass what God has said.

Elijah spoke the word of God to King Ahab concerning the absence of rain for three and half years. Elijah spoke the word that God had given him in faith and he understood the consequences of the word that he was speaking. He was making himself an enemy of the king with those words. But Elijah knew that there were greater issues at stake in God's bigger picture. This was about something more than rain. It was about the battle for the souls of the people of God.

There is a battle going on for the souls of the future generation and the people of faith are being called upon to stand in the gap as intercessors. Could it be that you and I are called upon to be the Elijah's of our day to speak the word of faith to principalities that threaten the souls of our people? Then we need to rediscover earnest prayer that calls into being things that are not.

Be blessed as you boldly speak the word of faith.

MARCH DAY 31

18 Again he prayed, and the heavens gave rain, and the earth produced its crops. James 5:18

The narrative of how Elijah prayed for rain after three and half years of drought started with the contest at mount Carmel. Elijah challenged the prophets of Baal to a contest in which each group should pray to their supreme being to answer by sending fire to consume their offering. This was to show that it was possible to receive answers to prayer.

In short, Elijah's God did answer by fire in a miraculous way. At the conclusion of that challenge the people of Israel responded with the words: "The Lord, he is God! The Lord he is God!" That was the whole purpose of the holding off rain and the contest. It was to draw the hearts of the people to their God. The God who can stop the rain and send fire is the God of Israel. The events that were unfolding were not mere coincidence but answers to prayer.

The word of God through the prophet did hold off rain for three and half years and the same word of the Lord was going to bring about rain. Elijah prayed and spoke the word of faith. There was no sign of rain at the time when Elijah spoke. But God has a way of honoring his word. So the mighty downpour of rain came as the prophet had said. The earth produced crops again, and natural cycle continued as if nothing had happened.

God answers prayer!

We conclude our daily compass readings through the book of James with admitting the inevitable that there will be backsliders in the community of faith. How do we restore such persons with minimum collateral damage? Then we will move on to finding our bearings in the book of Proverbs.

April Day 1

[19] My brothers and sisters, if one of you should wander from the truth and someone should bring that person back, James 5:19

The Christian community has always been an inclusive one. That is not to say that it did not have signs of patriarchy. But when considered alongside the surrounding environment, the Christian community was head and shoulders above the secular society in terms of gender inclusiveness. James found it fitting to address the community as brothers and sisters instead of any other term that could be interpreted to include both genders.

When Paul says: "In Christ there is neither male or female" that is precisely the way things ought to be. The Christian church is gradually regaining that voice "in Christ". It is only in Christ that slave and master can worship together. It is only in Christ that people of all racial backgrounds can and should discover their common identity.

What does it mean to wander from the truth? The implication here is that someone who has known the truth and been part of the community of faith decides to take a hike and slowly drift away from the tenants of the faith. As long as there are distortions of the message of the gospel out there, there will be people who will be led astray. And so long as the devil prowls around like a roaring lion, there would be some who will wander away from the faith.

James accepts the inevitable that there will be backsliders in the community of faith. He wanted the community to find ways of handling such situations when they arise. Many Christians who have fallen prey to sin have been pushed away into the deep end by the unchristian attitudes of the community.

Some do conveniently forget that it is the grace of the Lord Jesus Christ that keeps all of us in the faith. Mercy and love will always triumph over judgment.

The love that will not let us go our own ways is still drawing us.

April Day 2

[20] *remember this: Whoever turns a sinner from the error of their way will save them from death and cover over a multitude of sins. James 5:20*

Rescue the perishing and care for the dying. Part of the mission of the Christian church is to care for those who have sinned. There will always be sinners in the body of Christ because we are all saved sinners. The work of the Holy Spirit in the Christian is to sanctify and present them blameless before the throne of grace.

The fact that the Holy Spirit works in the life of the believer and through the Christian to bring about sanctification cannot be disputed. For after all, it is God who is at work in us to bring about praise and glory to God's name. James picks on this theme by involving the Christian in the process. Christians for most part are not passive by-standers in what God is doing. We are challenged not only to be evangelists and witnesses to the good news, but also to allow ourselves to be used by God in rescuing the perishing in our midst.

How do you know that you have been called by God to help the brother or sister who has fallen into sin? This is a task to be taken with great humility with the full understanding that for the grace of God we could be in worse situations. There is a verse that allows me to keep things in perspective for me when it comes to sin. "Simon, Simon, Satan demanded to sift you like wheat but I have prayed for." I thank God for the prayers of my Lord and that of the saints. I know that our fight is not against flesh and blood. With that in mind, let us be in the task of restoring sinners to the kingdom with all the gentleness that God supplies.

Oh! Yes, there are a multitude of sins to be covered as we enter into the mission of restoration to the fold.

April Day 3

[1] The proverbs of Solomon son of David, king of Israel: [2] for attaining wisdom and discipline; for understanding words of insight for acquiring a disciplined and prudent life, doing what is right and just and fair; Proverbs: 1-3

The book of Proverbs is part of the wisdom literature (Writings) in the Hebrew Bible. Other books classified with it are: Psalms, Job, and Ecclesiastes. In the book of Proverbs, we find wise sayings that relate to human behavior, relationships and the natural order. The goal of this body of work is to develop a proper set of values and to drive home truth that would turn sinners from their wicked ways. The Book is generally attributed to King Solomon but internal evidence suggests that several wise folks could have made contributions.

The prologue does summarize the purpose or the book. Wisdom and discipline are listed as virtues to be attained in reading this book. Wisdom is presented to the reader in different ways. It is a way for understanding words of insight. The suggestion is that it is possible for people to ignore words of insight because they have not been trained or prepared to recognize and understand what is right in front of their noses.

A disciplined life is not something that just happens by accident. People need to acquire the wisdom that is from above or imparted to those who are open to it so that they may do what is right, just and fair. We can enter into a long debate and discourse concerning what is right, just and fair. This is because we live in a society that has reduced everything to relative terms. In other words, there are no absolutes and there are no standards. Those who are inclined to hold this view would find the book of Proverbs to be something that does not agree with that way of thinking.

The suggestion in the first three verses is that the author wanted to impart some guidelines to those who are open to acquiring a prudent and disciplined life. It will benefit all of us to listen to these wise sayings from of old and ask ourselves: "What is God saying to us through these words of wisdom?"

April Day 4

The proverbs of Solomon son of David, king of Israel:

⁴ for giving prudence to the simple, knowledge and discretion to the young ⁵ let the wise listen and add to their learning, and let the discerning get guidance ⁶ for understanding proverbs and parables, the sayings and riddles of the wise. Proverbs 1:4-6

We continue with the prologue of the book of Proverbs and what Solomon, son of king David, intended them for. It was intended to give prudence to the simple. Those who believe that they know enough already may find that the words of wisdom in this book are not for them. It is targeted at the simple or at least those who recognize their need for instruction. Prudence means good judgment. There are many situations in life when we will all do well to exercise good sense. How often have we said to ourselves: "What made me do that or say that?" We can all use some good judgment in the choices we make in life.

The young and old alike could do with some knowledge and discretion. It is sad to observe how discretion and caution have been thrown out of the window in the way we carry out human discourse. Unfortunately, it seems the desire to shock one another in our language and actions has come to stay and people are try to outdo one another in how much they can shock society.

It is true that whatever state in life we find ourselves we can never rule out the need to add more wisdom to life.

April Day 5

⁷ The fear of the LORD is the beginning of knowledge, but fools despise wisdom and discipline. Proverbs 1:7

What does it mean to fear the Lord? In our contemporary society fear has a negative connotation that does not attract people. We shun and stay away from things that we fear because they do not appeal to us. The writer of Proverbs had a different idea when he spoke of the "fear of the Lord". This notion became the theme of the whole book to which the author returned to now and again.

The author had in mind the loving reverence of God that included submission to the Lordship of Jesus Christ. It is the type of fear that is born out of respect and love. When people come to understand who God is and what God has done for them they are moved to ask: "what have I done to deserve all this? We stand in awe of this God who will go all lengths to secure our pardon and our salvation.

More so, when we come to appreciate who God is and that there was no obligation on the part of God to extend so much kindness to us. When the creator of the whole universe takes an interest in a creature like you and I, we are bound to respond with reverence. That is truly the beginning of Knowledge.

The author wants us to understand that it is that attitude of seeing ourselves in the bigger picture of God that will open doors for us into the corridors of knowledge. It takes humility for any one of us to admit that we are not the center of what God is doing but God has nonetheless focused enough attention on us for us to respond in awe.

On the other hand, those who despise the revelation of God find themselves fighting a losing battle all the time. It is possible to live in such a way as to exclude God in daily deliberations. But only time will reveal that a life outside the realm of God is a life without discipline and wisdom.

Why would anyone despise the wisdom of God to his or her peril? Only those who are shortsighted would embark on such a reckless adventure.

April Day 6

[8] Listen, my son, to your father's instruction and do not forsake your mother's teaching. [9] They will be a garland to grace your head and a chain to adorn your neck. Proverbs: 1:8-9

The role of Godly parents is emphasized in these verses. Fathers and mothers have been instrumental in guiding and teaching the next generation about what life is all about. It is true that people cannot impart a light that they do not have. The expectation here is that parents who have come to understand the fear of the Lord would be able to impart the same to future generations.

We cannot therefore point the blame of what is happening around us to others without admitting that we partly share in the situations we see around us. The children are supposed to listen to the instructions of parents. But at the same time the parents must accept the responsibility of imparting the teachings and instructions that would mold the next generation.

The author described the instruction and teaching of mothers and fathers as something that in the long run would be a garland of grace around head and a necklace around the neck. The implication is that Godly teaching is what is going to turn these young people into victors. The victors garland is not something that comes by accident. The garland takes a lot of proper discipline and paying attention to a lifelong of instructions.

A garland of grace is a reminder that God is at work in any instruction and teaching that parents do. God is able to turn the humble efforts of parents into something that is far beyond any expectation.

April Day 7

[10] My son, if sinners entice you, do not give in to them. [11] If they say, "Come along with us; let's lie in wait for someone's blood, let's waylay some harmless soul; [12] let's swallow them alive, like the grave, and whole, like those who go down to the pit; [13] we will get all sorts of valuable things and fill our houses with plunder; [14] throw in your lot with us, and we will share a common purse"- Proverbs 1:10-14

The instructions of a God fearing parent to a child are the pillars of a disciplined life. In this instance, the lesson is on enticement by others. So many people have fallen prey to the enticements by sinners and friends. These individuals prey on the inability of people to say no! The invitation to join the crowd is as simple and innocent as "come along with us". Most of the time, those invited are sucked in by peer pressure and the desire to conform. By the time they become aware of the real scheme they have been invited to be a part of, it is too late.

The plot is to destroy an innocent person for no good reason. Sometimes what is promised is just fun or some worldly gain that amount to nothing. The invitation to throw in our lot with sinners who do not share our values is being sent out to those who will not listen to instructions from God-fearing parents.

Valuable things to fill our houses should not be the motivating factor. Neither should it be to share a common purse with those who are bent on destroying others. There is only a thin line between paying attention to what we know to be right because of the instruction we have received and going along with the crowd. What would it be in our particular circumstance today?

April Day 8

¹⁵ my son, do not go along with them, do not set foot on their paths; ¹⁶ for their feet rush into sin, they are swift to shed blood. ¹⁷ How useless to spread a net in full view of all the birds! ¹⁸ These men lie in wait for their own blood; they waylay only themselves! ¹⁹ Such is the end of all who go after ill-gotten gain; it takes away the lives of those who get it. Proverbs 1: 15-19

"Do not go along with them". This is the type of advice we will do well to heed at all times when we understand that the "them" in this case refers to sinners who are bent on destroying others. Such people are always looking for those who would join them in their plots against unsuspecting individuals. We are told not to set foot on their paths for a good reason.

It is not that easy to stay away from people we love but know that they are always plotting evil for gain or just for the fun of it. When we become aware of the schemes that are being plotted, we have no other option but to stay far away from such individuals. The temptation has been that Christians feel that they are strong enough to overcome being drawn into such evil plots. But sooner or later these Christians find out that they are caught in a web they cannot escape. It is safer and better not to start down that slippery road.

The end result of going along with evildoers is self-destruction and making a shipwreck of our faith. The word for today is to stay away from all appearances of evil before we get too deeply entangled in the sin that accompanies such endeavors. We will not be at peace with ourselves when we know that what we have is ill-gotten gain.

April Day 9

[20] *Wisdom calls aloud in the street, she raises her voice in the public squares;* [21] *at the head of the noisy streets she cries out, in the gateways of the city she makes her speech:* [22] *"How long will you simple ones love your simple ways? How long will mockers delight in mockery and fools hate knowledge?* [23] *If you had responded to my rebuke, I would have poured out my heart to you and made my thoughts known to you.* [24] *But since you rejected me when I called and no one gave heed when I stretched out my hand,* Proverbs 1: 20-24

"Wisdom calls aloud in the street". Why is no one paying attention? Is it because people have tuned out the words they hear? Or they have simply refused to listen? The point being made here is that we find ourselves in our current predicament not because of a shortage of wisdom. It is also not because of a lack of communication. Everything possible is being done to make sure that God's wisdom is put out there for people.

The author laments a situation that is often too real. There is nothing so heart ranching as to watch a young person on a path to destruction and yet they would not heed any words of wisdom or advice because they think they know it all. It seems such individuals just hate knowledge. They would rather pursue the path they have chosen and suffer the consequences than listen to the instructions of God.

The rejection of rebuke is often associated with rejection of wisdom. It is not easy for any one of us to admit that we are wrong. But sometimes that is exactly what is needed to enable us to turn and go in a different direction. Rebuke can be a way of calling us back to the right path.

God has been waiting for us to turn around and accept God's rebuke so that we can receive the abundant blessing that has been promised. The outstretched hand of God is waiting to pour into us something that we cannot get any other way. But it starts with a turning around and paying attention to God's rebuke.

Receive all that God has for you!

April Day 10

^{25} since you ignored all my advice and would not accept my rebuke, ^{26} I in turn will laugh at your disaster; I will mock when calamity overtakes you- ^{27} when calamity overtakes you like a storm, when disaster sweeps over you like a whirlwind, when distress and trouble overwhelm you. ^{28} "Then they will call to me but I will not answer; they will look for me but will not find me. Proverbs 1:25-28

When Proverbs speak of the simple it is referring to people without a moral compass. Those who have chosen to ignore the advice and instructions of God to their own peril. It is a choice that people make sometimes knowing the consequences fully well, but at times counting on chance to settle scores for them.

The author paints a picture of people having made their beds and being asked to lie in it. The calamity that they were warned of would certainly overtake those who ignore the advice and rebuke of the Lord. When things become unbearable then people would call on the Lord and realize that things have gone too far to be salvaged.

How terrible it would be for one to keep calling on the Lord and receive no answer. It would seem as if God is silent to our plight. During those moments the tendency is to blame the Lord for being so distant. I cannot even wrap my mind around what it would feel like when the realization dawns that the period of grace is over.

It is better to call upon the Lord now that God may be found. As we hear the voice of God beckoning us to heed that gentle knock, there is no need to postpone our response.

Lord be merciful to me a sinner, and I confess all the ways that I have not listened to your instructions. Thank you for the gift of Jesus Christ who died for my sin. I receive you as my Lord and savior today.

April Day 11

²⁹ Since they hated knowledge and did not choose to fear the LORD, ³⁰ since they would not accept my advice and spurned my rebuke, ³¹ they will eat the fruit of their ways and be filled with the fruit of their schemes. ³² For the waywardness of the simple will kill them, and the complacency of fools will destroy them; ³³ but whoever listens to me will live in safety and be at ease, without fear of harm." Proverbs: 1:29-33

Those who lack a moral compass because they did not choose the fear of the Lord are bound to make decisions that reflect their choice. As the saying goes: "The apple does not fall too far from the tree." The grace of God is extended to all people but the truth is that not all people would accept the free gift that is given. People would rather scheme their way into disasters rather than accept the offer of God because they have convinced themselves that there is no God.

"For the waywardness of the simple will kill them". As indicated earlier, the word simple is used here to refer to those who lack a moral compass by choice. Living a life without God is like attempting to fix or operate a machine without the maker's instructions. That is a recipe for disaster. On some days it may seem that we are making progress but eventually reality will catch up to us.

The author reminds us the patient and longsuffering God does not give up on any one of us. Whoever listens to God and turns to God finds that the opportunity to live in peace and live without fear is always there for those who would turn to God.

In the midst of all the talk about disaster and destruction we hear the offer of grace loud and clear.

APRIL DAY 12

¹ My son, if you accept my words and store up my commands within you, ² turning your ear to wisdom and applying your heart to understanding, ³ and if you call out for insight and cry aloud for understanding, ⁴ and if you look for it as for silver and search for it as for hidden treasure, ⁵ then you will understand the fear of the LORD and find the knowledge of God. Proverbs 2:1-5

It is one thing hearing the words of God and accepting them. In one case we hear the words as audible sounds that could be understood and nothing more than that. On the other hand, the words of the Lord could be accepted and stored up in the heart as guidelines for living.

The author is suggesting a living approach to the instructions of the Lord. When the hearers allow the commands and words of the Lord to come alive to a degree that they could be applied to daily living. The daily turning to the word of the Lord for instruction and guidance is what shapes an individual into the type of person that has a heart of understanding.

This posture of living does not come easily. It comes to believers who are not satisfied with the ordinary Christian life. They decide to search for the silver and the treasure of their walk with God. It may take some calling out for insight and crying out for understanding. That means it takes some prayer and some discipline. But it will come to those who search patiently.

If it were that easy everyone would be boasting of the treasure of a disciplined life in the Lord. What I find interesting is that, it has been God's will all along to give the fear and knowledge of the Lord to all who seek. "You will find me when you seek me with all your heart." Just open yourself to what God is seeking to pour into your heart today.

Seek ye first the kingdom of God and God's righteousness. And all these things will be added to you.

April Day 13

⁹ Then you will understand what is right and just and fair—every good path. ¹⁰ For wisdom will enter your heart, and knowledge will be pleasant to your soul. ¹¹ Discretion will protect you, and understanding will guard you. Proverbs 2:9-11

There is a by-product to wisdom that comes as a gift of the Lord. It is the ability to live in awe of what God has done and what God is doing. The steadfast love of the Lord is all around us but unfortunately, we are not able to take it in until something has been established in the deep recess of our beings. It is that awesome revelation of God's love that prompts us to see everything with a brand new set of eyes. That is the gift of wisdom.

The author of proverbs says that: "Then you will understand what is right and just and fair". Just pause and think about that for a minute. People spent years pondering over those ultimate questions in life. What is right? What is just? And what is fair? We are told that when we pay attention and allow wisdom from above to engulf our way of thinking and action then we will understand what is right, just, and fair.

In other words, those who forsake the wisdom of God find themselves struggling to understand what is right and just and fair. To put it another way they will be asking the questions "Who is my neighbor?" and "What does the Lord require of me? These are no longer questions to be asked but they become a way of living and a path made for us to walk in. How so? It is because the wisdom of God has come to reside in the heart of the individual.

"For wisdom will enter your heart, and knowledge will be pleasant to your soul. ¹¹ Discretion will protect you, and understanding will guard you". That is all that we need to hear. For wisdom will enter our hearts and the rest would be us co-operating with the Lord who has come to take residence.

April Day 14

[12] Wisdom will save you from the ways of wicked men, from men whose words are perverse, [13] who leave the straight paths to walk in dark ways, [14] who delight in doing wrong and rejoice in the perverseness of evil, [15] whose paths are crooked and who are devious in their ways." Proverbs: 2:12-15

We live in societies that are filled with people who are bent on doing evil. Sometimes when one reads of some of the atrocities that are being committed, one wonders how perverse the human heart could be. At the same time, we have to mention that there are several people whose hearts have been filled with the wisdom of God and have assimilated what God has been doing in their lives.

The Holy Spirit of God is still at work in our world leading people in the way of wisdom. There is always good news in the midst of the negativity that surrounds us. Unfortunately, people are eager to spread and broadcast the bad news than they are to accentuate the positive work that God is doing.

"Wisdom will save you from the ways of wicked people". The reason why God sent wisdom into our world was to save us from ourselves and the evil that we love peddle. Evil will not win at the end of the day. Those are the words in the book of Revelation that the enemy prevents many Christians from reading. All the perverse plans and words around us will be swallowed up by God's wisdom.

The plan of God is to level the hills and valleys so that all the crooked ways that lead people astray will be over ruled by the wisdom that has come to abide in the people of God. It is an awesome responsibility to be a recipient of God's wisdom. We are called to declare the way of God that rejoices in the right. We are ambassadors to God's new way of living and acting. Thanks to God who reminds us that we are unable to live out our calling without God's wisdom.

All things are possible to them that believe!

April Day 15

[16] It will save you also from the adulteress, from the wayward wife with her seductive words, [17] who has left the partner of her youth and ignored the covenant she made before God. [18] For her house leads down to death and her paths to the spirits of the dead. [19] None who go to her return or attain the paths of life. Proverbs 2:16-19

Wisdom will save you from the adulteress. How does that happen? Wisdom from above allows an individual to discern the will of God concerning every situation that confronts us. One needs help to listen to seductive words and be able to put them in their proper context.

Anyone who buys into the idea that someone who is unfaithful to their partner would be faithful to them is deceiving himself or herself. Unfortunately, deceptive and seductive words have been used to sway people into making decisions that they have regretted later. The example given is one who had left a partner of her youth. They have also ignored the covenant she made with God. The author of Proverbs is saying that wisdom will save us from falling into the trap of someone who has spurned the covenant of God.

For one reason or the other Christians are being swayed by the standards of the world. The instructions and wisdom provided by God are being pushed aside because of the seductive powers of people who do not have the same compass in life. When the people of God compromise their standards then they are on a slippery road to destruction.

There is a way that leads to life. It is a way that is under girded by wisdom from above.

April Day 16

[20] *Thus you will walk in the ways of good men and keep to the paths of the righteous. Proverbs 2:20*

This is a promise for all those who decide to accept the wisdom that the Lord gives. These folks seek after wisdom, desire it and make it their own. In so doing they stumble on a treasure that people have longed for all their lives. Some have tried so hard and have waited so long for this wisdom that comes as a gift of God.

Those who embrace wisdom are destined to walk in the ways of good men. What did the author mean by this? God has prepared a way for all those who have a relationship with God. They embark on a lifelong spiritual journey with God. They are not alone on this journey. Others have gone ahead of them and have left their marks on the trail. There will be others behind them and one thing is common with all of them. They walk on the way of "good men and women".

These people also keep to the paths of the righteous. It means right relationship with God and with neighbor. This is something that should not be taken lightly. For it is by grace that we are made righteous or are able to keep to the path of the righteous. Thank God for Christ who has become our righteousness. Thank God for the Holy Spirit who keeps us on the paths of the righteous. In our own selves we have no righteousness but in Christ all of us have been placed in God's family.

April Day 17

²¹ For the upright will live in the land, and the blameless will remain in it; ²² but the wicked will be cut off from the land, and the unfaithful will be torn from it. Proverbs 2: 21-22

"For the upright will live in the land." The vision of Gods' kingdom is one in which people are at peace with one another, the animals are also at peace with humanity and with the environment. It is the perfect society that is out of this world. The realization of God's perfect plan for all humanity is something in the future. Each time Christians pray: "Your kingdom come on earth as it is in heaven", they are hoping for God's will to be done to hasten the coming kingdom.

There cannot be a perfect plan of God without people who have been transformed by God to fit that environment. Since the fall of humanity, God has been at work redeeming and transforming people for God's earth. The intention of God is to bring into harmony all creation so that the lion and the lamb could lie together and not harm each other under one roof.

First of all, humans have to learn to live with each other in peace for the kingdom of God to be realized on earth. The lions in our midst have to be transformed to live with the lambs and the wolves. None of us can claim to be blameless in that matter. It is precisely for that reason that Jesus Christ came to earth. He came to turn sinners into blameless people who eventually could live in God's earth. What a thought! People who do not have the qualities for living in God's kingdom have been given the right to be called the children of God.

Those who are unfaithful and wicked would realize that they have excluded themselves from God's kingdom by choice. Refusing to accept the wisdom of God will put people outside God's kingdom for no good reason. Why will anyone make that choice?

Receive all that God has for you by making the right choice!

April Day 18

[1] My son, do not forget my teaching, but keep my commands in your heart, Proverbs 3:1

The advice of a parent to a child could be likened to what God has been trying to communicate to us all along. It is proper for God to address us as children. The relationship between parents and children are special when the feeling is mutual. All those who have put their trust and faith in God have been given the right to be called children of God. So it is in order to be addressed as sons and daughters of God. Indeed, it is a joy and privilege to be considered God's children.

The title "child of God" does not come cheaply. It comes with a responsibility. This is something that is shared in all families. To really avail oneself of the sense of belonging, one would have to ask: "what is expected of me in this family?" The same is true for those who belong to the family of God. There is something that identifies all those who belong to God's family.

It is loyalty to the one who called us. Our names are inextricably tied to the one who called us and set our feet upon a rock. We were given a new family name and everything we do has a bearing on that name. It is for that reason that we are told: "Do not forget my teachings." The teachings that brought us to the faith and marked us as the people of God are to be central to whatever we do.

"But keep my commands in your heart". What is being said here appears to be basic and unnecessary? But history has shown that we are a people of short memory. We are prone to wander away from what we have learned from the Lord. Thus a reminder here and then is in order for all of us.

April Day 19

² for they will prolong your life many years and bring you prosperity. Proverbs: 3:2

We are talking about the commands and the instructions of the Lord in this context. Sometimes God is made out to be a "joy killer" who is only interested in making his followers miserable. Those who believe this understanding of God walk around with long faces to prove their piety. Little do people know that all along God has been planning to bring the joy of the Lord to all those who believe. In-fact it is the joy of the Lord that becomes our strength.

How often do we hear the exultation "rejoice in the Lord always!" and just gloss over it and move to the task to be done? What we forget is that, rejoicing in the Lord is also a witness for the Lord. The commands of the Lord are designed for the welfare of those who place their trust in the Lord. "I know the plans I have for you, plans for good and not for evil; to give you a future and a hope". When we keep that in mind we realize that God has more for us than we can see at any particular time.

The God who has promised good to us has plans to prolong the life of everyone who walks by faith. After all, eternal life has been promised to those who believe in the Lord Jesus Christ. Is there any other prolongation of years that could be compared with life everlasting? Certainly not! We have a reason to depend on the commands of God even when we do not see the immediate outcome.

We are informed that "prosperity" will come our way as we keep the instructions of the Lord in our hearts. When God says prosperity, we have to understand it not only in one dimension. God's prosperity is all encompassing. It is both now and the future. Any attempt to limit or expand it in one sphere is dangerous. God promises prosperity that includes a good name and honor. When God prospers us we will know that we have been blessed. Just like everything, it is going to be by the grace of God.

I am standing on the promises of God.

April Day 20

³ Let love and faithfulness never leave you; bind them around your neck, write them on the tablet of your heart. Proverbs 3:3

Why would anyone allow love and faithfulness to leave them? That could happen when the two virtues are superficial. Love that is genuine has its roots in God who is love. We are able to love to the degree that we have experienced love. The Bible puts it this way: "We love because God first loved us." Those who have tasted the unconditional love of God are able to understand that they have no obligation but to love.

How can one separate love and faithfulness? It cannot be done where that love is genuine. God loves the world so much that God is faithful to the promises given to all of us. To be faithful is to be a promise keeper and to do all that is in one's power to be true to those one loves. These are not just words to be spoken or exchanged. They have to be translated into action and deeds.

The writer of Proverbs says: "bind love and faithfulness around your neck. And write them on the tablet of your heart". The message is that they have to be a part of us so that they become obvious wherever we find ourselves. The writer is suggesting that there has to be outward as well as inward evidence of love and faithfulness. Whatever is written on the heart cannot be erased. It is a permanent branding of the individual.

Oh! that our hearts would be stamped with love and faithfulness!

April Day 21

[4] Then you will win favor and a good name, in the sight of God and man. Proverbs 3:4

When love and faithfulness become vital ingredients of a person's life something happens. They become transformed. The change that started in the heart gradually and steadily permeates all the dealings of this individual. The originator of the process is God who is the source of love. In God we find the depository of the width, length, depth and height of love. This is the love that surpasses knowledge.

Those who embrace this love find that they are on the same wavelength with God. Others begin to notice that there is something special happening in these people. Winning the favor that is associated with a good name does not come easily. It takes time and discipline to cultivate. But more importantly, it takes grace from God.

Some have tried to pay money for a good name and others would give anything to win favor with God. But we learn that these virtues are gifts from God. They are associated with love and faithfulness. It is more important to win favor with God than with people. But what is interesting is that those who win favor with God find that their neighbors and sometimes their enemies are at peace with them.

Let us get our priorities right and win favor with God through love and faithfulness.

April Day 22

⁵ Trust in the LORD with all your heart and lean not on your own understanding;
Proverbs 3:5

There are going to be situations and experiences that will shake your trust in the Lord. Some of these would come as observations that you make relating to what is happening to others in the world. Take for example the natural disaster that shook Haiti not too long ago. Some of the pictures may still be ingrained on your mind as it is on mine. Several of us asked the question: "Why Lord? How much can one nation take? Where were you Lord?"

There were no answers for our questions. All that we could hear back was "Trust the Lord with all your heart". Probably you have found yourself in a similar spot because of a personal tragedy or that of loved one. Things happened that did not make sense and you wondered: "Where was God in all that?" Yes, we may not have the answers presently, but we believe that we would understand them by and by.

The temptation is to lean on human understanding when the going gets tough. Some of us may be tempted to follow the suggestion of Job's wife: "Curse God and die!" But we know better to trust God with all our hearts. The one who will do everything for our salvation will come through for us in those critical moments.

Leaning on our understanding might mean going with popular culture instead of trusting the Lord. These days, there are people ready to tell you what to do without your asking. They operate from a different world-view. It is not based on what Christ would do. That is why it is important to trust in the Lord fully and not partially. This half–hearted approach to faith does not bring eternal results.

"The arm of flesh will fail you and you dare not trust your own"

Trust in the Lord!

April Day 23

⁶ in all your ways acknowledge him, and he will make your paths straight. Proverbs 3:6

One of the temptations that Christians encounter in life is to depart from the Lord under some circumstances. The advice I have given to people young and old alike is that they should make every effort to identify themselves as Christians in any new environment that they find themselves. This is so important when people move from one community to another. The same applies when people change jobs. Of course this should be done in a humble way without calling unnecessary attention to oneself.

Christians would save themselves from unnecessary headaches and pain when "they come out of the closet" and acknowledge that they belong to God and to Jesus. First and foremost, the Christian is aware that their witness for their Lord is at stake and therefore they have to stand up for the right. Secondly, the people around them may either tease them or apologize when they make unwholesome comments around them. They are aware of what these Christians stand for.

"Acknowledging the Lord in all your ways": that is another way of saying that one should live by the principles of God in every situation. It is very easy to abandon what we know the Lord would want us to do and follow a different path because that is what every-one is following. When it comes to spiritual things it is not the "majority rules" principle. The Lord has the final say.

After all, it is the Lord who has the ability to straighten our paths. When we decide to stick with the Lord who holds the future, we can rest assured that God would level the crooked paths. It is a promise that can be trusted because many who have gone ahead of us have found that the steadfast love of the Lord would never change.

Just acknowledge the Lord in everything!

April Day 24

[7] Do not be wise in your own eyes; fear the LORD and shun evil. Proverbs: 3:7

What does it mean to be wise in your own eyes? The issue here is the standard that is being used to determine wisdom. When we start creating our own standards for what is wrong and what is right, it does not take long for anarchy to take hold. At that point everything becomes subjective and we can find ways to justify every action or inaction.

When we admit that our knowledge is limited and our vision is also limited, we open ourselves for someone who is higher than us. We turn to the Lord for wisdom and direction knowing that we will be instructed to do the right thing.

That is what fearing the Lord is all about. To fear the Lord is to accept that we do not have the last word on everything. More importantly, we are accountable to the Lord. When people know that they are accountable to God, they are careful about the decisions that they make and what they get involved in. Those who have the impression that they are accountable to no one, live in a manner that reflect their way of thinking.

To be able to shun evil, one has to know what evil is all about. Evil is doing what displeases the Lord. To know that, one has to have a reference point that is Jesus Christ and God.

In all your ways acknowledge God!

April Day 25

⁸ This will bring health to your body and nourishment to your bones. Proverbs 3:8

"Oh, what needless pain we bear because we do not carry everything to God in prayer." There are many instructions given in scripture that are directed at the well-being of those who trust in the Lord. These instructions relate to our physical and spiritual well-being. It is common to observe people allowing resentment and anger to eat at them to the point that they are unable to enjoy a good night sleep. The sad part is this, the person we may be angry with is enjoying their sleep and we are suffering unnecessarily for something that could be avoided.

The other one is being anxious about so many things. "What if this happens?" Those who suffer from this dilemma are trying to keep tight controls over everything. They are unable to turn things over to God. In so doing they find out that there are many uncertainties that are beyond their control. The result is high blood pressure and unnecessary worrying.

The word is: "Do not be anxious about anything, but in everything by prayer and supplication let your requests be known to God." Another way of saying this is, trust the Lord at all times and do not be wise in your own eyes. This will bring health to your bodies. And the word of the Lord will nourish your soul and bones.

God is the source of all true nourishment. I pray that we would trust the Lord to provide the nourishment that is eternal.

April Day 26

⁹ Honor the LORD with your wealth, with the first fruits of all your crops; ¹⁰ then your barns will be filled to overflowing, and your vats will brim over with new wine. Proverbs 3:9-10

How does one honor the Lord with wealth? After all, God does not need anything from mortals. To honor the Lord with our wealth is to declare that all human achievement is a gift from God. Just the mere fact that one is willing to admit that any gain or wealth they have is not because of their intellect or special abilities but rather it is a gift of grace, is the key.

But the honoring does not end with accepting that God is the source of any blessing that we have received. Rather, it goes a step further in using that wealth in advancing the work of Christ or God. In an agricultural culture, it is common for Christians to use the first fruits or the best of their crops as an offering to God.

The idea of tithing or sacrificial giving is something that honors God. Several people have found ways of circumventing the principle of tithing with wise arguments. Even some would say everything that they have belongs to God but when it comes down to where the rubber hits the road they are not able to honor God with a tithe.

There is a big difference between knowing what to be done and honoring God with our wealth. One does not have to be wealthy to give sacrificially. One only has to understand the principle to reap the benefits that come out honoring God with your wealth. *"Then your barns will be filled to overflowing, and your vats will brim over with new wine"*. Several people have proved God to be faithful to God's word in this regard.

Honor God with your substance and see what happens!

April Day 27

¹³ Blessed is the one who finds wisdom, the one who gains understanding. Proverbs 3:13

Wisdom is personified in the following verses. The attributes given to Wisdom leave no doubt as to who is being talked about. Wisdom is placed above everything in the world and it is safer to assume that we are talking about God and about Jesus Christ.

The person who finds wisdom is called blessed. We know that all those who find God are blessed. To be blessed is to receive favor. When we do what pleases the Lord we open ourselves to all the favors of God. The question that is often asked is do we find Wisdom or does Wisdom find us?

The truth is that Wisdom has been searching for us all along. Wisdom has never been lost we are the ones who have strayed and gone our own ways. The love that will not let us go has been extended to humanity down the ages. The question has always been when will people turn and find the outstretched arm of the Lord waiting for them.

So when one finds Wisdom, they are responding to a loving God who has made herself available to all those who seek. It is true that those who seek the Lord are not disappointed in what they find. We come to understand the unfolding drama of salvation history revealed in Jesus Christ who is our wisdom and righteousness.

God is waiting for us, let us turn and be blessed in what we find.

April Day 28

¹⁴ for she is more profitable than silver and yields better returns than gold ¹⁵ She is more precious than rubies; nothing you desire can compare with her. Proverbs: 3:14-15

In the midst of economic crisis, people do not have confidence in the currencies of the world. Investors turn to precious metals as safe havens for investment. There are those who believe that the best place to invest at all times is in the gold and silver markets. The people of God on the other hand have adopted a different strategy and approach to investments that are not temporary.

Wisdom has been suggested as the safest commodity for one to fully and totally place their investment in. The experience has been that people could let you down. Sometimes churches and preachers have let many believers down. But those who have placed their trust in God the source of wisdom have found that there are benefits for now and the future. The words of the Lord are: "I will never leave you nor forsake you".

These are words that one can take to bank anytime, any day, anywhere and cash it in. That is what the author of Proverbs meant when he said: "For she is more profitable than silver and yields better returns than gold".

I know that the gold market seems to going through the roof at the moment but the word of God still stands supreme. Those who find Wisdom have a better investment that these precious metals. The author throws in rubies to sweeten the pot and that does not to change the conclusion.

When one finds Wisdom, they have found the purpose for which God created humanity. The deep longing in the hearts of all of us can only be filled with that peace that passes understanding. That is Wisdom indeed.

Nothing that the human heart desires could be compared with what God offers for now and eternity.

April Day 29

[16] *Long life is in her right hand; in her left hand are riches and honor. Proverbs 3:16*

The benefits promised to those who find wisdom are complete. They fill both the right hand and the left hand. That is another way of saying that one would have more than enough. All that one could desire would be supplied when one finds this Wisdom.

The preoccupation with long life was not something reserved to those of old. We find the same dilemma today as people search for anti-aging medications. Others would go as far as paying to preserve their dead bodies just in case a remedy was found to resuscitate dead bodies. The author says all that is unnecessary because in the right hand of Wisdom one finds long life. Oh, yes! It is a life that goes beyond this earthly life into eternity. That is a promise worth paying attention to.

Just in case you are wondering what is in the left hand of Wisdom? One finds riches and honor. These are two commodities that do not come together without a price. Some of those who are rich often fail in their responsibility to justice issues. And because of that they do not attain the honor that they desire before God. Wisdom has a way of making people rich and honorable in the sight of God.

Wisdom provides the perspective that is needed for one to prioritize. In that way we are able to discern what is important in the overall scheme of things. Wisdom gives the ability to people to ask: "What does God want me to do at this time and this place with all the gifts that I have been given?"

April Day 30

*"When I am afraid,
I will trust in you."* Psalm 56:3

I have had many reasons to be afraid. I have had to make decisions on the spot that have affected others; I have been stranded at airports in the United States; I have been faced with the dilemma of providing for the needs of 54 orphans in Africa; our mission team was faced with the challenge of how to free one of our vans that was stuck in the mud. Time will not permit me to mention in detail the teeming crowds pressing forward for physical and spiritual healing. In all these circumstances, God was with our mission team helping us to overcome one obstacle after the other.

The Psalmist makes an interesting point when he says: "When I am afraid". He affirms the reality of fear in daily life. He also expects that there will be times when he will be afraid. The point that is emphasized is that fear should not cause us to move away from God or make us give up hope. Instead, fear should cause us to trust all the more in God.

There are going to be situations that will seek to rock the foundations of our faith. But the way forward is to trust in God. What determines our future is the solid relationship that we have with Jesus Christ. God has given us a way out in every situation and that is to trust God. Abraham did that and he was not disappointed. All the women and men of faith have found that to be true, and we are not to be the exception.

Join with me in trusting God for a wonderful day full of the presence of Christ.

The book of Proverbs is a store house for "compass for daily living". Several conditions of life are addressed to drive home the point that we should seek the wisdom that God gives. We will continue to look for our bearings in this book.

May Day 1

17 Her ways are pleasant ways, and all her paths are peace. Proverbs 3:17

Wisdom is personified in this passage and the feminine pronoun is used for Wisdom. It is important to point out that God is gender neutral although some of us have been brought up in the tradition of scripture that refers to God as masculine. It is also important to note that Jesus referred to God as "Father". Be that as it may be, the feminine gender is assigned to wisdom in Proverbs.

The ways of wisdom are definitely the ways of God and they are described as pleasant. There is another way that is broad and leads to wickedness. The psalmist calls that the counsel of the wicked. We are advised not to walk or sit in that way. The reason being that there is no peace in walking in ways that are contrary to our maker. The one who made us has the blue print for living. So it would be expected that the ways of God are preferable and commendable.

And all the paths of Wisdom are those of peace. In a world full of strife and acrimony, it is refreshing to hear and know that there are paths of peace available. We do hurt ourselves and other people when we try to depend on our understanding. There is another way available to humanity. It is the path of peace that God offers.

Oh what peace we often forfeit because we fail to take our cares and burdens to the Lord in prayer. There is a way out of our predicament today. It is turning it over to the Lord and saying: "Lord I need your help"

May Day 2

[18] *She is a tree of life to those who embrace her; those who lay hold of her will be blessed. Proverbs 3:18*

The psalmist talks about a tree that is planted by the water. This tree gets nourishment at the appropriate time and it is supplied with abundance of water. That tree will bear green leaves all the time and it would produce its fruit in season.

Trees like humans are made for a purpose. We are all at our best when we find the purpose for which God made us and live to fulfill that destiny. You and I were called by God to bear fruit and to bear fruit that would abide. This is not a temporary situation. There is eternity attached to this call. And that is what makes our call different from any other.

The life that God has for each one of us can be lived to the fullest to the extent that we embrace Wisdom. This life is found in Jesus Christ who is the Way, the Life and the Truth. Proverbs puts it slightly differently. "Wisdom is a tree of life to those who embrace her."

The key is finding Wisdom and embracing her. What a relief to know that wisdom has been seeking us all along. When we embrace Wisdom we find that the tree of life that has eluded many becomes a part of us. Jesus said: Abide in me and I in you for apart from me you can do nothing.

Indeed, those who embrace her are blessed!

May Day 3

[19] *By wisdom the LORD laid the earth's foundations, by understanding he set the heavens in place;* [20] *by his knowledge the deeps were divided, and the clouds let drop the dew. Proverbs 3:19-20*

In the prologue to the gospel of John we read these words: "Through him all things were made; without him nothing was made that has been made." We know that this passage was referring to Jesus Christ, the Word made flesh. And now we read in Proverbs that by wisdom the Lord laid the foundations of the earth. The implication is that Wisdom was there at creation.

It is comforting to know that our Lord was deeply involved in the creation of the universe and of humanity. There is nothing about us that the creator who divided the deeps cannot fix and make new. If by his knowledge dew is formed in the clouds, then I submit to you that the Lord understands every "tear drop" that is shed today.

He has the whole world in his hands. He has you and me in his hands and by Wisdom God is going to do something special with our lives today.

MAY DAY 4

²¹ My son, preserve sound judgment and discernment, do not let them out of your sight; ²² they will be life for you, an ornament to grace your neck. Proverbs: 3:21-22

Sound judgment and discernment come from God. In fact, they are gifts of the Holy Spirit. It is God who gives these gifts to those who call God Abba. So we are reminded that these gifts are to be preserved; in other words, they are to be put in use.

Unfortunately, Christians have tended to throw sound judgment out of the window and operated on what they thought was appropriate for the occasion. Whenever that has been the case we have discovered to our shame and sorrow that we were operated outside the will of God.

The fact that we are children of God does not mean that we will always employ sound judgment and discernment in our day-to-day dealings. We have to learn how to preserve these gifts and bring them to bear when needed. The writer says we should not put them out of sight. That is another way of saying that we are going to need these gifts daily. We should not be caught off guard without them.

These gifts of discernment are going to be lifelines as we enter situations that we may not know what to do. They are going to be at our disposal, as we have to respond to people who attack us for no apparent reason.

When you do not know what to do or say, remember that you have these ornaments of God around your neck. They are called sound judgment and discernment.

You will hear a voice saying "This is the way, walk in it."

May Day 5

²³ Then you will go on your way in safety, and your foot will not stumble; ²⁴ when you lie down, you will not be afraid; when you lie down, your sleep will be sweet.
Proverbs 3:23-24

The suggestion is that we should embrace Wisdom and put sound judgment and discernment around our necks like ornaments. When that is in place then we will go on our way in safety. The foundation that people build is the key to living a fulfilling life.

Jesus talked about building a house on the rock instead of the sand. Those who lay a firm foundation, find out later that they are able to live in safety. There is one thing that we can all be sure of and that is there will be storms in life that will threaten the foundations of our faith. Embracing Wisdom, sound judgment and discernment would ensure that our feet would not stumble and our anchors would hold during turbulent times.

Not only that, there is a promise: "When you lie down, you will not be afraid; when you lie down, your sleep will be sweet." The suggestion here is that one is able to cast all their cares on the Lord to the degree that they know God will take care of them. That is what it means to embrace wisdom.

God gives sleep to those who trust in Him. In all your ways acknowledge him and enjoy your sleep. Your God is able to carry you through this one too.

May Day 6

[25] *Have no fear of sudden disaster or of the ruin that overtakes the wicked,* [26] *for the LORD will be your confidence and will keep your foot from being snared.* Proverbs 3:25-26

"Have no fear of sudden disaster". There are some things that many people are scared that might happen to them. It is the fear of the unknown. These are things that happen without any warning. If you have lost a job or a source of income suddenly you might understand what I am talking about. It seems like the bottom has fallen out on you and you imagine that it is a dream that would soon pass away.

These sudden disasters come to the righteous and the wicked alike. We are all exposed to these events. The difference is that for the people of God, the promise is that the disasters would not ruin them. The same event that would crush a person without hope may be the stepping-stone to greater things for a person of faith. It is for that reason that we are told to have no fear.

The other reason not to have fear is the confidence we have in God. Those who know that God will make a way for them in every circumstance are those who are able to smile at the storm that is brewing all around them. I know that our God is a promise keeper and no matter what happens the one who lives in us is greater than who is outside. We may not know how but we are certain that God will make a way.

MAY DAY 7

^{27} Do not withhold good from those who deserve it, when it is in your power to act. ^{28} Do not say to your neighbor, "Come back later; I'll give it tomorrow" when you now have it with you. Proverbs 3:27-28

If there is any good we can do today, we might just as well be on to that task instead of procrastinating. The work of God sits undone because several of us have made a profession out of postponing what should be done today. There are those who are still waiting for a lightning from the sky to affirm what they know God has been calling them to do now.

Each day that we procrastinate what the Lord is telling us, we are in fact withholding good from several people who would be the recipients of God's blessing. How do you know that that single step of faith is what is going to lead somebody to accept the Lord Jesus? How do we know that somebody who is depressed and on the point of suicide would not benefit from your action?

It is for that reason that we walk and act by faith not knowing exactly what God is going to do with the random acts of kindness that we perform in the name of our Lord. I have been richly blessed by the words of encouragement from several of you who have taken the time to let me know how these few words that the Lord gives me each day blesses you.

"Do not say to your neighbor come back later when it is in your power to give it to them now." I pray that we would not hold back our love and kindness when we can extend them to someone today.

No good thing does the Lord withhold from those who love Him. We should do the same because God has shown us the way.

May Day 8

²⁹ Do not plot harm against your neighbor, who lives trustfully near you. ³⁰ Do not accuse a man for no reason— when he has done you no harm. Proverbs 3:29-30

The "golden rule" is to love the Lord your God with all your being and to love your neighbor as yourself. Our Lord Jesus Christ tells us that this simple rule sums up all the law and the prophets. That is the least we can all do to honor the fact that all are created in the image of God.

Plotting against a neighbor is an indication that something has gone wrong in the relationship. Most often the other person is not even aware of what is going on. Plotting harm against any person is an indication that things have gone a step further in the wrong direction. It would seem bad enough not to be on good terms with a neighbor, but to plot harm is an indication that bitterness, hardness of heart and vengeance have taken root. These should not even be mentioned among the people of God.

Unfortunately, things happen to cause these situations to arise when people find it necessary to plot and scheme. How many people have lost their jobs because of schemes and plots of others? And how many unsuspecting pastors have left their parishes because of slanders and unguarded words being spoken in secret by Christians.

The sad part of all this is the pretense that is used for a cover up for unchristian plotting behind the scenes. I know this does not happen in many Christian groups because it is the way of the world.

The word is "Do not plot against a neighbor". And do not accuse anyone when they have done you no harm.

MAY DAY 9

[31] Do not envy a violent man or choose any of his ways, [32] for the LORD detests a perverse man but takes the upright into his confidence. Proverbs: 3:31-32

What is there to envy about a violent man anyway? Unfortunately, we live in a world that has become so violent that we glamorize violence. You only have to turn on the television or watch a film and notice that what is called an action scene is all violent. Even those who have disciplined themselves not to get exposed to these gadgets quickly find out that we encounter them in everyday living and interactions.

The real issue addressed by the writer of Proverbs is this: How do the people of God view this tendency for violence around us? Who are the role models who influence our thinking and our living? Do we envy those who become powerful through the barrel of the gun? Probably we are being asked to contemplate another form of power.

It may be true that we have grown up in a society that only knows power and violence as might. But another way of approaching life is suggested by the life, teaching and death of Jesus Christ. It is a way of service and suffering for others. That is the way that we are challenged to emulate.

The reason given is this: "The Lord detests those who are perverse. On the other hand, the Lord takes into his confidence those who are upright." The real question is this: whom are we trying to please? We can either please the Lord or those seem to have power in this world.

May Day 10

³³ The Lord's curse is on the house of the wicked, but he blesses the home of the righteous. ³⁴ He mocks proud mockers but gives grace to the humble. ³⁵ The wise inherit honor, but fools he holds up to shame. Proverbs 3:33-35

The way of the wicked has been likened to chaff that the wind blows away. There is nothing permanent about it and it is destined to perish. To embrace wickedness is to incur the wrath of God. Why would anyone identify with a situation that results in the curse of God? Could it be that they have not been taught a better way? Or could it be that those who have been called to speak out boldly for Jesus have refused to bear witness?

The alternate way is placed before us. It is the way of the righteous. You and I know that we have no righteousness of our own. And all our righteous deeds are like filthy rags before the Lord. So when we speak of the home of the righteous we are talking about a situation that has been made possible only by the grace of God.

It is therefore not surprising that the writer of Proverbs would say that God gives grace to the humble. It takes humility to admit that we are sinners. How often do we fight that simple thought? We go to all lengths to explain to ourselves that we are not that bad. We will do everything to convince ourselves that there are worse people than us. But that is not the point; it takes humility to admit that we are sinners before God. And we stand in need of the grace of God to be righteous before God.

The fear of the Lord gives us that wisdom to say we are not our own and we have been loved by God. God seeks to honor our feeble steps of faith.

May Day 11

¹ Listen, my sons, to a father's instruction; pay attention and gain understanding. ² I give you sound learning, so do not forsake my teaching. Proverbs 4:1-2

Is a father's instruction worth anything these days? Well, I will leave that to your own observations. But what if the father is God? What if the father has attained the Wisdom that is talked about in the book of Proverbs? That certainly changes everything. We are now talking about instructions that have been informed by wisdom from above.

One has to pay attention to instructions that come from Abba. Those who are able to call God Abba have established a life transforming relationship with God. At the core of that relationship is paying attention to the instructions that come from God. That is the only way to gain understanding.

Listening to the instructions of God seems like an easy and simple thing to do. But in practice we find that obedience does not come easily. The human nature is disposed to rebellion and trying to go our own way. God's directions for living are often seen as attempts to curtail our freedom and steal our joy. On the contrary those who listen to the instructions of God find out that these instructions are meant for our own good.

Our "Heavenly Father" knows tomorrow from today and therefore the instructions of God do work out for our good in the final analysis. If we are sincerely looking for sound learning and doing what God expects, then we should not forsake the teaching of God.

MAY DAY 12

³ When I was a boy in my father's house, still tender, and an only child of my mother, ⁴ he taught me and said, "Lay hold of my words with all your heart; keep my commands and you will live. Proverbs 4:3-4

When we remember our youthful days, we are reminded of all the things that made impressions on our delicate minds. Some of those things never leave us and they become part and parcel of who we are. Sometimes we remember the environment with all the sounds and even the smells. It is for that reason that we are encouraged to teach the young ones the way of the Lord with the assurance that they will not depart from it when they grow old.

The writer of the Book Proverbs testifies how he was taught at a tender age to lay hold of the words of God. The command was stronger than what I have indicated. The author was instructed to lay hold of the words of God with all of the heart. This suggests a deliberate and active participation in the process.

The suggestion required more than getting to know or possess the instructions of God. The exhortation was to obey the commands. There are those who have "head knowledge" of the instructions of God. They can quote it backward and forward. Obedience to the instructions of God or a parent is the issue in these verses. Those who keep the commands of God find life in abundance.

May Day 13

⁵ Get wisdom, get understanding; do not forget my words or swerve from them. Proverbs 4:5

My father used to tell us that wisdom is common in the market place. But it is those who seek wisdom that find it. I do not know how far I can stretch this wise saying of my earthly dad. There is a sense that wisdom is all over the place because the true source of wisdom is God. Since it is the will of God to reveal the riches of God to all people, it will be fair to say that there is a universal availability of the wisdom of God. It is another way of saying that God is available to all who seek.

It is for that reason that the writer of Proverbs would say: "Get wisdom, get understanding; do not forget my words or swerve from them." We are not being asked to do the impossible. Wisdom and understanding are items within our reach. Those who come to believe that it is possible to reach out to God because God is so near are the ones who are surprised by joy. The word says: "you will find me if you seek me with all your heart."

So my brothers and sisters, it is possible to get the wisdom and understanding that comes from above. The exhortation is that those who find wisdom must do all that is in their power to stay on course. Swerving to the left or right would not benefit us in the long run. Some have sought to cut corners and found out that the only things they have to show for it are scars. Thank God for the everlasting love of God that brings us back to the straight and narrow.

MAY DAY 14

⁶ Do not forsake wisdom, and she will protect you; love her, and she will watch over you. Proverbs: 4:6

Why would anyone decide to forsake wisdom? Especially when they have come to understand the source of wisdom. We may take that thought a step further and say that especially so when we have come to identify Wisdom with God. It is true that for Christians, all wisdom is deposited in Jesus Christ according to the will of God. So we can read what the writer of Proverbs is saying in this verse and hear a clear and loud message that affirms the promises of Jesus Christ.

"Do not forsake wisdom, and she will protect you." God has promised that we will never be left alone or forsaken as the people of God. But we also have a part to play in not walking away from under the protection of God. God has never forced any one to serve Him. You and I would not be the first either. We can use our free will to walk away and become like the prodigal son. But even there, the God of compassion would be waiting every day hoping that we would return and embrace wisdom.

Love Wisdom and you will be protected and she will watch over you. God has done all that is necessary for humanity to live in peace. It begins with living under the shelter of God's love. Let us respond to that love of God that leads to finding Wisdom.

May Day 15

7 Wisdom is supreme; therefore, get wisdom. Though it cost all you have, get understanding. Proverbs 4:7

"Wisdom is supreme" That sounds like one of those sound bites that could be used in an advertisement or in a campaign. We all know that there is only one who is supreme although there is no short supply of imposters. It is not enough to claim supremacy it has to be demonstrated through action and deeds. The history of our world and the testimonies of those who have gone ahead of us do bear witness to the supremacy of God.

Humans are good at identifying precious commodities and then going after them. There is no point in spending all your energies searching for something precious only to turn around and leave it there. Our thirst and our desire for God should not culminate in a fruitless endeavor. Those who have been led by scripture, experience, tradition and reason to conclude that Wisdom is supreme, are encouraged to get wisdom.

It is one of those pearls that it is all right to sell everything that one has just to acquire it. At all cost we are encouraged to get wisdom. We used to sing a song in Scripture Union camps in the early sixties that went like this: "He is all I need. He is all I need; Jesus is all that I need." After decades of walking with this Jesus I can honestly say that I have not been disappointed. He is supreme. It is worth selling everything and banking on the Christ the wisdom of God.

Wisdom is Supreme!

May Day 16

⁸ Esteem her, and she will exalt you; embrace her, and she will honor you. ⁹ She will set a garland of grace on your head and present you with a crown of splendor." Proverbs 4:8-9

"Esteem wisdom and she will exalt you;" Those who have learned the secret of esteeming God above all things have testified of the faithfulness of God. Those who have stood on the fence and have not gone all out for God have remained unsure of the steadfast love of the Lord. God desires to exalt nations and individuals who are sold on God.

Those who go all out for God find out that they are swimming against the tide in the human opinion poll. The world sees them as unenlightened and even some will call them fools. Embracing God and God's wisdom will not win anyone the popular vote. What it does is to win the God's honor. The choice has always been clear. To be a "Human pleaser" or to be exalted and honored by God.

It is needless to say that sometimes our struggle comes from trying to get a little of both. It is as if we want enough of God for insurance just in case things do not pan out. Then we want as much of the world as we possibly can and not jeopardize our stand with God. Unfortunately, when things do not work out as we expect we turn around and blame God.

God has more grace and splendor for all those who set out to esteem and embrace wisdom. A crown awaits you and I in our endeavor to be faithful.

MAY DAY 17

¹¹ I guide you in the way of wisdom and lead you along straight paths. ¹² When you walk, your steps will not be hampered; when you run, you will not stumble.
Proverbs 4:11-12

Who else could guide us in the way of Wisdom? It has to be the one who is the source of wisdom. It is always good to have a guide walk alongside us as we go through life. Jesus did promise all those who follow him that he would send a guide who would have the principal responsibility of taking what belonged to God and teaching those who enter into a covenant relation.

Many of us would be ecstatic to know that there is a promise of God specifically directed to lead us along straight paths. If that is the case, then how come we sometimes struggle so much to discern the way we should go? There must be a breakdown in communication somewhere. More than often the problem is with us. We have not been able to listen and take the Lord at his word.

The challenge comes down to how much we are willing to be totally dependent on God. The world would call us weak people and sometimes something worse. But that is a small price to pay for what our Lord has done for us.

"When you walk your steps will not be hampered" Who is out there seeking to hamper the steps of the people of God? Those who underestimate the struggle against principalities and powers find out when it is too late. The Lord is not only the guide but also our protector through every situation.

Our guide and protector is patiently waiting for a prayer from us.

May Day 18

¹³ Hold on to instruction, do not let it go; guard it well, for it is your life. Proverbs: 4:13

There are some things that are worth holding on to at all cost. There are other things that we should let go of. It is important to know the difference between the two. The writer of Proverbs reminds us of what we should hold on to. Included in this category are instructions from the Lord.

There are pearls of wisdom that could be gleaned from the instructions from the Lord. When one finds this treasure, it is important to hold on to it and not allow it to slip out of our hands. People have come so close to taking hold of the Wisdom of God and they have for one reason or the other refused to hold on to it. Such individuals did not appreciate the importance of what they had received from God.

Those who come to understand the preciousness of what they have received from God and from the Lord Jesus Christ, guard the gift with all of their might. The question is how do we guard the instructions from the Lord? We decide to obey and live according to the directives as the Lord that gives us strength. It is the resolve to allow the directives of God to be our watchword that keeps us on the straight and narrow. The truth is that real life depends on holding on to the instructions of God.

Thinking about it, I know that the Lord is able to keep all those who are sold on the instructions of the Lord. No one is able to snatch us from God's hands.

I want to walk with the Lord Jesus Christ all the days of my life. I have been invited to follow him and give my life to the Holy Spirit's instruction every day.

MAY DAY 19

¹⁴ Do not set foot on the path of the wicked or walk in the way of evil men. ¹⁵ Avoid it, do not travel on it; turn from it and go on your way. Proverbs 4:14-15

What will qualify as the path of the wicked? It is important to identify this particular path if we are going to attempt to avoid it. In its simplest form, this is a path that is at odds with the instructions of God. Anything that distracts from the worship of God or leads people away from God could be classified with the path of the wicked.

The writer knows exactly what would happen to those who attempt to flirt with the path of the wicked. There is nothing like claiming to be so strong that one could withstand the drawbacks on the path of the wicked. Those who have attempted to walk on the edge of the path of the wicked have found the current to be too strong for them and thus have been drawn into the center of its currents. It is that type of scenario that makes the writer of Proverbs so adamant about any attempt to go near the path of the wicked.

People who are evil can seduce us into their way of life and thus the warning to avoid those who will lead us to compromise our faith. We are told to flee from them and avoid them. There is a way that is mapped out for those who will follow the guidance of the Holy Spirit. The admonishment is that we should pay attention to the promptings of the Holy Spirit and keep on the way.

What is the Holy Spirit of the Lord telling us to avoid this day? God is interested in our futures more that we may know! It is time to avoid the paths that enemy has been trying to place in front of us.

Dr. Seth Asare

May Day 20

¹⁶ For they cannot sleep till they do evil; they are robbed of slumber till they make someone fall. ¹⁷ They eat the bread of wickedness and drink the wine of violence. ¹⁸ The path of the righteous is like the first gleam of dawn, shining ever brighter till the full light of day. ¹⁹ But the way of the wicked is like deep darkness; they do not know what makes them stumble. Proverbs 4:16-19

Yesterday we were considering the path of the wicked and the ways of evil persons. It is interesting to observe that when people are sold on doing evil, every thought and imagination have at their root how to accomplish evil designs. Our passage says they cannot sleep till they do evil. That must be a terrible state for anyone to be in.

Unfortunately, we live in a society where people specialize in pulling others down. People seem to enjoy seeing others brought down for one reason or the other. It is described so well with these words: "They eat the bread of wickedness and drink the wine of violence." We are told that misery likes company. But the situation described here is one that enjoys destruction of anything that is related to God.

The contrast points to the path of the righteous. It is like the first gleam of dawn. The serenity and the peace on the path of the righteous are indescribable. The path shines as a beacon to all those seeking to know God. The intensity of the light grows with the passing of day.

God does not want anyone to stumble in the light of Christ. Jesus is the light that shines on the path of those who have a relationship with God.

In the light of Christ, we shall see light.

MAY DAY 21

[20] My son, pay attention to what I say; listen closely to my words. [21] Do not let them out of your sight, keep them within your heart; [22] for they are life to those who find them and health to a man's whole body. Proverbs 4:20-22

Here again we encounter a parent pouring her or his heart to their child. It is a pleading that comes with urgency because the parent has had enough experience in life to point the child in the right direction.

It is for those very reasons that we pay close attention to the words of the One who was, is and will come gain. When someone has been through all that we are going through and has come out victorious, it goes without question that we ought to pay attention to what this individual has to say.

As a pastor, I wished my congregation would agree with me on the words of scripture outlined here. Specifically, that the words of the Lord should not be let out of our sight. They should be kept closely to the heart. It is true that those who hide the words of God in the heart are mindful of sin and the presence of God.

Oh! the peace that our savior gives. Peace that the world would never know. Indeed, our ways will grow brighter as we learn to trust God's word all the more. The Word became flesh and dwelt among us. The truth is that the Word continues to become flesh to all those who open themselves to an unapologetic embrace of Jesus.

"For they are life to those who find them and health to a man's whole body." Oh that we may regain the health that God has promised us all along.

May Day 22

^{25} Let your eyes look straight ahead, fix your gaze directly before you. Proverbs 4:25

Distraction! Distraction! Distraction! Many a Christian has started this spiritual journey and has fallen by the wayside because of distraction. Their eyes wandered to the left and to the right because there was nothing to focus on. Or to put it another way, they took their eyes off the Lord Jesus Christ.

What will make people look away from what has been set in front of them? It does not take much to make people start wondering if there is a better way to the left or to the right. When we start looking at other human beings and start comparing ourselves with them we will soon find out several things.

We could come to the conclusion that their way is not that bad. We may even rationalize and say that all roads lead to the same place eventually and forget the calling we have received. Those who are double minded are not able to receive what the Lord has promised them in Christ Jesus.

Sometimes those who look to the left and to the right come to the conclusion that they are not that bad after all. They can always see others who are worse off in their spiritual walk. That has led to complacency in many quarters in the Christian realm. The call is to fix our eyes on the one who called us. What God is doing with another sister or brother is not your business and my business. We were called to follow Jesus Christ.

Those of us who have heard the call to follow Jesus Christ are admonished to fix our gaze directly on the author and finisher of our faith. This does not mean that we are not concerned about others. Rather the emphasis is on avoiding distractions that cause us to be out of focus.

Do you see Christ, when you look straight ahead of you to the goal?

MAY DAY 23

²⁶ Make level paths for your feet and take only ways that are firm. ²⁷ Do not swerve to the right or the left; keep your foot from evil. Proverbs 4:26-27

How do we find level paths for our feet in a world filled with crooked ways? We will need all the help from God and the power of the Holy Spirit. The psalmist says:" Thy word is a lamp unto my feet and a light unto my path". Therefore, to make level paths for our feet will call for knowledge and obedience in the word that directs us in the "Way Everlasting".

When we establish our feet on the way that is life and truth, then we can honestly say that we have found level paths for our feet. Anything short of that is still struggling to find our way in this world. God has revealed to us in Jesus Christ the path that leads to everlasting life.

The author calls us to take steps that are firm in the way that we have found. Those who have received assurance of salvation, in Jesus Christ, do not have to guess where they are going. Jesus put it this way: "I give them eternal life and they shall not perish, no one is able to snatch them out of my hand; because my father who gave them to me is greater than all."

It is important to remember that those who have received this call must not swerve to the right or to the left. Neither should they follow any evil path.

MAY DAY 24

[1] My son, pay attention to my wisdom, listen well to my words of insight, [2] that you may maintain discretion and your lips may preserve knowledge. Proverbs 5:1-2

There are some important truths that have to be repeated several times for them to sink in. One of those is the call to pay attention. We miss a lot because we fail to pay attention. It does not take much for us to realize that we have not been paying attention all along.

The question is what are we supposed to pay attention to? In this context it is the Wisdom of God or the wisdom of a parent. The reason given is that insight does not come cheaply. It is gained through a lot of sweat and experience. So the words that are passed on from those who have insight have to be treasured as precious gem.

Those who have walked the road we are on right now have something to teach us. They have years of accumulated insight about life that could make a difference in our living today. When this is understood in terms of God, we come to the conclusion that there is nothing that we are going to confront in life that is outside the knowledge of God. With that in mind, it will serve us well to pay attention to the insight offered by God.

If we wish to maintain discretion and preserve knowledge, then we have to heed to the call to listen to the words of wisdom that come from rich experience and from God. Teachable spirits do not come by accident. They are the result of paying attention to what God has been trying to say to humankind all along. Do we hear what God is trying to say to us in our circumstances?

MAY DAY 25

³ For the lips of an adulteress drip honey, and her speech is smoother than oil; ⁴ but in the end she is bitter as gall, sharp as a double-edged sword. Proverbs: 5:3-4

We are given an example of a word of wisdom that needs our attention. Someone has had the experience of witnessing seduction by deceptive words and a piece of advice is given to all those who would listen. A parent realizes that there is danger ahead for those who would run ahead without caution. So a warning sign is posted for those who would want to pay heed.

What is the parent trying to get across with the words "the lips of an adulteress drip honey"? The issue here is deception that comes through words. Listening and believing smooth talk has led several people astray. People have been promised the moon and they have bought it only to realize that it is all vanity.

The truth is that those who refuse to listen and pay attention to what God is saying sooner or later find out that they have been taken in by the smooth took of this world. The issue is not only an adulteress, but it is about everything that seeks to draw us away from the path of God. The end result is never pleasant.

The disappointment in the end is always bitter. We find out to our shame that we left the security of a relationship with God for something that is worthless. Our hearts get pierced with pain that take a long time to heal.

We cannot take what we have for granted. There is nothing worth exchanging for a relationship with God.

May Day 26

⁵ Her feet go down to death; her steps lead straight to the grave. ⁶ She gives no thought to the way of life; her paths are crooked, but she knows it not. Proverbs 5:5-6

The sad commentary that can be given about anyone is that they are sincerely convinced of the wrong thing that they are doing. How else can you describe anyone who is sincerely convinced that there is no God? They so strongly believe it that their actions and words reflect that notion. For any bystander watching, it is obvious that this individual is on a wrong trajectory. But what can anyone do when this person can give you the classic arguments to convince anyone that there is no God.

All that one has to do is to watch the path that has been taken by those with these high sounding arguments against God. The writer of the Book of Proverbs describes them as people who are walking on the path of death. There is a way that seems right to humans, but the end is the way of death. It is not so much about what you and I think. It is about what God has given to humanity.

There is a way of life that God has laid down for all people. It is a covenant relationship with God. Those who are in relationship with God see themselves as a small part of God's bigger picture. We are no more at the center of things. God has loved us and that makes all the difference. We know what life is all about because we are connected to the giver of life.

It would be sad to keep walking on a crooked way and not know it. How else would people know, if they were not prepared to open themselves to the convicting power of the Holy Spirit?

May Day 27

⁷ Now then, my sons, listen to me; do not turn aside from what I say. ⁸ Keep to a path far from her, do not go near the door of her house, Proverbs 5:7-8

There is a way that seems right to people but the end of that road is not pleasant. How do we know how to keep away from that road? We will know it by listening to the instruction of God and guarding it because our lives depend on it. There are several voices out there seeking to draw Christians away from the saving grace of our Lord and savior.

Some of these voices have become crafty in our day. So it has become more and more difficult to separate the seductive voices from that of the good shepherd. Some have even clothed themselves as angels of light and they operate in the churches. Jesus warned us of all these many years ago. "My sheep hear my voice, they follow me." The key is listening to the voice of Jesus no matter what happens and no matter what is dangled in front of us.

The author calls us to keep to a path that is far away from the seductive words that would lead us astray. In fact, we are told to literally run away from anything that would lead us away from the Lord. We are not supposed to go anywhere near the door of her house. This is not escapism. Rather, when we know what we are dealing with, it will be safer to flee into the arms of our Lord. There is no need to underestimate the power of evil.

Lord, lead us in the paths of righteousness.

May Day 28

⁹ lest you give your best strength to others and your years to one who is cruel, ¹⁰ lest strangers feast on your wealth and your toil enrich another man's house. Proverbs 5:9-10

The result of being seduced is that we discover our folly when it is too late. The Lord has a plan for each one of us when we enter into a relation with God. The plan is never forced on anyone. Those who rebel and go their own way find out that they have given the best years of their lives to causes that did not profit anyone. The people who entice us to this life apart from God do not have any purpose that is of eternal significance. They cannot promise us something that they themselves do not have.

Jesus promised his followers eternal life that was purchased with his own sacrificial death. The way of obedience may not be an easy road. But we know the one who has gone ahead of us. So we follow with an assurance that the one who called us is faithful.

The author wants us to understand that it is possible to toil in this life to no avail. It would seem like we are waiting for someone to tell us at the end that "tonight your soul would be demanded of you and all the toil on earth would belong to another". That is what happens when we live without keeping eternity in view.

It helps to keep in perspective what God is calling us to do in making a difference through Jesus Christ. God has a plan for us.

May Day 29

[11] At the end of your life you will groan, when your flesh and body are spent. [12] You will say, "How I hated discipline! How my heart spurned correction! [13] I would not obey my teachers or listen to my instructors. [14] I have come to the brink of utter ruin in the midst of the whole assembly." Proverbs 5:11-14

Discipline and correction were words we did not want to hear in boarding school. We did everything possible to prevent discipline. We wanted to get away with the breaking of school rules under the guise of freedom. We were convinced that the religious boarding school was imposing foreign standards on us.

But now I look back and see that all the rules and instructions were for our own good. The school was seeking to shape us into responsible adults. The same applies in the spiritual realm. Those who hate spiritual discipline miss out on the promises of God. "At the end of your life you would groan, when your flesh and body are spent." We do not have to wait till the end of life to realize that it would have been beneficial to accept discipline and correction.

It is not easy for most people to accept that they are wrong and they need correction. It is for that reason that even some churches are avoiding the word "sin". Talking about sin and repentance is becoming a taboo in some circles. But there is no way we can be healed without the forgiveness and correction of God.

The question is how do you correct anyone who does not see that that they need correction. We all need to humble ourselves before God so that the Holy Spirit would lead us in the way everlasting.

May Day 30

[15] Drink water from your own cistern, running water from your own well. [16] Should your springs overflow in the streets, your streams of water in the public squares? [17] Let them be yours alone, never to be shared with strangers. [18] May your fountain be blessed, and may you rejoice in the wife of your youth. Proverbs: 5:15-18

We encounter in these verses a unique way of saying that people should be satisfied with what God has given them. Especially, when it comes to life partners. The subject being addressed here is fidelity in marriage. Married folks are being exhorted to drink water from their own cisterns or be content with what they have.

Those who keep looking over their shoulders thinking the grass is green on the other side would never appreciate what God has given them. A rhetorical question is asked about springs flowing into the streets and public places. The answer is that there are some things that should not be shared. Marriage is one of those things: "Let them be yours alone".

Those who have learned how to rejoice in the wife of their youth have mastered what it takes to have a happy relationship. God would bless all those who cultivate the habit of saying: "thank you" to God for the gifts that they have received. Whatever God has given to us ought to be received with joy and thanksgiving. In so doing we open ourselves to more of God's blessings.

May Day 31

[19] A loving doe, a graceful deer— may her breasts satisfy you always, may you ever be captivated by her love. [20] Why be captivated, my son, by an adulteress? Why embrace the bosom of another man's wife? [21] For a man's ways are in full view of the LORD, and he examines all his paths. [22] The evil deeds of a wicked man ensnare him; the cords of his sin hold him fast. [23] He will die for lack of discipline, led astray by his own great folly. Proverbs 5:19-23

The theme of contentment with what God has given continues in these verses. People have pierced their hearts with much sorrow because they failed to appreciate the gifts that the Lord has given them. Not only that, they decided to lust after what belonged to another. When we are captivated by the love of our partners we do not make room for others who come calling for love.

Two questions are asked here that pertain to be captivated by the love of an adulteress and the love of another's wife. The answer is the same in both cases. There is no reason for anyone to toy with the idea of pursuing an adulteress or embrace the bosom of another's wife. This is a sound warning for all to heed because it leads to a slippery road of sin.

We are also reminded that nothing can be hidden from the Lord because a person's ways are in full view of the Lord. Sometimes people can deceive themselves with the notion that the Lord does not see. But we know better. "The Lord examines all their paths".

There will always be situations that will seek to ensnare the children of God. But the way out is sticking to the discipline of the Lord under all tempting conditions. Giving in to selfish desires is a matter of lack of discipline and as the writer says, it amounts to great folly. The Lord provides a way of escape from those tempting situations.

We turn now to the Book of Joshua for our compass bearings. Transition from a great leader like Moses to Joshua was not going to be easy. Moses was the only leader the people of Israel had known. But with God all things are possible. God gave Joshua the same words of assurance that had been given to Moses. And the young man took the words of God to heart when he was told to be courageous. "As I was with Moses I will be with you" became his watchword. There is so much to learn.

June Day 1

[1] Then Moses went out and spoke these words to all Israel: [2] "I am now a hundred and twenty years old and I am no longer able to lead you. The LORD has said to me, 'You shall not cross the Jordan.' [3] The LORD your God himself will cross over ahead of you. He will destroy these nations before you, and you will take possession of their land. Joshua also will cross over ahead of you, as the LORD said. Deuteronomy 31:1-3

New situations demand new leadership. The Lord had spoken to Moses and he had accepted the rational of God that it was time for a new person to lead into the promise land. Moses did mention his age as being hundred and twenty but that was not the reason given by God. There was nothing preventing Moses to cross the Jordan into the Promised Land except for the word of God.

The real reason was because of sin. Moses did not honor God before the people. He was angry with the people of Israel and struck the mountain to bring forth water. He was commanded by the lord to speak to the rock in front of the assembled Israelites. "[37] Because of you the LORD became angry with me also and said, "You shall not enter it, either. [38] But your assistant, Joshua son of Nun, will enter it. Encourage him, because he will lead Israel to inherit it." (Deuteronomy 1:37-38). As we can see it was not because of physical disability that Moses was disqualified from entering the promise land.

All along the people of God were given the assurance that it was God who did the fighting for them. It was a matter of who was the warrior leading them into battle. What made the people of Israel unique was their God who led them through every circumstance of life. That still remains true for all those who wish to be part of the "People of God". It will never be because of might or power. It will be by the Spirit of God.

June Day 2

⁹ Now Joshua son of Nun was filled with the spirit of wisdom because Moses had laid his hands on him. So the Israelites listened to him and did what the LORD had commanded Moses. Deuteronomy 34:9

Joshua the son of Nun was one of the ten spies who were sent to spy out the Promised Land. Joshua and Caleb were the two people who came back with the minority report that went against the fear and doubt of the majority. "⁶ Joshua son of Nun and Caleb son of Jephunneh, who were among those who had explored the land, tore their clothes ⁷ and said to the entire Israelite assembly, "The land we passed through and explored is exceedingly good. ⁸ If the LORD is pleased with us, he will lead us into that land, a land flowing with milk and honey, and will give it to us. ⁹ Only do not rebel against the LORD. And do not be afraid of the people of the land, because we will swallow them up. Their protection is gone, but the LORD is with us. Do not be afraid of them." Numbers 14:6-9. This report caused the assembly of Israel think about stoning Joshua and Caleb. But that did not shake the confidence of Joshua and Caleb in what the Lord would do for Israel.

Joshua believed that if the Lord were to be pleased with the people, then the Lord would lead them into the Promised Land. According to Joshua and Caleb, the protection of the people living in Canaan was gone. On the other hand, the Lord was with the people of Israel. This was the man Joshua who was to take over from Moses in leading the people of God into the Promised Land.

What qualified Joshua for this extraordinary task of leadership was not his past experiences as a spy. The real reason was that he was filled with the Spirit of wisdom. This happened when Moses laid his hands on him. This is an interesting statement. It is one of the early references to the power of the Holy Spirit being associated with the laying on of hands. God is able to do all things in every age and nothing will limit the power of God. The people of Israel listened to Joshua because they recognized the power of God upon him.

June Day 3

¹ After the death of Moses the servant of the LORD, the LORD said to Joshua son of Nun, Moses' aide: ² "Moses my servant is dead. Now then, you and all these people, get ready to cross the Jordan River into the land I am about to give to them—to the Israelites. Joshua 1:1-2

Moses the servant of the Lord died on the mountain after he had been given a "bird's–eye" view of the Promised Land. He received orders to commission his aide, Joshua, as the new leader of the people of God before his death. He carried this out with the laying on of hands and Joshua was filled with the Spirit of wisdom. The Israelites spent some time mourning for their fallen leader. They also knew that the mission was not yet accomplished.

As usual God took the initiative in calling upon Joshua to fulfill the role that Moses had commissioned him to. Why did Joshua wait for the Lord to prompt him to the task ahead of him? Could it be a sign of humility on the part of Joshua? Yes, it was true that he had been prepared for this very task. But he was also aware of how easy it was to be presumptuous. After all, he knew that he was not Moses. The shoes of Moses were not to be stepped in without much trepidation. Joshua knew and had learned this lesson from his mentor. It always pays to wait for the Lord.

Those who wait for the Lord find out that God would come through and speak so clearly that the way forward would be clear. God spoke words to Joshua that seemed obvious. "Moses my servant is dead". But that was not the end of the story. Many people make the mistake of quickly dismissing what God is saying because they think what is being revealed seem obvious and a waste of time. But those who tarry to hear the full revelation do come to the conclusion that God has more to teach them.

Yes, Moses was dead but Joshua now received the mantle to take the people to the Promised Land. It was important for Joshua not carry out a vision that belonged to Moses. God has a fresh vision for every generation and for every person. Sometimes it may be a repackaging of the same great commission but what is different is that it comes to us directly from God.

Joshua had to receive the word from God to take the people of Israel across the Jordan into the Promised Land. This was certainly a new vision for Joshua from God. Has God been preparing your heart for something fresh.

June Day 4

"³ I will give you every place where you set your foot, as I promised Moses. ⁴ Your territory will extend from the desert to Lebanon, and from the great river, the Euphrates—all the Hittite country—to the Great Sea on the west. Joshua 1:3-4

The directions of God to Joshua were clear and unambiguous. He was to get ready to cross the Jordan River with all the people of Israel. They were to enter a land that God was about to give to his people. This was not the time to ask questions because God was supplying the answers before anyone had an opportunity to ask a question. All that Joshua had to do was to listen and pay attention to the words of God.

Joshua had served as second in command to Moses for several years. He knew what it meant to receive a promise from God and a mission from God. He understood that when God sends anyone on a mission, it was God who accomplished the task. So one can imagine the excitement of Joshua as he heard the words: "I will give you every place where you set your foot, as I promised Moses".

The implication was that Joshua was not going to be alone in this mission of taking the Israelites into the Promised Land. All that Joshua had to do was to literally set foot on a piece of property across the Jordan and the Lord will add that territory to the people of God.

The promise of God was extraordinary. God will give to his people whatever was ahead of them. All they had to do was to obey and move forward in the strength of the Lord. What I find interesting is that the territory they were to occupy had already been mapped out by God. "⁴ Your territory will extend from the desert to Lebanon, and from the great river, the Euphrates—all the Hittite country—to the Great Sea on the west." God was aware of what was ahead of them and the details had been taken care of.

God has gone ahead of all of us in the coming year and God has mapped out the whole territory. Just listen, trust and obey.

June Day 5

5 No one will be able to stand up against you all the days of your life. As I was with Moses, so I will be with you; I will never leave you nor forsake you. Joshua 1:5

One of the realities that will confront all those in leadership position is the number of people who will challenge their authority. Joshua had witnessed a few instances in his role as the aid to Moses. There will always be those who think they have equal abilities to do the job of a leader. Unfortunately, this attitude pertains in the secular world and also within the Christian community.

God decided to give Joshua an assurance of the authority that had been invested in him. When God says: "No one will be able to stand up against you all the days of your life." One cannot ask for anything better. God had not only surveyed the territory that Joshua and the people of Israel were going to possess, God had weighed the people who were going to confront Joshua in all manner of situations. The verdict of God was simple and straightforward. None of the situations or the people will be able to prevail.

The reason for this verdict was because God was going to be with Joshua in every situation. All that Joshua had to do was to take the authority that had been given to him and move forward with it. Joshua was reminded of something that would bring so much assurance to his heart. "As I was with Moses, so I will be with you". If I were Joshua, that would be all I would want to hear.

Then as if to put the icing on the cake, God says "I will never leave you nor forsake you". Joshua had received enough assurance to carry out the mission of God. The same assurance has been given to Christians. We were promised the Holy Spirit to be with us forever. Wherever we go the presence of the Lord walks with us. "For lo, I am with you always even to the end of the age."

This is a promise to us as we continue in the New Year. God will not forsake you or leave you. You will never be alone.

June Day 6

⁶ "Be strong and courageous, because you will lead these people to inherit the land I swore to their forefathers to give them. Joshua 1:6

The name Joshua means "The Lord saves". Now, God has defined the mission of Joshua for him. The mission was in line with his name. The Lord was going to save his people and Joshua was to be the leader to lead the people into the Promised Land beyond the Jordan River.

God has assured Joshua in so many ways that God was going to be with him and the words "I will be with you" took on a new meaning for this new leader of the people of God. Humanly speaking, the task that was being asked of Joshua was enormous. When one considers the hard time that the rebellious people of God gave to Moses, one is not surprised by the multiplicity of assurances that Joshua received. They all carried the message: "I will direct you, sustain you, and assure success.

Those are the very words that God has for all of us as we continue in this New Year in the power of the Holy Spirit. God has not withdrawn his promise to direct, sustain and assure success for all those who would put their faith and trust in the Lord Jesus Christ. That should include you and I. These are promises waiting to be cashed in by all those who believe. I have decided to take God at his word and say: "Lord I believe, please help my unbelief".

Then comes the word that has been given to all the servants of God who dare to stand in the gap in an attempt to reconcile people to God. "Be strong and courageous". The task ahead is not for the weak and fainthearted. But at the same time, the strength be alluded here is not human strength. It is not a question of who is a better fighter. What is being asked of Joshua is a resolve to trust God against all odds.

There was no question about who was going to lead the people into the Promised Land. Joshua was assured of that mission. But the leader had a part to play and that was being strong and courageous. We are being asked to be strong and courageous so that we can accomplish the Lord's work in this year.

Nehemiah reminds us that: "the joy of the Lord is our strength"

JUNE DAY 7

⁷ Be strong and very courageous. Be careful to obey all the law my servant Moses gave you; do not turn from it to the right or to the left, that you may be successful wherever you go. Joshua 1:7

The people of God had waited several generations to see the fulfillment of a promise made to Abraham in Genesis 15: "I am the LORD, who brought you out of Ur of the Chaldeans to give you this land to take possession of it." Jacob received a renewal of the same promise at Bethel when God appeared to him in a dream: "I am the LORD, the God of your father Abraham and the God of Isaac. I will give you and your descendants the land on which you are lying. ¹⁴ Your descendants will be like the dust of the earth, and you will spread out to the west and to the east, to the north and to the south. All peoples on earth will be blessed through you and your offspring. ¹⁵ I am with you and will watch over you wherever you go, and I will bring you back to this land. I will not leave you until I have done what I have promised you."

Now, Joshua stands on the shoulders of all those who have gone ahead of him to bring to pass the fulfillment of the promise made to Abraham. This was an awesome task with a lot of responsibilities. No wonder that God tells Joshua to be strong and very courageous. The fulfillment of God's word may take hundreds of years or a day but whatever it is God is never late concerning promises.

Besides being strong and courageous God expected Joshua to be careful to obey all the law that Moses gave to him. God had outlined what God would do for Joshua and now it was time for Joshua to know his responsibilities. We are not talking about cheap grace when it comes to our dealings with God in a new territory.

Success was not guaranteed unconditionally. God expected obedience to the commands of God given through Moses. The same expectation is true for all of us. Obedience should never be separated from the promises of God.

If we would obey, God would prove faithful.

June Day 8

⁹ Have I not commanded you? Be strong and courageous. Do not be terrified; do not be discouraged, for the LORD your God will be with you wherever you go." Joshua 1:9

What happens when God says something to you three times? It is either you are not getting the message or it is for emphasis. In verse six we read the words "Be strong and courageous". Then in verse seven we read again: "be strong and very courageous. And now verse nine repeats the same phrase. What is going on here? We know the history of Joshua as a very courageous man who was taken by Moses to the foot of the mountain when Moses was going to receive the commandments. Joshua was a warrior who had led the people into battle and won victories.

So could it be that another type of strength and courage was being referred to here? Could it be that Joshua was asked to contemplate a type of strength and courage that required reliance on God in the face of people seeking to depart from the Book of the Law?

Joshua was told not to be terrified or discouraged in the mission ahead of him. Leaders of God's people are often faced with discouragement because they find themselves marching to God's drumbeat while the people they serve march to a different tune. But the word is that when the vision tarries, do not be discouraged or terrified because God is still with you.

The one who is speaking to Joshua is God Almighty and he promises to be with him wherever he goes. Where are you going to be in this coming year? You may not know yet, but God does know and says he will be with you. That is all we need.

Be strong and very courageous in the Lord!

June Day 9

¹⁰ So Joshua ordered the officers of the people: ¹¹ "Go through the camp and tell the people, 'Get your supplies ready. Three days from now you will cross the Jordan here to go in and take possession of the land the LORD your God is giving you for your own.'" Joshua 1:10-11

Joshua believed all the words that the Lord had spoken and he did not waste time in laying out the implementation plan. How many people have received directions from the Lord and have failed to carry out God's mission? There is a difference between believing the word of the Lord and acting on the word of the Lord. Saul had to be jolted with the words "To obey is better than to sacrifice and to hearken than the fat of rams."

Joshua was the type of leader who delegated responsibilities and he also believed in preparing the people for the mission of God. People do want to be included in what God was doing and a little preparation would go a long way to prevent alienation. Joshua asked the officers or representatives of the people to go through the camp to prepare them for the task of crossing the Jordan River to possess the Promised Land. The officers were leaders who knew their people and were trusted by their tribe members. Their task was simply to convey the message of God given through Joshua.

Joshua spoke words of faith to the officers. There was no wavering or doubting what God was going to do. He spoke with confidence as he announced that in three days the people of Israel would cross the Jordan River and enter the Land that God had promised to give to them. Joshua made the point that it was God who was giving the land. The words of Joshua were so reassuring that it made the work of the leaders of Israel look easy. How are we transmitting the words of faith that we have received?

The way we convey the message from the Lord impacts how the message is received.

June Day 10

² But to the Reubenites, the Gadites and the half-tribe of Manasseh, Joshua said, ¹³ "Remember the command that Moses the servant of the LORD gave you: 'The LORD your God is giving you rest and has granted you this land.' ¹⁴ Your wives, your children and your livestock may stay in the land that Moses gave you east of the Jordan, but all your fighting men, fully armed, must cross over ahead of your brothers. You are to help your brothers ¹⁵ until the LORD gives them rest, as he has done for you, and until they too have taken possession of the land that the LORD your God is giving them. After that, you may go back and occupy your own land, which Moses the servant of the LORD gave you east of the Jordan toward the sunrise." Joshua 1:12-15

The Reubenites, the Gadites and the half tribe of Manasseh had been allotted their place of residence on the east side of Jordan by Moses. These tribes have settled their families and livestock in the places apportioned to them. Now it was time to move forward and settle the remaining tribes of Israel on the other side of the Jordan River.

The temptation was for those who have been settled on the east side of the Jordan to find reasons why they should stay behind and protect their wives and little children. Joshua handled this situation with much diplomacy by appealing to the communal spirit that existed among the people of God. They were one people who cared for each other's welfare. None of the tribes of Israel could be at peace so long as the others did not enjoy a place of their own.

The same is true for Christians all over the world. The body of Christ was purchased at a cost to God. We are who we are because God gave us a great High Priest who has opened the way for all of us to obtain access into the presence of God. This is the "rest" that God has purposed for all those who would dare to believe in Jesus Christ. But all have to understand that our "rest" is not complete until all those who are called by God do enter the "rest" prepared for them.

The Reubenites and the Gadites and the half tribe of Manasseh were admonished to consider their "rest" incomplete until all the people of God enter the Promised Land beyond the Jordan River. These tribes were not forced to take up arms with their brothers. The appeal of Joshua considered their unique situations and allowed women and young ones to stay behind as the fighting men went ahead to fight alongside their brothers.

Joshua assured the tribes on the east side of the Jordan River that they would be allowed to return safely to their families. These tribes had to see and understand what God was doing to be able to buy into the plan of God to build a community of faith.

God is asking all of us to sacrifice something for the sake of the body of Christ. How much comfort and convenience are we willing to sacrifice so that the plan of God will come to fruition?

June Day 11

[16] *Then they answered Joshua, "Whatever you have commanded us we will do, and wherever you send us we will go. Joshua 1:16*

Joshua had challenged the tribes who had settled on the east side of the Jordan to take up the challenge of sacrificing for the sake of the whole community of faith. It was time for the people to respond to the words of Joshua.

The response of these tribe members was straight to the point. That should be the response of all of us. "Whatever you have commanded us we will do". The words demonstrated the confidence and trust that the Reubenites had placed in their new leader. They had come to accept the words from Joshua as the word of the Lord.

The people of Israel were giving their unqualified support to the ministry and leadership of Joshua. We do not often hear people providing such a blank check to a leader. That is because so many leaders have abused the trust that people have placed in them. That includes people who bear the name of God.

The people were not only ready to do but also to go wherever they are sent. This was indeed a bold declaration because the mission ahead of them was conquering foreign lands under the direction of God and Joshua. The people making this bold statement were not naïve to think that there would be no casualties in the mission ahead. There was the possibility that some of them would not return to their families. But they knew that this was a sacrifice to be made for the purposes of God to come to fruition.

We are called to follow wherever Christ leads us. We may not fully know what that means for each one of us but one thing is sure: "The one who has called us is faithful". Wherever Jesus leads us we will follow and go with Him all the way".

JUNE DAY 12

17 Just as we fully obeyed Moses, so we will obey you. Only may the LORD your God be with you as he was with Moses. Joshua 1:17

Joshua's leadership credentials were tested when he had to call upon the tribes that had already settled on the east side of the Jordan to take up arms with their brothers. Joshua came out of the situation unscathed after the Reubenites and the other tribes affirmed that they were willing to go wherever Joshua asked them to go.

These Israelites went ahead to promise obedience to Joshua as a leader. They said: "Just as we fully obeyed Moses, so we will obey you." Joshua did not solicit these words from the people. They voluntarily vowed their obedience to the leadership of Joshua. One cannot be a leader if they did not have followers who were willing to obey the directions of the said leader.

The Israelites promised to fully obey Joshua just as they did with Moses. We know that for most part these people obeyed the directives of Moses. That was the only way that this group of people had come to settle on the east side of the Jordan River. Now they were ready to transfer the same allegiance to Joshua as he prepares to lead the same group of people to settle on the west side of the Jordan River.

The people were very much aware of the role The Lord God played in using Moses to bring them to the brink of The Jordan River. So they did not only pledge their allegiance but prayed that the same God who was with Moses would be with Joshua. That was another way of saying that we are confident that you are going to be successful because of the Lord God. Praying for our leaders is something that the people of God cannot afford to ignore. Leaders in our Churches, communities and nations need the prayers of the saints. Let us pray for one another.

God calls people to leadership positions and God provides them with the tools to lead and accomplish the mission of God. We are going to be over comers to the degree that we are submissive to the Lord.

June Day 13

^{18} Whoever rebels against your word and does not obey your words, whatever you may command them, will be put to death. Only be strong and courageous!" Joshua 1:18

The people of Israel had taken the oath of allegiance to Joshua. They had indicated that they would obey him to the extent that they obeyed Moses. That was a big step for this group of people. There was no coaxing or arm-twisting on the part of Joshua. There were no threats from Joshua or from any other person on behalf of Joshua. All that their leader did was to lay before them the mission of God and waited for the people to respond.

Most of the time, that is all we can do. We just put forward the message of God and trust the Lord to do the rest. The Holy Spirit took the words of Joshua and used them to move the people to a place of accepting the leadership of Joshua. The people of Israel went beyond the call of duty by announcing what should be done to anyone who did not obey the words of Joshua.

They invoked capital punishment on anyone who refused to obey the command of Joshua. The people of Israel have come to accept the unique relationship between Joshua and God. Now, they were ready to receive the directives given by Joshua, as the perfect will of God that was being communicated. Under those conditions disobedience amounted to treason.

The people decided to encourage their new leader with the very words that God had used to encourage him. "Be strong and very courageous" That must have been reassuring to hear the same words again.

June Day 14

¹ Then Joshua son of Nun secretly sent two spies from Shittim. "Go, look over the land," he said, "especially Jericho." So they went and entered the house of a prostitute named Rahab and stayed there. ² The king of Jericho was told, "Look! Some of the Israelites have come here tonight to spy out the land." ³ So the king of Jericho sent this message to Rahab: "Bring out the men who came to you and entered your house, because they have come to spy out the whole land." Joshua 2:1-3

Joshua had taken over from Moses as leader of the people of Israel. God had given the new leader all the assurances that he needed to be able to lead the people of God into the Promised Land. The people had pledged their allegiance to Joshua and were ready to take possession of the territory ahead of them with the help of God.

Joshua sent two spies ahead of the group to go and spy out the land especially Jericho. That was an excellent leadership tactic. He knew that God was going to give the territory into his hands but he also wanted to encourage his fighting men. Sometimes we are called to use the gifts that God has given to all of us in practical ways. For Joshua, that meant using his mind to look at the best way to lead the people into the Promised Land.

The spies took refuge in the home of a prostitute. We are not told why this was the lodging that the spies preferred on this special mission. We would want to believe that the decision was part of God's direction. We also know that that was the most practical action for people in a foreign land. The home of the prostitute Rahab was open to any man who knocked at her door. The spies took advantage of a situation that existed to achieve their goal.

Unfortunately, word got to the King of Jericho that spies had come to Jericho. Not only that, the King had an idea where the spies were staying. So the king sent messengers to try and arrest the spies. The life of the prostitute Rahab was now in danger if the report reaching the king of Jericho was found to be true.

How far are we willing to endanger our comforts for the sake of the gospel?

June Day 15

"⁴ But the woman had taken the two men and hidden them. She said, "Yes, the men came to me, but I did not know where they had come from. ⁵ At dusk, when it was time to close the city gate, the men left. I don't know which way they went. Go after them quickly. You may catch up with them." ⁶ (But she had taken them up to the roof and hidden them under the stalks of flax she had laid out on the roof.) ⁷ So the men set out in pursuit of the spies on the road that leads to the fords of the Jordan, and as soon as the pursuers had gone out, the gate was shut." Joshua 2:4-7

Rahab took a step of faith in the direction of the God of Israel when she decided to hide the two spies and to redirect the Kings messengers. Did she know exactly what she was doing and the implications of her actions? Probably she did not fully understand her own actions. She could only surmise that she was doing the right thing.

Rahab was honest with the messengers of the King with her partial story. Yes, he admitted that the two men had come to her door but she did not know where they came from. She also added that she did not know where the men went. That was stretching the truth a little bit to save the lives of these two spies who had come from Israel.

Rahab had taken the men from Israel and hidden them under stalks of flax in her roof. She made sure that any attempts to ransack her house would not uncover these spies. Rahab made sure that Joshua's men were safe from any harm. She also sent the King's men on a chase that was not going to yield any results.

The actions of Rahab were part of her belief that nothing was going to stop the army of Joshua from over running Jericho. The news of what the God of Israel had done for them in Egypt and though the wilderness was spreading like wild fire. The hearts of Kings and peasants alike were melting at the news of God's actions on behalf of God's people. Those who are blessed by God are truly blessed and God paves a way for them.

God goes ahead of each one of us before we become aware of what God is doing. We may never be sure who is the next angel God is going to put in our path to rescue us. Rahab became God's messenger for the two spies. You can be God's agent of deliverance for someone today.

JUNE DAY 16

[8] Before the spies lay down for the night, she went up on the roof [9] and said to them, "I know that the LORD has given this land to you and that a great fear of you has fallen on us, so that all who live in this country are melting in fear because of you. [10] We have heard how the LORD dried up the water of the Red Sea for you when you came out of Egypt, and what you did to Sihon and Og, the two kings of the Amorites east of the Jordan, whom you completely destroyed. [11] When we heard of it, our hearts melted and everyone's courage failed because of you, for the LORD your God is God in heaven above and on the earth below. [12] Now then, please swear to me by the LORD that you will show kindness to my family, because I have shown kindness to you. Give me a sure sign [13] that you will spare the lives of my father and mother, my brothers and sisters, and all who belong to them, and that you will save us from death." Joshua 2:8-13

Can you imagine the feeling that came over the spies when Rahab knocked on their rooftop-hiding place? They were not sure of the message that Rahab was bringing to them. They were surprised by the message that the woman brought. "I know that the Lord has given this land to you. And that a great fear of you has fallen on us". The spies heard all that they needed to hear. But there was more, Rahab had heard how the mighty hand of God had led the people of Israel since they left Egypt.

When the people of Canaan heard about how God had defeated the enemies of Israel, their hearts melted within them. Rahab did not only make a confession but she also declared her faith in the God of Israel. She said: "The Lord your God is God of heaven and earth." There was no doubt that this woman had forsaken the gods of Canaan for the God of Israel.

Rahab had a request to make of the spies. The request showed her faith in the mission of the spies and the fact that God was going to give the whole territory into the hands of the people of Israel. She wanted the spies to give her an assurance that they were going to spare her life and that of her family.

Just think about this these two men who were sent to spy out Jericho. All they could find out was being hidden in the roof of a prostitute and listening to the testimony of this woman. But that was all that they needed to hear to accomplish their mission. It is amazing the way God works. Sometimes God does things in ways we cannot plan if we were given the opportunity.

God has a plan for you.

June Day 17

14 "Our lives for your lives!" the men assured her. "If you don't tell what we are doing, we will treat you kindly and faithfully when the LORD gives us the land." 15 So she let them down by a rope through the window, for the house she lived in was part of the city wall. 16 Now she had said to them, "Go to the hills so the pursuers will not find you. Hide yourselves there three days until they return, and then go on your way." Joshua 2:14-16

The spies from Israel listened attentively to what Rahab was saying. She gave them all the information they needed to report back to Joshua and the people of Israel. There was no need for the spies to go through the length and breadth of the region assessing the mood of the people. It was obvious from what Rahab said that the morale of the nations beyond the Jordan was low for fear of the people of Israel.

Rahab requested that in exchange for the help that she was giving, her family should be spared when Israel ultimately overrun Jericho. The spies responded positively to the request of Rahab under certain conditions. The spies gave her assurance with these words: "our lives for your lives." They promised to treat her and her family kindly when the Lord gave the land into the hands of Israel. But there were a few conditions attached to the promise given by the spies.

The first was that she would not give them away as spies. The truth was that the two men could have been betrayed at this point. The gate of the city had been shut and there was no way of escape for them. Even at this crucial moment Rahab had could have alerted the authorities secretly. The king's people would have gone after the spies and could hunt them down.

Rahab believed the assurances given by the spies so she showed them a secret way of escape that looked so obvious. She let them down through a window over the wall of Jericho since her house was on the wall. She gave them a sensible route and advice so they could escape those who had gone out in search of them.

Thank God for people like Rahab. She was trustworthy and she had placed her faith in the God of Israel. She was willing to risk everything for God's people.

June Day 18

[17] The men said to her, "This oath you made us swear will not be binding on us [18] unless, when we enter the land, you have tied this scarlet cord in the window through which you let us down, and unless you have brought your father and mother, your brothers and all your family into your house. [19] If anyone goes outside your house into the street, his blood will be on his own head; we will not be responsible. As for anyone who is in the house with you, his blood will be on our head if a hand is laid on him. [20] But if you tell what we are doing, we will be released from the oath you made us swear."
Joshua 2:17-20

Rahab's house was strategically situated on the city wall. So she conveniently used a scarlet cord to let the spies down to safety. When the men were safely out of Jericho they were sure that the prostitute (Rahab) had kept her end of the bargain so far. It was the turn of the spies to nail down their final conditions for the woman.

The first was that the same cord that had been used to let them down into safety should be tied to the same window. All the warriors from Israel would be asked to look out for the scarlet cord. The second condition was that all the family members should be brought into the house. The last condition was that those who had come under the safety of Rahab should not venture into the street when the conquering army is in town.

The implication was that Rahab and his household had now come under the shadow of the Almighty. There is something to be said for being under the shelter of God. There is safety under the wings of the God of Israel. This is a promise that God has given to all of humanity. People have to take advantage of living under the protection of God. Rahab made that choice after considering all the options available to her. She was not forced to make that choice. We all have a similar opportunity to decide to be counted with the people of God.

The spies expected Rahab to be faithful to the covenant that they had made. It is not enough to make a promise. We have to follow through with faithfulness.

June Day 19

21 "Agreed," she replied. "Let it be as you say." So she sent them away and they departed. And she tied the scarlet cord in the window. 22 When they left, they went into the hills and stayed there three days, until the pursuers had searched all along the road and returned without finding them. 23 Then the two men started back. They went down out of the hills, forded the river and came to Joshua son of Nun and told him everything that had happened to them. 24 They said to Joshua, "The LORD has surely given the whole land into our hands; all the people are melting in fear because of us." Joshua 2:21-24

"Agreed, she replied." Rahab listened carefully to the instructions that were supposed to lead to the salvation of her family when Israel took possession of her city. She was told that she had a part to play and she agreed to keep her end of the bargain. What I find interesting is the action of Rahab when the two spies left her. "She tied the scarlet cord in her window". That was an act of faith. She had no doubt that the words related to her would come to pass. One would have expected her to wait a few days, but "no' Rahab act with faith as the men were leaving. I am sure the men turned their heads and saw the scarlet cord hanging in the window. Yes, Rahab had identified herself with the people of Israel and the God of Israel.

The spies also followed the advice of Rahab and stayed in the hills for some days before returning to the camp of Israel. They narrated to Joshua everything that had happened to them. God had led them to the home of a prostitute and she became the agent of God. It was a story full of miracles and the leading of the Lord that kept them safe throughout their journey. But that was not the point of emphasis. The spying trip was successful because they gathered some useful information about the morale of the people in Jericho and the nations beyond.

The spies reported that: "The LORD has surely given the whole land into our hands; all the people are melting in fear because of us." That was what Israel needed to hear and the message of the spies renewed the strength of the people of Israel.

Have you realized that the same report is true for you and for me? The Lord has given the whole land into our hands. The real question is what are we going to do with that knowledge?

JUNE DAY 20

¹ Early in the morning Joshua and all the Israelites set out from Shittim and went to the Jordan, where they camped before crossing over. ² After three days the officers went throughout the camp, ³ giving orders to the people: "When you see the ark of the covenant of the LORD your God, and the priests, who are Levites, carrying it, you are to move out from your positions and follow it. ⁴ Then you will know which way to go, since you have never been this way before. But keep a distance of about a thousand yards between you and the ark; do not go near it." Joshua 3:1-4

Joshua and the people of Israel heard the report of the two spies. They paid attention to the act that the nations beyond the Jordan River were dreading the arrival of the armies of Israel. Joshua concluded that it was time for the people of Israel to move forward without any delay. Early in the morning they set out from Shittim and made their way to the crossing at the Jordan River. There comes a time when all of us have to set out from "Shittim". There may be an unknown ahead but with the help of God we can face it.

It was time to give instructions that would facilitate an orderly crossing. The ark of the covenant of the Lord was going ahead into the water, and the rest of the people were to follow. They were expected to move out of their positions and know that the Lord was leading the way. None of these people knew exactly which was the best route to take to cross the River Jordan and they also did not know what was waiting for them on the other side of the Jordan. Their confidence was in the leading of the Lord.

The people of Israel were reminded of something that was so true. "Since you have not been this way before". The Christian journey and our walk with the Lord required a similar attitude. It is a journey of faith that cannot rely on past experiences. When one has not ventured out on a particular route before, we are left with few options. One has to walk by faith.

The people had to follow the ark of the covenant of the Lord to know which way to go. We have to follow our Lord Jesus Christ if we are going to find our way.

June Day 21

⁵ Joshua told the people, "Consecrate yourselves, for tomorrow the LORD will do amazing things among you." ⁶ Joshua said to the priests, "Take up the ark of the covenant and pass on ahead of the people." So they took it up and went ahead of them. ⁷ And the LORD said to Joshua, "Today I will begin to exalt you in the eyes of all Israel, so they may know that I am with you as I was with Moses. ⁸ Tell the priests who carry the ark of the covenant: 'When you reach the edge of the Jordan's waters, go and stand in the river.'" Joshua 3:5-8

"Consecrate yourselves!" These were the words of Joshua to the people of Israel. To consecrate is to set apart for the work of the Lord. Anything that was set apart for God was considered to be Holy. Holiness is an attribute of God and all that came in close proximity of God were made holy or prepared for that purpose. Joshua acknowledged that the people of Israel were not ready to come into the presence of the mighty God. Joshua on the other hand was expecting the powerful presence of God in the midst of the people the next day. So he called on his people to take away any thing that defiled them and be ready for the in breaking of God.

God had promised to do an amazing thing in the midst of the people. Some of the people entering the Promised Land had heard about the miraculous things that the Lord had done at the time of Moses. Now God was ready to do similar things in front of the present generation of Israelites. The parting of the red sea was part of the history that was narrated to adults and children alike. Could it be that there was going to be another parting of the Jordan River? All eyes were fixed on Joshua and what God was going to ask to do.

Joshua commanded the Priests to take the Ark of the Covenant into the water. And the LORD said to Joshua, "Today I will begin to exalt you in the eyes of all Israel, so they may know that I am with you as I was with Moses". Those were words of assurance for Joshua and also for the people to know that God had not changed. The unchangeable God was in the midst of the people. The Priests obeyed the command given by Joshua and the people followed. It is God who exalts individuals. And when God does it everyone comes to know of it.

God is giving the same assurance to each one of us who have come to consecrate ourselves in the blood of the Lord Jesus Christ. The God who is and was and would be is at work in our midst. Open your eyes and take a step into the waters of Jordan.

June Day 22

⁹ Joshua said to the Israelites, "Come here and listen to the words of the LORD your God. ¹⁰ This is how you will know that the living God is among you and that he will certainly drive out before you the Canaanites, Hittites, Hivites, Perizzites, Girgashites, Amorites and Jebusites. ¹¹ See, the ark of the covenant of the Lord of all the earth will go into the Jordan ahead of you. ¹² Now then, choose twelve men from the tribes of Israel, one from each tribe. ¹³ And as soon as the priests who carry the ark of the LORD -the Lord of all the earth—set foot in the Jordan, its waters flowing downstream will be cut off and stand up in a heap." Joshua 3:9-13

God had spoken to Joshua and informed him of the amazing thing that was to happen in the sight of all Israel. A new generation of Israelites was on the brink of witnessing the mighty work of God. Joshua invited them to hear what God was going to do before it happened so that they would know that the living God was among them.

According to Joshua, the miracle of God would be an indication that God would certainly drive out the Canaanites and the other nations beyond the Jordan before Israel. The nations may seem numerous and powerful and settled in their land but it was the will of the Lord to give that land to Israel.

Each tribe was to select a representative to be a witness and also to be close to what God was going to do. The ark of the Lord and the priests carrying it would be first to set foot in the water. As soon as the ark of the Lord enters the water the Jordan River would stop flowing downstream. The waters would be heaped on the side of the ark of God and the priests. This would be a sight for all Israel to observe and narrate to posterity.

God was once again going to part the waters for God's people. The surrounding nations would hear about this and know that their gods would be no contest for the God of Israel. God continues to part the waters of life for those who place their confidence in the Lord.

God is still in the business of rolling back the waters.

June Day 23

14 So when the people broke camp to cross the Jordan, the priests carrying the Ark of the Covenant went ahead of them. 15 Now the Jordan is at flood stage all during harvest. Yet as soon as the priests who carried the ark reached the Jordan and their feet touched the water's edge, 16 the water from upstream stopped flowing. It piled up in a heap a great distance away, at a town called Adam in the vicinity of Zarethan, while the water flowing down to the Sea of the Arabah (the Salt Sea was completely cut off. So the people crossed over opposite Jericho. 17 The priests who carried the ark of the covenant of the LORD stood firm on dry ground in the middle of the Jordan, while all Israel passed by until the whole nation had completed the crossing on dry ground. Joshua 3:14-17

It is one thing being told what is to happen and another thing witnessing a miracle take place. The people broke camp and prepared themselves to follow the directives given by their leader. Yes, they have heard the salvation history of how the Lord parting the red sea when Moses was the leader. Now, Joshua has announced to them that there was going to be another parting of the waters. This time it was the River Jordan.

It would be needless to say that there were a few doubters who were not sure if Joshua was up to the task. The situation was complicated by the fact that the river was in a flood stage. But that did not change the word of the Lord given by Joshua. The ark of the Lord was to go forward and the people were to follow.

In obedience, the first steps were taken and people were surprised at the results. We read this account: *"Yet as soon as the priests who carried the ark reached the Jordan and their feet touched the water's edge, 16 the water from upstream stopped flowing. It piled up in a heap a great distance away, at a town called Adam."* So the people of Israel crossed over on dry ground opposite the city of Jericho. The priests bearing the ark of the Lord stood on dry ground in the middle of the river as the people crossed.

The people had experienced an amazing thing indeed. Now they know for sure that their God could and should be trusted. Note what it said about the priests planting their feet on firm ground until all the people of Israel had crossed the river. That did not mean that fear and doubt did not attempt to creep in. But the priest planted their feet on the firm ground of the word of the Lord.

God is still doing amazing things in our day. Plant your feet on firm ground because of the word of the Lord.

June Day 24

¹ When the whole nation had finished crossing the Jordan, the LORD said to Joshua, ² "Choose twelve men from among the people, one from each tribe, ³ and tell them to take up twelve stones from the middle of the Jordan from right where the priests stood and to carry them over with you and put them down at the place where you stay tonight." ⁴ So Joshua called together the twelve men he had appointed from the Israelites, one from each tribe, ⁵ and said to them, "Go over before the ark of the LORD your God into the middle of the Jordan. Each of you is to take up a stone on his shoulder, according to the number of the tribes of the Israelites, ⁶ to serve as a sign among you. In the future, when your children ask you, 'What do these stones mean?'⁷ tell them that the flow of the Jordan was cut off before the ark of the covenant of the LORD. When it crossed the Jordan, the waters of the Jordan were cut off. These stones are to be a memorial to the people of Israel forever." Joshua 4:1-7

The whole group of Israelites crossed the Jordan on dry ground. The Lord commanded Joshua to choose twelve men from among the people one from each tribe. These twelve people were to go down into the Jordan River and pick up stones according to the number of tribes. Each one was to carry the stone on their shoulder and take it to the camp.

These stones were to serve as a sign among the people. The stones were supposed to be a reminder to future generations of the amazing thing that the Lord had done in the midst of the people. In the future their children would ask for the meaning of this stone. That would present a teaching moment. They were to tell posterity about how the flow of the River Jordan was cut off before the ark of the Lord. So the stones were to be set up as a memorial.

The need for memorials for the people of God is something that Christians in the 21st century need. We all need to be reminded of the mighty works of God in our midst. When we are surrounded by pain and uncertainty, it is so easy to forget that the same God of the past is still at work. We all have our Ebenezer moments when we can recount ways in which the Lord has helped us.

Those moments have to be reminders of the faithfulness of God.

June Day 25

[18] And the priests came up out of the river carrying the ark of the covenant of the LORD. No sooner had they set their feet on the dry ground than the waters of the Jordan returned to their place and ran at flood stage as before. [19] On the tenth day of the first month the people went up from the Jordan and camped at Gilgal on the eastern border of Jericho. [20] And Joshua set up at Gilgal the twelve stones they had taken out of the Jordan. [21] He said to the Israelites, "In the future when your descendants ask their fathers, 'What do these stones mean?' [22] tell them, 'Israel crossed the Jordan on dry ground.' [23] For the LORD your God dried up the Jordan before you until you had crossed over. The LORD your God did to the Jordan just what he had done to the Red Sea when he dried it up before us until we had crossed over. [24] He did this so that all the peoples of the earth might know that the hand of the LORD is powerful and so that you might always fear the LORD your God." Joshua 4:18-24

Joshua commanded the priests carrying the ark of the Lord to come out of the water. And no sooner had they set their feet on dry ground than the waters of the Jordan returned to their place and ran at flood stage as before. In essence things returned to normal so far as the River Jordan was concerned. When God does something amazing there is no doubt as to who did it and to what purpose. The waters of the River Jordan returned to flood stage. The people of Israel witnessed the powerful hand of God at work. I pray that we witness God at work in our day.

There was the temptation to linger on the bank of the Jordan and celebrate the miracle of God. But that was not the reason for God leading the people across the Jordan River. The vision and the mission had to be kept at the forefront. So Joshua commanded the people to move forward to Gilgal on the eastern border of Jericho.

At Gilgal, the twelve stones that had been picked up from the Jordan River were set up as a memorial. Joshua told the people that: "In the future when your descendants ask their fathers, 'What do these stones mean?' [22] tell them, 'Israel crossed the Jordan on dry ground.' That was the message to be passed on to future generations.

There was a reason for this amazing method used by God. It was a reason that the people of Israel would not forget. In addition, it was to demonstrate that the God of the whole earth who walked in the midst of the people was mighty and powerful. Joshua put it this way: *"He did this so that all the peoples of the earth might know that the hand of the LORD is powerful and so that you might always fear the LORD your God."*

The fear of the Lord is truly the beginning of wisdom.

June Day 26

[1] Now when all the Amorite kings west of the Jordan and all the Canaanite kings along the coast heard how the LORD had dried up the Jordan before the Israelites until we had crossed over, their hearts melted and they no longer had the courage to face the Israelites. [2] At that time the LORD said to Joshua, "Make flint knives and circumcise the Israelites again." [3] So Joshua made flint knives and circumcised the Israelites at Gibeath Haaraloth. Joshua 5:1-3

News traveled very fast, something had happened that was unheard of. The Israelites had crossed the River Jordan on dry ground. That became top news in the region. If the God of Israelites had parted the water for them then what could stand in the way of this great people. So the Amorite kings west of the Jordan and all the Canaanite kings along the coast heard what God had done for his people and their hearts melted and they no longer had the courage to face the Israelites.

These kings had been planning for the arrival of these wandering Israelites. They wanted to band together to fight and destroy the Israelites. Now, the Israelites had crossed the Jordan River and the fighting was supposed to begin. But the kings were gripped by fear and they did not know what to do. The element of surprise that these kings wanted to use as the Israelites crossed the Jordan was gone because of fear.

At that time God gave instruction to Joshua to circumcise the Israelites. It was time for covenant renewal. It was time to bring the people of God back to basics. What was unique about the people of Israel was their covenant relationship with God. That relationship had been sealed with the covenant of circumcision of all male children.

So the instruction to Joshua to circumcise the male Israelites was a command to renew the covenant.

It is time for covenant renewal. The people had to be reminded that they were a peculiar people who belonged to God.

You are a child of the Covenant.

June Day 27

⁴ Now this is why he did so: All those who came out of Egypt—all the men of military age—died in the desert on the way after leaving Egypt. ⁵ All the people that came out had been circumcised, but all the people born in the desert during the journey from Egypt had not. ⁶ The Israelites had moved about in the desert forty years until all the men who were of military age when they left Egypt had died, since they had not obeyed the LORD. For the LORD had sworn to them that they would not see the land that he had solemnly promised their fathers to give us, a land flowing with milk and honey. ⁷ So he raised up their sons in their place, and these were the ones Joshua circumcised. They were still uncircumcised because they had not been circumcised on the way ⁸ And after the whole nation had been circumcised, they remained where they were in camp until they were healed. Joshua 5:4-8

We are given the reason for the command to circumcise the people of Israel. It was related to the reality of wandering in the desert. All the people that came out of the desert had been circumcised but all the people born in the desert during the journey from the Egypt had not. For forty years the people had moved around until all those who came out of Egypt had died. So a brand new group of Israelites were entering the Promised Land

Moses had done his best to keep the people of Israel in constant communion with God. He had always pointed them to the God of the Exodus. The God who had revealed himself to Moses at the burning bush led the people to the Promised Land. Unfortunately, the men who crossed the Jordan River were not circumcised. They were foreign to the covenant of God.

Joshua listened to God and circumcised all the male people of Israel.

The people were not in any mood to move on. So they stayed in camp until they were healed. The action of Joshua was a bold one. He knew how vulnerable his fighting men would be under such circumstances. But Joshua knew that it was better to obey the God who parts the waters.

Thank God for people like Joshua.

June Day 28

⁹ Then the LORD said to Joshua, "Today I have rolled away the reproach of Egypt from you." So the place has been called Gilgal to this day. ¹⁰ On the evening of the fourteenth day of the month, while camped at Gilgal on the plains of Jericho, the Israelites celebrated the Passover. ¹¹ The day after the Passover, that very day, they ate some of the produce of the land: unleavened bread and roasted grain. ¹² The manna stopped the day after they ate this food from the land; there was no longer any manna for the Israelites, but that year they ate of the produce of Canaan. Joshua 5: 9-12

The Israelites who left Egypt always looked back at their time in slavery as the most settled phase in their history. One is not surprised that several of them wanted to return to bondage instead of a life of wandering in the desert. When the people renewed their covenant with God on the west side of the Jordan, it was a way of saying that they have put their slavery past and all that went with it behind them.

At Gilgal the reproach of Egypt was truly removed from God's people. They were no longer a people who used slavery as a reference point.

Sometimes Christians find themselves in circumstances where the scars or negative experiences in their lives become what define them.

But in Jesus Christ we enter into a new covenant that gives us meaning. We are no longer defined by sins that held us bondage. Christians are a new creation in Jesus Christ.

The other thing that happened at Gilgal was the celebration of Passover. The event that was pivotal in the Exodus story could not be properly remembered in the wilderness. Now that the people had entered the Promise Land it was time to remember the institutions that defined them and gave them meaning. On the plains of Jericho, the Israelites celebrated the time when God in his mercy did pass over the Hebrew people in Egypt. Do you have a place where you remember the past mercies of God?

The day after the Passover celebration, there was no need for the manna that had been their daily ration in the wilderness. Now they could grow their crops and eat the fruit of the land. It is important to realize that God makes other provision when the manna stops.

God will take care of you no matter where you find yourself.

June Day 29

¹³ Now when Joshua was near Jericho, he looked up and saw a man standing in front of him with a drawn sword in his hand. Joshua went up to him and asked, "Are you for us or for our enemies?" Joshua 5:13

The people of Israel had celebrated Passover on the other side of the Jordan. The Exodus from Egypt had taken on a new meaning for God's people. The people of Israel had also witnessed the crossing of the Jordan River on dry land. The waters of the river parted before them by the mighty hand of God. Now they were ready to fulfill their mission of taking possession of The Promised Land.

Joshua was ready to lead the people to conquer the territories beyond the Jordan. He saw his first mission to be capturing Jericho. He looked up and saw a man standing in front of him with a drawn sword in his hand. Joshua understood the significance and the consequence of the event that he was confronted with. There was no turning back for him as far as the task ahead.

Joshua was a warrior who did not entertain any fears when confronted with difficult situations. He understood that the Lord who had brought them across the Jordan River would not give them into the hand of a lonely man standing in front of him with a drawn sword. Joshua went straight to the man with a drawn sword and asked a question that revealed bravery and confidence in the Lord.

Some people looking at the action of Joshua would think that his action in confronting the man with the drawn sword was foolhardy. But he demonstrated a confidence that said God was leading us and anyone who stood in our way was not going to amount to anything. Those who are not on the side of God would be fighting for the enemies of God. The question was simple. "Are you for us or for our enemies?

June Day 30

14 "Neither," he replied, "but as commander of the army of the LORD I have now come." Then Joshua fell facedown to the ground in reverence, and asked him, "What message does my Lord have for his servant?" Joshua 5:14

Joshua remembered the commission that the Lord gave him to be courageous because every place that he sets his feet would be given to him and the people of Israel. So he walked up to this man with a drawn sword standing in his way. Many people would have turned and gone the other way. Not so with Joshua. He walked up straight to the man with the drawn sword and asked a confrontational question. "Are you for us or for our enemies?"

I do not know the answer Joshua was expecting but one thing was certain. Joshua knew that whatever was going to happen, he had to go through this man with the drawn sword. The man with a drawn sword replied Joshua with an answer he was not expecting. He simply said: "Neither". I can imagine what was going through the mind of Joshua. "What do you mean by neither?" Joshua might have asked in his mind. Then why do you have a drawn sword? And why are you standing in my way?

The next sentence of the man with the drawn sword did clarify the issue at hand. He said: "but as the commander of the army of the Lord I have come". Joshua was surprised by the words he heard because he only saw those who were on his side or on the side of his enemies. Now he learns that there is another category. Those who are on the side of the Lord are far more than Joshua could have imagined. Those on the side of the Lord could possibly include angels and commanders of the army of the Lord of hosts. Joshua thought that he was the commander of Israel's army. He realized quickly that this was not about him at all. God has a way of raising commanders without the knowledge of those who believe to be earthly commanders.

Joshua immediately realized that the right thing to do was to fall prostrate before the Lord's messenger. He spoke from a lowly position and requested to know what message the Lord has for him.

He recognized that he was a servant of the Lord. He was ready and willing to do whatever the Lord said.

When God intervenes all we have to do is to learn to listen.

June Extra

Then Joshua fell facedown to the ground in reverence, and asked him, "What message does my Lord have for his servant?" ^{15} The commander of the Lord's army replied, "Take off your sandals, for the place where you are standing is holy." And Joshua did so. Joshua 5:14b-15

Falling face down was a sign of respect and acknowledging that we are before someone who is greater and more powerful. Joshua sent that message without second thoughts because he realized that he had been presumptuous in confronting the man with the drawn sword. He quickly came to terms with the fact that the real commander of the army of Israel was the Lord God.

The question of Joshua, as he lay on the ground, conveyed the sense of a repentant and humble individual. The question was this: "What message does my Lord have for his servant?" Joshua was expecting some specific instructions about battle plans and strategies to capture the city of Jericho. He called himself a servant who was ready and willing to carry out the orders of his Lord.

The commander of the Lord's army replied: "Take off your sandals for the place where you are standing is holy." Joshua was standing in the presence of God without realizing it. Wherever the Lord appears becomes holy ground. Falling prostrate before the commander of the army of the Lord was not enough. Joshua had to remove the sandals from his feet. One can imagine the desperate attempt of Joshua to remove his sandals without getting up from the ground.

The whole episode recalls the encounter Moses had at the burning bush before he was commissioned by God to lead the Israelites from slavery into the Promised Land. It was important for Joshua to get a perspective of who and what he was dealing with.

Just when we think we have everything figured out. God has a way of bringing us to the place where we know there is more to know about this God who has called us to follow Him.

We are standing on holy ground.

Brother Seth

July Day 1

¹ Now Jericho was tightly shut up because of the Israelites. No one went out and no one came in. Joshua 6:1

Joshua had sent two spies to Jericho earlier. The report of the spies was favorable in the sense that the kings on the west side of the Jordan River were living in fear of the advancing Israelites. The spies had an accomplice by the name of Rahab who was hoping that the advancing Israelite army would spare her and her family. The report did not reveal any weakness in the city wall. So there was no definite plan on how to mount an attack on Jericho apart from laying siege for as long as possible.

To make matters worse, the people of Jericho had got an advance warning of the conquering army under the leadership of Joshua. The King of Jericho also heard about the two spies who were in his city and managed to escape. Therefore, the people of Jericho did not have any alternative but to shore up their defenses. The biggest advantage of the city was that it was walled around and they had posts on the city wall.

The king therefore ordered the city wall to be tightly shut up to prevent any enemy from entering. That meant that no one was allowed to exit or enter the city. Most likely they hoped that Joshua's men would camp on the outskirts of the city for a while then they would be able to attack them from time to time and run back into the city. Whatever strategy the people of Jericho hoped to deploy had to be based on the fact that they had enough supplies stored up in the city so that there would be no need to venture out the city walls.

We are told that the city was shut up because of fear of the Israelites. Sometimes fear can make people short sighted. They could not way all their options because they were operating from fear. The citizens of the city who had farms and businesses outside the city wall were now at a disadvantage. The biggest question was "how long could the city stay shut tightly?"

Fear does not allow people to think straight.

July Day 2

² Then the LORD said to Joshua, "See, I have delivered Jericho into your hands, along with its king and its fighting men. ³ March around the city once with all the armed men. Do this for six days. ⁴ Have seven priests carry trumpets of rams' horns in front of the ark. On the seventh day, march around the city seven times, with the priests blowing the trumpets. ⁵ When you hear them sound a long blast on the trumpets, have all the people give a loud shout; then the wall of the city will collapse and the people will go up, every man straight in." Joshua: 6:2-5

The Lord did not leave any doubt concerning who was going to win the victory in the battle ahead. The Lord said to Joshua, "See, I have delivered Jericho into your hands along with its king and its fighting men." It seemed that God had done everything that was needed to assure victory. Joshua did not have to worry about the battle strategy. He had no problem concerning himself with the walled city of Jericho, its king or its fighting men.

The commander of the army of Israel had truly taken charge of the details on how Jericho was going to be defeated. The details of the battle plan were a little bit unusual. The strategy was unfamiliar to Joshua and he had never heard of that type of battle plan used before in the history of Israel. Joshua however knew that the source of the strategy was God and he had no reason doubting or questioning the directives of God.

The army was to march behind the ark of God with seven priests blowing trumpets ahead of the ark of the Lord. The route of the march was to go around the wall of Jericho once a day without much fanfare and noise. On the seventh day, they were to march around the wall seven times before sounding the victory shout. When this is done the wall of Jericho would fall flat and the army of Israel would have to rush straight in and take the city.

We dare not question the directives of the Lord who is the commander of the army of Israel. Even when what God is saying does not make sense to our human minds, it will serve us well to trust the Lord.

July Day 3

⁸ When Joshua had spoken to the people, the seven priests carrying the seven trumpets before the LORD went forward, blowing their trumpets, and the ark of the Lord's covenant followed them. ⁹ The armed guard marched ahead of the priests who blew the trumpets, and the rear guard followed the ark. All this time the trumpets were sounding. ¹⁰ But Joshua had commanded the people, "Do not give a war cry, do not raise your voices, do not say a word until the day I tell you to shout. Then shout!" ¹¹ So he had the ark of the LORD carried around the city, circling it once. Then the people returned to camp and spent the night there. Joshua 6:8-11

The whole exercise must have seemed strange and partly ridiculous to the people of Jericho who had shut themselves tightly within their city walls. If they had not heard of the miraculous ways that God had used on behalf of Israel they would have had no reason to be concerned. What they witnessed the people of Israel circle the wall of their city, it seemed like children playing.

Seven priests carrying the seven trumpets before the Lord went forward blowing their trumpets. The ark of the Lord's covenant followed them. There was an armed guard that marched ahead of the priests who blew the trumpets. All that could be heard was the sound of the trumpets. The people of Israel were faithfully carrying out the directives of the Lord given through Joshua.

The people of God did not miss the symbolism. They had their Lord present and leading them in battle. That was more than they could ask for. The presence of the Lord in their midst gave the people a level of confidence that was infectious. Joshua had taken the precaution of providing armed guard for the priests who were ahead of the whole group. The first day must have been the most difficult as the people marched around the wall once. They did not know what to expect. All they had going for them was that the commander of the army of the Lord was in their midst.

What would happen if Christians took seriously the presence of the Lord in their midst? That would mean the unleashing of a great potential to accomplish the work of God. There is so much God seeks to do with people like us if we are prepared to put on the back burner our own ideas and seek what God wants us to do.

The most difficult thing for Christians to do is living in that period between the promise and the fulfillment of the word of God. At some level things seem non eventful. But we always have to remember that God is still working in the moments that we return to camp thinking that nothing happened.

God is still working behind the scenes.

July Day 4

[15] On the seventh day, they got up at daybreak and marched around the city seven times in the same manner, except that on that day they circled the city seven times. [16] The seventh time around, when the priests sounded the trumpet blast, Joshua commanded the people, "Shout! For the LORD has given you the city! Joshua 6:15-16

For six days the people of Israel had been faithful to the directives of the Lord with no apparent results. The people in the city of Jericho were by this time accustomed to the daily march around their city once with a whole army in tow but not doing anything. On the seventh day, it seemed things were going to be different. The instructions were that the people should rise early because there was an important task at hand.

The first task was to circle the city of Jericho seven times. Just when the army of Israel thought it was settling into a daily routine, the order came that things were to be different. Sometimes God finds it necessary to wake us up from our comfortable routines. Oh! That the people of God would be open to the surprises of God instead of a fixation on what we know or what we have seen done by someone. My prayer is that God would shake things up for all of us. Lord, do something new in our lives!

There were more words of instructions for the people after the breaking of their routine, there was going to be a command to shout for the Lord. The priests with the trumpets were to give a loud blast. Then Joshua would follow with a command to shout for the Lord. It was going to be a shout of victory. The type of victory that is announced before it comes to pass. It is a "prevenient shout". God has already gone ahead and accomplished the unthinkable.

I invite you to join me today for a victory shout of our own. There are walls and barriers that must come down. But we need a shout of faith that can be heard by every problem or situation in our lives.

July Day 5

17 The city and all that is in it are to be devoted to the LORD. Only Rahab the prostitute and all who are with her in her house shall be spared, because she hid the spies we sent. 18 But keep away from the devoted things, so that you will not bring about your own destruction by taking any of them. Otherwise you will make the camp of Israel liable to destruction and bring trouble on it. 19 All the silver and gold and the articles of bronze and iron are sacred to the LORD and must go into his treasury." Joshua 6:17 -19

The promise was that the city was going to be given to the people of Israel after the victory shout. Just imagine how things were going to change overnight. Suddenly, the people of Israel were going to be in command of the first major walled city that seemed unconquerable. If Jericho could fall at the approach of Israel under the leadership of the Lord, then what could stand in the way of the commander of the army of the Lord?

The instructions that followed were as important as the promise of an overwhelming victory. "The city and all that was in it were to be devoted to the Lord." The people were to keep away from the devoted things. Anything that was taken from the city and brought to camp of Israel would defile the camp. The instructions about devoted things were so serious that the people of Israel were put on notice that violating the ban would amount to breaking faith with God.

The silver, gold and other precious metal were to go to the treasury of the Lord. Any attempt to be greedy by an individual or a group would be considered as a serious breach of trust. The people of Israel were also given instructions about Rahab who was faithful to the two spies who went out to survey the city of Jericho.

There is always a temptation to be greedy. God did not want these people who have lived all their lives in the wilderness to be suddenly overcome by their exposure to the wealth of Jericho. They needed some guidelines to put things in perspective.

There is a reason behind every command of God.

July Day 6

20 When the trumpets sounded, the people shouted, and at the sound of the trumpet, when the people gave a loud shout, the wall collapsed; so every man charged straight in, and they took the city. 21 They devoted the city to the LORD and destroyed with the sword every living thing in it—men and women, young and old, cattle, sheep and donkeys. Joshua 6:20-21

The instructions on how to take the city of Jericho captive were clear. The people of Israel had marched around the city seven times on the seventh day. They had also been given a stern warning concerning the whole city. It had been devoted to the Lord. "But keep away from the devoted things, so that you will not bring about your own destruction by taking any of them. Otherwise you will make the camp of Israel liable to destruction and bring trouble on it." Any attempt to go against this command would surely bring about disaster.

So when the trumpets sounded, the people shouted and the wall of Jericho collapsed. So every man charged straight ahead and the city did not have a chance. The people of Jericho were not expecting their great wall to collapse and so they were taken by the surprise when they saw fighting men charging straight at them. Everything happened too quickly and the people of Israel did not receive any resistance from the armies of Jericho.

The army of Israel considered everything in sight as devoted to the utter destruction and they carried that out without fail. When one reads this passage, one is surprised by the extent of the destruction. There are serious questions to be asked in our day when we read about the destruction of Children. But it is also important to understand what it means to have a whole city devoted to destruction. In other words, when the instruction is given not to spare anything devoted to destruction, the command must be carried out. There must be more to this than we can see or understand. Saul was given a similar command and he tried to spare a few sheep and the king of the Amalekites. He received a sharp rebuke from the prophet Samuel. He was told that to obey was better than to sacrifice.

Lord, even when we do not understand, we still trust you.

JULY DAY 7

22 Joshua said to the two men who had spied out the land, "Go into the prostitute's house and bring her out and all who belong to her, in accordance with your oath to her." 23 So the young men who had done the spying went in and brought out Rahab, her father and mother and brothers and all who belonged to her. They brought out her entire family and put them in a place outside the camp of Israel. 24 Then they burned the whole city and everything in it, but they put the silver and gold and the articles of bronze and iron into the treasury of the Lord's house. 25 But Joshua spared Rahab the prostitute, with her family and all who belonged to her, because she hid the men Joshua had sent as spies to Jericho—and she lives among the Israelites to this day. Joshua: 6:22-25

It pays to be a promise keeper. Rahab promised the two spies that she was not going to give them away. She requested the spies on the other hand to spare her family when the Lord gave the city into the hands of Israel. Now it was the turn of the people of Israel to keep the promise that they made to Rahab. Note that her house was on the city wall and most likely was damaged by the collapse of the wall. I am not sure if the scarlet cloth in her window was going to be any help. But the important is that the spies located the family with or without the scarlet cloth. And they were brought to safety.

The entire family of Rahab was brought to the camp of Israel and that meant that they came under the shadow of the Almighty God. That must have been a difficult experience for Rahab's family. They watched everything they have known and loved destroyed before their very eyes. But Rahab had spoken of this earlier. She knew that God was going to give the city into the hands of Israel. Now that it had happened Rahab was counting on the faithfulness of the people of Israel and the God of Israel to keep them safe.

When both parties kept promises they had made things worked out better for all concerned. Christians are also called to keep the promises they made to the Lord Jesus Christ when they entered into a relationship with God. We know God is faithful and would keep His end of the bargain. After all, it was God who took the initiative to extend love to us in Christ Jesus.

He has said I will never leave you nor forsake you!

God will keep that promise to you.

July Day 8

¹ But the Israelites acted unfaithfully in regard to the devoted things; Achan son of Carmi, the son of Zimri, the son of Zerah, of the tribe of Judah, took some of them. So the Lord's anger burned against Israel. ² Now Joshua sent men from Jericho to Ai, which is near Beth Aven to the east of Bethel, and told them, "Go up and spy out the region." So the men went up and spied out Ai." Joshua 7:1-2

"But the Israelites acted unfaithfully in regard to the devoted things." How could that be when one considers the zeal with which the people took Jericho and condemned everything to utter destruction? It took the unfaithfulness of one man to bring the whole nation into disrepute. It is surprising how the secret action of one man could have such a devastating condemnation of a whole nation.

We often forget how our actions could affect the whole body of Christ. In this case a whole nation. Achan presumed that he could get away with taking some items that were devoted to the Lord during the conquest of Jericho. He believed that what he took was so insignificant in the large scheme of things that it would not be noticed let alone be missed. But he was wrong! God noticed what Achan did.

Achan managed to deceive Joshua. The head of his tribe had no idea what he had done, but the actions of Achan did not go unnoticed by the Lord. It was business as usual in the camp of Israel. Joshua was making plans for the next town to attack. He did not pay attention to the spiritual state of the nation. After all, God had led the Israelites to a mighty victory. It is important for all of us to stay alert spiritually after we have won some victories in the spiritual journey.

If Joshua had paused to seek the face of the Lord, he would have learned that all was not well at the home front. How often do we plunge ahead without pausing to reflect and wait on the Lord for direction? Joshua was using the same methodology that had worked for him previously and had worked for Moses also. He sent out spies to scout out the next town that they were to enter.

Folks, no strategy or methodology would ever replace seeking the face of the Lord and being in good relationship with the Lord.

July Day 9

³ When they returned to Joshua, they said, "Not all the people will have to go up against Ai. Send two or three thousand men to take it and do not weary all the people, for only a few men are there." ⁴ So about three thousand men went up; but they were routed by the men of Ai, ⁵ who killed about thirty-six of them. They chased the Israelites from the city gate as far as the stone quarries and struck them down on the slopes. At this the hearts of the people melted and became like water Joshua 7:3-5

The men who went out to spy that little town called Ai came back with a favorable report. They indicated that the experiences of the Israel army indicated that a couple of thousand men could defeat the town. There was no need for the whole army to go into battle. That was the strategy required to defeat a town of that size according to the scouts. Joshua listened to the scouting report and acted on it accordingly.

The problem with this report and the action of Joshua was that the God factor was missing. Everything was predicated on the strength of the army of Israel and its past experiences. The hymn writer says: "The arm of flesh will fail you and you dare not trust your own." Joshua and his spies had forgotten what had given them the victories in their previous encounters. They were missing the commander of the army of Israel. The sad thing about the whole episode was that they did not even realize what was missing as they made preparations to go forward to battle against Ai.

How often do we find ourselves acting in a similar fashion? We go forward with our human agendas, presuming that God would always be there because of what God has done in the past. It may be time to pause and pray and ask: Is God leading us in this endeavor or are we doing it because we believe it is the right thing to do?

The army of Israel learned the hard way. They were defeated by a small army and they had to retreat before this small town suffering thirty-six casualties. They were surprised by the outcome. Usually, when the people of God encounter such results they tend to put they blame on God. They ask where was God? When they had forgotten to include God at the center of their decision-making.

In this particular instance God was completely out of the loop because of sin. Yet Joshua and his army were not aware of the sin in the camp of Israel. The psalmist says: "if I regard iniquity in my heart the Lord will not hear."

It may be time to put some things right with God.

July Day 10

They chased the Israelites from the city gate as far as the stone quarries and struck them down on the slopes. At this the hearts of the people melted and became like water. ⁶ Then Joshua tore his clothes and fell facedown to the ground before the ark of the LORD, remaining there till evening. The elders of Israel did the same, and sprinkled dust on their heads. ⁷ And Joshua said, "Ah, Sovereign LORD, why did you ever bring this people across the Jordan to deliver us into the hands of the Amorites to destroy us? If only we had been content to stay on the other side of the Jordan! Joshua 7:5-7

The Israelites were chased from the city gates of Ai. The men had to run for their lives. We are told that: "At this the hearts of the people melted and became like water." That is a good description of a people who had been humiliated by their defeat and were in no shape or form to go and possess the Promised Land. Fear had taken the place of a "victory shout", and people were beginning to doubt the promises that God had made to them.

Joshua took responsibility for what had happened. After all, it was Joshua who sent the men to go and die in battle and also to be chased by their enemies as they run from the battle. So Joshua tore his clothes and prostrated himself before the ark of the Lord. How come that it so easy to fall face down in the presence of the Lord when our backs are against the wall than when things are going so well? Well, that was what Joshua and the elders of Israel did after their terrible loss to Ai and the humiliation of the fighting men of Israel. They went as far as sprinkling dust on their heads as a sign of mourning and repentance.

Joshua lamented the defeat of Israel in his prayer. He was concerned that God had brought his people across the Jordan River only to hand them into the hands of the Amorites and the kings on the west side of the Jordan. It seemed that Joshua was blaming God for what had happened. He was saying that God had let his people down by not keeping the promises made to Joshua.

Joshua could have analyzed the situation differently with the assumption that God was faithful and the defeat of the Israelites could have been the result of the unfaithfulness of the people of God. Let us not be hasty in apportioning blame to God when things do not go as expected.

God is faithful to the promises that have been made to us in Christ Jesus.

July Day 11

"Ah, Sovereign LORD, why did you ever bring this people across the Jordan to deliver us into the hands of the Amorites to destroy us? If only we had been content to stay on the other side of the Jordan! 8 O Lord, what can I say, now that Israel has been routed by its enemies? 9 The Canaanites and the other people of the country will hear about this and they will surround us and wipe out our name from the earth. What then will you do for your own great name?" Joshua 7:7b-9

The human side of Joshua seemed to have gotten the upper hand. He was heavily involved in the blame game without the critical reflection that is called for when things go wrong. He indicated that he would have preferred dying on the other side of the Jordan River (Wilderness) than being handed over to the kings on the west of the Jordan River.

One would say: "That does not sound like Joshua at all!" But that was the same Joshua who had shown courage as a spy and had brought a minority report with the confidence that the people of Israel were able to take possession of the Promised Land. He had been given exhortation to be courageous and to be afraid because God was going to be with him just as God was with Moses. So what changed? It was a reality check and a confidence that had been badly shaken.

The other problem that Joshua had was his obsession with what the nations and the kings in the Promised Land would think or interpret the defeat of Israel by Ai. He was in a way more concerned about defending the name of God before the nations of the world instead of asking: "Could we have done something wrong? Could there be the possibility that it is not God's fault?"

Fear can make even the greatest of us begin to think irrationally. Joshua could already see a scenario in which the Canaanite people have surrounded the people of Israel and wiped them out from the surface of the earth. At least that was the complaint that Joshua brought to the Lord as he lay face down before the ark of the Lord.

I am glad that Joshua took his problems to the Lord instead of quitting. Many have thrown in the towel in the face of defeat or humiliation. Others have decided to have nothing to do with God when things do not work out the way they expected.

Joshua went to the Lord in prayer with his problems, fears and uncertainties. Let us do the same.

July Day 12

¹⁰ The LORD said to Joshua, "Stand up! What are you doing down on your face? ¹¹ Israel has sinned; they have violated my covenant, which I commanded them to keep. They have taken some of the devoted things; they have stolen, they have lied, they have put them with their own possessions. ¹² That is why the Israelites cannot stand against their enemies; they turn their backs and run because they have been made liable to destruction. I will not be with you anymore unless you destroy whatever among you is devoted to destruction. Joshua: 7:10- 12

Joshua had prostrated himself before God after the defeat of the Israelites by an inferior army. What happened was unthinkable in the camp of Israel. The spies who scouted Ai were distraught because it seemed their assessment of the situation was wrong. Joshua was the leader and he took responsibility for the defeat.

The Lord asked Joshua an obvious question. "What are you doing down on your face?" God did not want Joshua to continue lying on the ground when there was work to be done. He was told to stand up and pay attention to what God had to stay. Sometimes people enjoy playing the blame game instead of facing the introspection that is called for. We cannot continue to blame God, others or ourselves for what is happening in our lives. We have to listen to what God is saying to us. There is so much work to be done and it was time for Joshua to get up from the ground.

The message to Joshua was simple: "There is sin in the camp of Israel." Someone had violated the covenant by taking some of the items devoted to God during the conquest of Jericho. Although there was nothing apparent outwardly, the sin of this individual had weakened the covenant relationship that Israel had with God. The stolen items had become a stumbling block for Israel. God had removed the protection that they had and the commander of the army of Israel was no longer present in their camp. All they had left were human ideas and human strategies. These may be good only to a point.

The remedy for the situation was given to Joshua. It was this: "I will not be with you anymore unless you destroy whatever among you is devoted to destruction." The first task was to find the devoted things that had been stolen. There was no doubt that Joshua was determined to remove the stumbling block so that Israel could enjoy the protection of God again.

Sin has to be dealt with drastically if we are going to enjoy our relationship with God.

JULY DAY 13

13 "Go, consecrate the people. Tell them, 'consecrate yourselves in preparation for tomorrow; for this is what the LORD, the God of Israel, says: That which is devoted is among you, O Israel. You cannot stand against your enemies until you remove it." Joshua 7:13

"Go, consecrate the people". Joshua was commanded to get up from the floor and stop all the series of lamentations. It was time for action. God wanted Joshua to prepare the people for an encounter with the Lord. Each time God requested a meeting with the people of Israel, there was a need for consecration. That scenario has not changed. We have to consecrate ourselves when we come to the presence of the Lord. In essence the term (Consecration) means being set apart for a special task. In this case it was a meeting with a Holy God.

God requested this type of consecration before the meeting at Sinai, and also before the crossing of the Jordan River. Usually the ritual involved washing all their garments and also their bodies. Sometimes consecration would require abstinence from all sexual relations. Appearing before the Holy God was a big thing that was not to be taken lightly. In this particular instance, God summoned all his people before him for judgment.

The reason for consecration was given to the people of Israel: "That which is devoted is among you". In other words, there was sin in the camp. As long as the status quo persisted, no amount of structural adjustments or strategic planning could remedy the situation. The people who were called by that name of the Lord were expected to humble themselves and repent of their sin so that they could enjoy the protection of the Lord and the leading of the Lord again.

First and foremost, the sin must be identified and confessed or dealt with. It is for that reason that prayers of confession are not to be taken lightly in the Church of Jesus Christ. During those moments we plead the cleansing blood of Jesus Christ for ourselves and for our communities. Yes, it is all by grace, but it is not cheap grace.

We thank God for the once and for all sacrifice of our Lord Jesus Christ. That is the only reason that we dare to stand against our enemies spiritually and also in our daily walk.

July Day 14

14 "'In the morning, present yourselves tribe by tribe. The tribe that the LORD takes shall come forward clan by clan; the clan that the LORD takes shall come forward family by family; and the family that the LORD takes shall come forward man by man. 15 He who is caught with the devoted things shall be destroyed by fire, along with all that belongs to him. He has violated the covenant of the LORD and has done a disgraceful thing in Israel!'" 16 Early the next morning Joshua had Israel come forward by tribes, and Judah was taken. 17 The clans of Judah came forward, and he took the Zerahites. He had the clan of the Zerahites come forward by families, and Zimri was taken. 18 Joshua had his family come forward man by man, and Achan son of Carmi, the son of Zimri, the son of Zerah, of the tribe of Judah, was taken. Joshua 7:14-18

The instructions were that all the people of Israel were to appear before the Lord, tribe by tribe. But prior to that, they all had to be consecrated and set apart for a meeting with the Lord. That was a good time for the culprit who had taken some of the devoted things into his tent to own up and confess what they had done. But nothing like that happened.

The instructions, communicated through Joshua, did outline not only the process, but also the punishment to be given to the individual or individuals who had violated the covenant of God. The culprit who is caught with the devoted things would be destroyed with fire. One would have thought that the severe punishment that was stipulated to be given would have caused the guilty party to come forward and saved time and embarrassment for the families and clans involved. But that did not happen. Was it because this individual thought that they still could get away from under the scrutiny of God? If that was the case, then this individual had calculated wrongly.

How often do we convince ourselves that God does not see what we are doing? That shows how limited our knowledge of God is. There is no place to hide from under the seeing eye of God. One by one the clans were asked to come forward until finally Achan the son of Carmi was selected as the man who had stolen some of the devoted things and hidden them.

Surely, the sins of Achan found him out. There was no more room for hiding. Either what God was saying was true or God was a liar.

July Day 15

[19] Then Joshua said to Achan, "My son, give glory to the LORD, the God of Israel, and give him the praise. Tell me what you have done; do not hide it from me." Joshua 7:19

Achan had been identified through the process of elimination. We are not told in specific terms how that process took place. But it was a reliable process that involved the Lord himself. After all, it was God who had called for a consecration of the people of Israel so that they could appear before him. One could still imagine a scenario in which some of the people of Israel could doubt if Achan had truly done anything wrong and if so what did he do?

Joshua was the type of leader who treated all the people of Israel with respect and he wanted to give Achan the same opportunity. Joshua himself had no doubts about the guilt of Achan but Joshua did not know specifically what the guilt of Achan was. So he approached Achan with all the wisdom and tact he could muster. Listen to the words of Joshua: "My son, give glory to the Lord, the God of Israel and give him praise …"

Joshua was saying in effect, this is what the God of Israel says, and our God does not lie so what are you going to do Achan? There were two choices before Achan. He could deny that he had done anything wrong and be punished. He could also accept what he had done and say exactly what he did and still be punished. The punishment had already been laid out and it was a matter of affirming the indictment of God to be true or not true.

Joshua used an approach that made the heart of Achan melt under the conviction of the Lord. He said: "Tell me what you have done; and do hide it from me." Now the ball was in the court of Achan and he had to come up with the truth. The sin had to be confessed; Achan had no way of escape.

If we say we have no sin, then the truth is not in us but if we confess our sin God is faithful and just to forgive and cleanse us.

July Day 16

[20] Achan replied, "It is true! I have sinned against the LORD, the God of Israel. This is what I have done: [21] When I saw in the plunder a beautiful robe from Babylonia, two hundred shekels of silver and a wedge of gold weighing fifty shekels, I coveted them and took them. They are hidden in the ground inside my tent, with the silver underneath." Joshua 7:20-21

This was the much-awaited time. It was time for Achan to come clean or continue to pretend that he was innocent. Achan spoke up and this time it was a confession of what he had done. He began by affirming what God had said. He was the culprit who had brought disaster to the whole nation. Achan realized and confessed that he had sinned against the Lord, The God of Israel.

It is important to note that the sin of Achan and for that matter any sin is against God. That was an important breakthrough, but the question is why did he not come forward and save the whole nation from the trouble of searching for the offender? Most people tend to be sorry for their sins when they are caught. That is different from one being sorry for their sins. In the latter there is genuine remorse while in the former the concern is more about the shame that accompanies being found out.

Achan told Joshua the real problem. It had to do with a beautiful robe from Babylon that he saw in the plunder and decided that it should not go to waste because he could find a good use for it. Then there were the two hundred shekels of silver and the wedge of gold weighing fifty shekels. These items were too precious to classify them as devoted things that should be burned or put into the treasury.

The only problem here was that Achan was playing God and defying the command of God. Moreover, the instructions were that that the gold and silver were to be consigned to the treasury of the Lord. So Achan was only trying to justify the fact that he stole the items. He went as far as saying that he coveted the items and buried them in the ground inside his tent.

Achan knew exactly what he was doing. He made an effort to hide the items securely so that anyone who visited him would not have noticed what he had done. He did not count on the "all searching eyes of God". I believe a burden was lifted off Achan after he had come clean. There was no need to hide again. Now everything was in the open.

There was no place for Achan to hide in the presence of the searching spirit of God.

July Day 17

22 So Joshua sent messengers, and they ran to the tent, and there it was, hidden in his tent, with the silver underneath. 23 They took the things from the tent, brought them to Joshua and all the Israelites and spread them out before the LORD. 24 Then Joshua, together with all Israel, took Achan son of Zerah, the silver, the robe, the gold wedge, his sons and daughters, his cattle, donkeys and sheep, his tent and all that he had, to the Valley of Achor. 25 Joshua said, "Why have you brought this trouble on us? The LORD will bring trouble on you today."

Then all Israel stoned him, and after they had stoned the rest, they burned them. 26 Over Achan they heaped up a large pile of rocks, which remains to this day. Then the LORD turned from his fierce anger. Therefore, that place has been called the Valley of Achor ever since. Joshua: 7:22-26

Achan did come clean with what happened after the capture of Jericho. Everything indicated that Achan was telling the truth this time. He even showed Joshua where the stolen items were hidden in his tent. Now, to confirm the clues given by Achan, people were sent into his tent to search for the items that would be proof that Achan was telling the truth. Also if the devoted items were recovered and destroyed then the sin that had caused Israel so much misery would be eliminated.

The men who ran into Achan's tent found the items just as he had indicated. They brought the garment, the silver and the gold and spread them before Joshua and the whole assembly of Israel. The stolen items and the tent and the family of Achan were all taken to the valley of Achor and eliminated with fire. A heap of stones was left as a reminder of how sin had impacted the people of Israel. Some would ask: "was the punishment of Achan and his family too severe?" This showed how serious God considered sin and also all who had come into contact with the devoted items.

When the sin was dealt with, the Lord turned from his fierce anger. Thank God for Jesus who has paid the price for sin.

July Day 18

[1] Then the LORD said to Joshua, "Do not be afraid; do not be discouraged. Take the whole army with you, and go up and attack Ai. For I have delivered into your hands the king of Ai, his people, his city and his land. [2] You shall do to Ai and its king as you did to Jericho and its king, except that you may carry off their plunder and livestock for yourselves. Set an ambush behind the city." Joshua 8:1-2

After Joshua had removed the sin of Achan from among the people of Israel, he faced a serious challenge. How was he going to motivate the army of Israel into battle against the same enemy that had defeated Israel? The painful defeat was still fresh in the minds of the people and the death of thirty-six soldiers was something that Israel had not experienced for a while.

God took the initiative to speak to Joshua. It was time to motivate the leader himself if Israel was going to step forward in battle again. The words spoken to Joshua were those of assurance of the presence of the Lord. "Do not be afraid; do not be discouraged. Take the whole army with you, and go up and attack Ai. For I have delivered into your hands the king of Ai, his people, his city and his land.

It was this type of instruction that was lacking in the first attempt to take Ai. It is always important to seek the face of the Lord so that we may get a clear direction as to the will of God. When the covenant community is in communication with God there is a clear sense of direction. In this particular instance God was assuring Joshua of victory before any attempt to retake Ai.

God promised victory in the same place where there had been defeat earlier. When we return to the Lord in repentance, we can be assured that the Lord would go ahead of us in all the areas where we have suffered defeat previously. In addition, the Lord promised to give the plunder of Ai to the people of Israel. That is where Achan missed out. If he had just been patient, the very things that he coveted in the defeat of Jericho would be promised to him without any repercussions.

We cannot put God in a box. We never know how God is going to bring about the next victory in our lives.

July Day 19

³ So Joshua and the whole army moved out to attack Ai. He chose thirty thousand of his best fighting men and sent them out at night ⁴ with these orders: "Listen carefully. You are to set an ambush behind the city. Don't go very far from it. All of you be on the alert. Joshua 8:3-4

The directions given to Joshua by God in the fight against Ai was very different from the first attempt to defeat Ai. This time it was not based on the scouting report of an overconfident army. It was rather the direct command of God on what to do every step of the way. God asked the whole army of Israel to go up against a city that was smaller than Jericho. One does not know why God gave that directive. Certainly, there was no doubt about who was in charge of this campaign.

The whole strategy was based on ambushing the people of Ai. So thirty thousand of the fighting men of Israel were sent out at night. They were ordered to stay very close to the city and they were not to go far from the city walls. The key words for the soldiers were "Listen" and "be on the alert". The whole strategy for victory was based on following the instructions of the Lord closely. They were also required to be ready to spring into action at the right moment.

The same instructions are given to Christians today in the battles that come their way. It is important to listen carefully to what the Lord is saying. All attempts to circumvent the word of God would fail. Those who have learned the secret of paying attention to the word of the Lord know what it means to hear what the Spirit is saying. Then there is the call to be alert. Christians need not be surprised by all the flaming darts that come at them. God is always doing something with those who dare to be alert to what is required.

Stay blessed today. Listen and be alert.

July Day 20

⁵ I and all those with me will advance on the city, and when the men come out against us, as they did before, we will flee from them. ⁶ They will pursue us until we have lured them away from the city, for they will say, 'They are running away from us as they did before.' So when we flee from them, ⁷ you are to rise up from ambush and take the city. The LORD your God will give it into your hand. ⁸ When you have taken the city, set it on fire. Do what the LORD has commanded. See to it; you have my orders." Joshua 8:5-8

What was the army of Israel supposed to listen and pay attention to carefully? It was the battle plan that was going to bring victory for the people of God. The enemy was going to count on the same plans that brought victory the other time. But God had something else in mind on how things were going to unfold. It was going to be an ambush and a surprise for the people of Ai.

Joshua and the men with him were to advance on the city of Ai. Then they were to draw the people of Ai out of their city by fleeing before them. Since the soldiers had seen the same thing happen in the first attempt by Israel to take Ai, the soldiers were bound to pursue the fleeing Israelites. In the meantime, the thirty thousand Israeli soldiers who were waiting in ambush would pounce on the fighting men from Ai and also go into the city to take it.

It looked so simple, but what happened was that God was turning a weakness in the first battle against the people of Ai, into strength. God continues to do that with his people. The very place where it seemed that defeat was inevitable could be God's opportunity for victory. There is nothing that God cannot use for God's glory.

The important thing is to remember that it is God at work and not us.

JULY DAY 21

14 When the king of Ai saw this, he and all the men of the city hurried out early in the morning to meet Israel in battle at a certain place overlooking the Arabah. But he did not know that an ambush had been set against him behind the city. 15 Joshua and all Israel let themselves be driven back before them, and they fled toward the desert. 16 All the men of Ai were called to pursue them, and they pursued Joshua and were lured away from the city. 17 Not a man remained in Ai or Bethel who did not go after Israel. They left the city open and went in pursuit of Israel. 18 Then the LORD said to Joshua, "Hold out toward Ai the javelin that is in your hand, for into your hand I will deliver the city." So Joshua held out his javelin toward Ai. 19 As soon as he did this, the men in the ambush rose quickly from their position and rushed forward. They entered the city and captured it and quickly set it on fire. Joshua 8:14-19

The king of Ai saw Joshua and his men camping in the open at the entrance of his city. He wanted to attack them early in the morning so that he could surprise the army of Israel. Little did he know that there was an ambush and the fact that Joshua and his men were widely exposed was part of the strategy to lure him out of the city! Joshua and his men allowed themselves to be driven back before the army of Ai and they fled in the direction of the desert.

This was exactly what happened in the last battle when Israel was defeated. So the king of Ai and his men felt confident that they were going to defeat Israel again. This time they were determined not to leave any of the Israelite army alive so that they could come back to fight another day. So they mustered as many people as people to chase the retreating army of Israel. In so doing they all left the city in pursuit of Israel thus making the city vulnerable to a counter attack.

The command came to Joshua to lift up his Javelin and hold it out toward Ai. The city was quickly captured and set on fire. The strategy had worked because the people obeyed the directions of the Lord this time. It all started with Joshua seeking the face of God before going out in battle.

It may be time for the Javelin to be raised in the direction of Ai. Each one of us should know what Ai represents in our spiritual journey. This time there is going to be victory.

July Day 22

14 When the king of Ai saw this, he and all the men of the city hurried out early in the morning to meet Israel in battle at a certain place overlooking the Arabah. But he did not know that an ambush had been set against him behind the city. 15 Joshua and all Israel let themselves be driven back before them, and they fled toward the desert. 16 All the men of Ai were called to pursue them, and they pursued Joshua and were lured away from the city. 17 Not a man remained in Ai or Bethel who did not go after Israel. They left the city open and went in pursuit of Israel. 18 Then the LORD said to Joshua, "Hold out toward Ai the javelin that is in your hand, for into your hand I will deliver the city." So Joshua held out his javelin toward Ai. 19 As soon as he did this, the men in the ambush rose quickly from their position and rushed forward. They entered the city and captured it and quickly set it on fire. Joshua 8:14-19

The king of Ai saw Joshua and his men camping in the open at the entrance of his city. He wanted to attack them early in the morning so that he could surprise the army of Israel. Little did he know that there was an ambush and the fact that Joshua and his men were widely exposed was part of the strategy to lure him out of the city! Joshua and his men allowed themselves to be driven back before the army of Ai and they fled in the direction of the desert.

This was exactly what happened in the last battle when Israel was defeated. So the king of Ai and his men felt confident that they were going to defeat Israel again. This time they were determined not to leave any of the Israelite army alive so that they could come back to fight another day. So they mustered as many people as people to chase the retreating army of Israel. In so doing they all left the city in pursuit of Israel thus making the city vulnerable to a counter attack.

The command came to Joshua to lift up his Javelin and hold it out toward Ai. The city was quickly captured and set on fire. The strategy had worked because the people obeyed the directions of the Lord this time. It all started with Joshua seeking the face of God before going out in battle.

It may be time for the Javelin to be raised in the direction of Ai. Each one of us should know what Ai represents in our spiritual journey. This time there is going to be victory.

July Day 23

20 The men of Ai looked back and saw the smoke of the city rising against the sky, but they had no chance to escape in any direction, for the Israelites who had been fleeing toward the desert had turned back against their pursuers. 21 For when Joshua and all Israel saw that the ambush had taken the city and that smoke was going up from the city, they turned around and attacked the men of Ai. 22 The men of the ambush also came out of the city against them, so that they were caught in the middle, with Israelites on both sides. Israel cut them down, leaving them neither survivors nor fugitives. 23 But they took the king of Ai alive and brought him to Joshua. Joshua: 8:20-23

The men of Ai underestimated the resourcefulness of the God of Israel. They assumed that things were going to be like the first attack of Israel. They had no way of knowing the spiritual condition of Israel when they mounted the first attack. They did not understand that they defeated the people of Israel because they had lost their protection. Now the city of Ai was facing an army of Israel that was under the full control of their God. And that made all the difference.

Just imagine the surprise on the faces of the men of Ai who had been pursuing the people of Israel into the desert; when suddenly the tables turned around and the pursued becomes the pursuer. The army of Israel turned around and started to face those who were following them in a battle. At that same moment the portion of the army of Israel who were hiding in ambush sprung to action behind the people of Ai. The latter found that they were trapped between the forces of Israel.

Moreover, when they turned around they saw their city on fire and burning. That must have been the last straw. They knew there and then that the battle was lost. The king of Ai was captured in battle and brought to Joshua. The soldiers of Israel were allowed to take as much of the plunder as they desired.

God had given them the victory over Ai. They knew that it was not because of the might of Israel. Rather the battle was the Lord's. Do you know that? Then why are you so anxious?

Dr. Seth Asare

JULY DAY 24

³⁰ Then Joshua built on Mount Ebal an altar to the LORD, the God of Israel, ³¹ as Moses the servant of the LORD had commanded the Israelites. He built it according to what is written in the Book of the Law of Moses—an altar of uncut stones, on which no iron tool had been used. On it they offered to the LORD burnt offerings and sacrificed fellowship offerings. ³² There, in the presence of the Israelites, Joshua copied on stones the law of Moses, which he had written. Joshua 8:30-33

After a glorious defeat, it was time for covenant renewal. The defeat of Ai was special in the history of Israel because there had been a reversal of fortunes under the guidance of God. Joshua did not call for covenant renewal after marching round the walls of Jericho and seeing it fall. However, the sin of Achan and the consequences for the whole nation called for a rededication.

The place that was chosen had historic significance. At the foot of Mount Ebal was a fortress town called Shechem. It was in this town that the Lord appeared to Abraham and promised that the land would be given to his offspring (Genesis 12:6-7). This promise was in response to a step of faith that Abraham had taken. Now, Joshua stood in that very place in fulfillment of the promise made to Abraham and decided to build an altar to the Lord.

This was not any ordinary altar but one that was built according to the specifications given by Moses. The people worshipped and sacrificed offerings to the Lord who was a promise keeper. Joshua also made sure that the law of the Lord was inscribed on the freshly cut stones. These were the laws that Moses had received from the Lord God.

We all have a need to renew our covenant with God from time to time. We should never forget who has brought us to such a place as this. The steadfast love of the Lord is new every morning. We give thanks for God's faithfulness.

July Day 25

³³ All Israel, aliens and citizens alike, with their elders, officials and judges, were standing on both sides of the ark of the covenant of the LORD, facing those who carried it—the priests, who were Levites. Half of the people stood in front of Mount Gerizim and half of them in front of Mount Ebal, as Moses the servant of the LORD had formerly commanded when he gave instructions to bless the people of Israel. ³⁴ Afterward, Joshua read all the words of the law—the blessings and the curses—just as it is written in the Book of the Law. ³⁵ There was not a word of all that Moses had commanded that Joshua did not read to the whole assembly of Israel, including the women and children, and the aliens who lived among them. Joshua 8:33-34

The Covenant Renewal at Mount Ebal involved all the people who were ready to identify themselves as the people of God. We learn that all the people were standing in the valley between Mount Ebal and Mount Gerizim. This was the very place where Moses the servant of the Lord had blessed the people of Israel.

Joshua decided to read the words of the Law in the hearing of all the people in the assembly. He decided not to leave anything out. It was important for Joshua that everyone was on the same page when it came to the Law of God. It was for that reason that women and children were included in this particular assembly of covenant renewal.

It was not enough to have the written record of the Law. Joshua believed that it was important for everyone to hear the word of God. These days there are Bibles in several homes and even hotels. But that is not enough to transform society. People should read it for themselves if they are going to be transformed by the written Word. My prayer is that we would all read the word of God and treasure it in our hearts so that we might not sin.

It is interesting to note that aliens were included in the assembly of Israel at this time. This showed that other people had associated with the citizens of Israel during their desert journey. God has a bigger tent for all people. We are all included in the plan of God.

July Day 26

¹ Now when all the kings west of the Jordan heard about these things—those in the hill country, in the western foothills, and along the entire coast of the Great Sea as far as Lebanon (the kings of the Hittites, Amorites, Canaanites, Perizzites, Hivites and Jebusites)- ² they came together to make war against Joshua and Israel. Joshua 9:1-2

The victories of Joshua and his men were bound to produce a reaction among the people living in the place. The reaction was two-fold. One was fear and dread of the God of Israel. The other was finding a way to fight and defeat Israel.

Each time God gives a victory to the people of God, the spiritual forces of wickedness are bound to react in a way that would chip away at the joy that results from God's victory. It is for that reason that the focus should always be on the one who is truly behind the victory.

All along Joshua and his men had received words of encouragement to the effect that entering the Promised Land was not going to be an easy venture. They were made aware of the fact that they would have to fight under the direction of God for every piece of land. Therefore, Joshua and his men did not have any illusions regarding the task ahead of them. It was God who was going to give them the Promised Land and their confidence had to be completely in God.

All the kings west of the Jordan decided that the only way to defeat the advancing army was to come together and fight Israel as a united front. These were nations and tribes that had been at war against each other. But they all saw Joshua and Israel as a common enemy that needed to be destroyed.

Do you sometimes feel that there are forces coming from different directions against you? That happens a lot when you make the God of Israel your God. You are not alone in this.

July Day 27

³ However, when the people of Gibeon heard what Joshua had done to Jericho and Ai, ⁴ they resorted to a ruse: They went as a delegation whose donkeys were loaded with worn-out sacks and old wineskins, cracked and mended. ⁵ The men put worn and patched sandals on their feet and wore old clothes. All the bread of their food supply was dry and moldy. ⁶ Then they went to Joshua in the camp at Gilgal and said to him and the men of Israel, "We have come from a distant country; make a treaty with us." Joshua 9:3-6

The saying is that "if you cannot beat them, then join forces with them". That was the attitude and the approach of the people of Gibeon. They decided to break ranks with the kings west of Jordan and make peace with the army of Israel. The only problem with the strategy of the Gibeonites was that they planned to use deception instead of coming to Israel honestly.

We are told that fear caused them to resort to a ruse or deception. They sent a delegation whose donkeys were loaded with worn-out sacks and old wineskins cracked and mended. The delegation also put on clothes and sandals that were worn and patched. They took with them food supply that was dry and moldy.

These deceptive men were pretending that they had traveled from a distant country. They knew that their words would not be credible if they did not carry these old clothes and worn shoes. They had a cleverly devised plan hoping that Joshua and his men would buy into what they were saying.

They came to Joshua with a simple story. "We have come from a distant land and we want you to make a treaty with us." Now it was the turn of Joshua and the leaders of Israel to ascertain the veracity of what was being said before entering into any treaty.

One can understand why Israel would enter into a quick treaty with a nation that does not want to fight them. Moreover, this nation was supposed to have come from a faraway place and would not be an immediate threat as neighbors. For Israel, that would be one less nation that they would have to fight. But that was not the issue. After all it was God who had been leading them into victories. The real question was: "What did God think of this treaty?"

Apart from God we can do nothing. What does God think of your situation?

JULY DAY 28

⁷ The men of Israel said to the Hivites, "But perhaps you live near us. How then can we make a treaty with you?" ⁸ "We are your servants," they said to Joshua. But Joshua asked, "Who are you and where do you come from?" Joshua 9:7-8

Have you ever heard someone narrating an incident and you felt that there was something not right with what you were hearing? That was what happened to the Israelites as they listened to the Gibeonites (Hivites). These people were going to be neighbors of the people of Israel in the Promised Land. They were only pretending to have come from a distant land. In those days there were no cell phones or e-mail to google and do a background check on the Hivites.

The people of Israel had a gut feeling that the story of the Gibeonites sounded too good to be true. But it seemed that the people had orchestrated things so well that their story matched up with the food they were carrying and their items of clothing. With all that evidence presented, the people of Israel and Joshua still were not sure so they made this statement: "But perhaps you live near us, how can we make a treaty with you?'

The people of Israel understood the seriousness of making a treaty. They knew that such a treaty could not easily be annulled. They also felt that there was something about the story of the Gibeonites that did not ring true. But the people of Israel failed to listen to the promptings that were telling them to be cautious of what they were hearing.

It is important for all Christians to be sensitive to the promptings of the Holy Spirit. It pays to spend time praying about what is before us and also not negating the part of us that tell us to be cautious even in circumstances where everybody is on board with the decision.

We all have to learn what it means to be at peace with a situation before moving forward. There is no need to hurry or to be pushed into making a quick a decision.

July Day 29

9 They answered: "Your servants have come from a very distant country because of the fame of the LORD your God. For we have heard reports of him: all that he did in Egypt, 10 and all that he did to the two kings of the Amorites east of the Jordan—Sihon king of Heshbon, and Og king of Bashan, who reigned in Ashtaroth. 11 And our elders and all those living in our country said to us, 'Take provisions for your journey; go and meet them and say to them, "We are your servants; make a treaty with us." ' 12 This bread of ours was warm when we packed it at home on the day we left to come to you. But now see how dry and moldy it is. 13 And these wineskins that we filled were new, but see how cracked they are. And our clothes and sandals are worn out by the very long journey." Joshua 9:9-13

I have learned to be cautious of people who are constantly talking and trying too hard to say the same thing over and over again. Here we have the Gibeonites responding to a direct question from Joshua. "Who are you and where do you come from?" These visitors narrated the same story that they have recounted earlier. They said they have come from a distant land. They have heard of the fame of the Lord, the God of Israel and all that the Lord had done in defeating the enemies of Israel. They talked about their clothing and their wineskins that proved that they were indeed coming from a distant country.

It seemed that the Gibeonites were buttering the Israelites with the hope that they would enter into a treaty with them. Now it was the turn of Israel to process all the information that they had received and make a decision. How does one discern the truth from all these words that had been spoken? Christians need help from the Holy Spirit to be able to have clear direction on what the Lord would have them do in every situation.

There is so much deception all around in our world today. We need a lot of help from the Lord to decipher truth from falsehood. Merely listening to what people are saying will not do it. It is time to seek help from above. Also we have to be careful when praises are heaped on us to the point that we fail to discern truth from fiction.

Do not be taken in by the praises that are aimed at extracting something from you!

July Day 30

^{14} The men of Israel sampled their provisions but did not inquire of the LORD. ^{15} Then Joshua made a treaty of peace with them to let them live, and the leaders of the assembly ratified it by oath. Joshua 9: 14-15

We are told that: "The men of Israel sampled their provisions but did not inquire of the Lord". Another way to put this is that: The men of Israel fell into the trap of the Gibeonites by buying into the lies that were presented to them. Note what the Israelites did to ascertain the veracity of what was presented to them. They went ahead and followed the suggestions of the Gibeonites by examining their bread and wineskins.

Israel decided to walk by sight and not by faith in the almighty God. Searching through the provisions could only produce results that were not different from what the Gibeonites had told them. Everything had been done to deceive the unsuspecting eye. Unfortunately, Joshua and his men were taken in by what they saw. They wanted so much to believe that these people would not go out of their way to plant the misleading evidence to make things appear that they came from a distant land.

The greatest indictment of Joshua and Israel was that they did not inquire of the Lord. Oh! That the people of God would know that "we are nothing apart from the Lord. And we can do nothing apart from the Lord." Our best intentions are not good enough and our critical assessment of situations should never be substituted for seeking the face of the Lord.

Israel had committed the same error when it came time to fight against Ai. Here again, God is relegated to the sidelines because human judgment has been deemed adequate and so there is no point in seeking God.

So Joshua signed a peace treaty that was ratified by oath. That was exactly what the Gibeonites wanted and Israel handed it to them without turning to the Lord in this whole matter.

July Day 31

^{16} Three days after they made the treaty with the Gibeonites, the Israelites heard that they were neighbors, living near them. ^{17} So the Israelites set out and on the third day came to their cities: Gibeon, Kephirah, Beeroth and Kiriath Jearim. Joshua 9:16-17

The leaders of the people of Israel went ahead and signed a peace treaty with the Gibeonites. The leaders of Israel went ahead and ratified the agreement with an oath. The Gibeonites went home laughing and rejoicing because they had fooled the people of Israel with their deception. The real mistake was that Israel did not listen to the promptings of the Holy Spirit or seek the direction of God.

It took three days after the signing of the treaty for the Israelites to find out that they have been deceived. That meant that if Israel had exercised a little bit of patience and sought the will of the Lord they would have found out the true character of the Gibeonites.

The lesson is clear for all of us. So often situations come along when it seems we are being rushed into making a decision. I am sure we have all heard these proverbial phrases: "This is your last chance!" "There will not be another opportunity like this one!"

Just imagine the feeling that came over the people of Israel when the Israelites realized that these people were neighbors. That is when people say out loud: "What have we done?" "Why did we not seek the face of the Lord?" But all that would be hindsight. The truth was that these people were neighbors and Israel had to find a way of living with them because they have given them a peace treaty that was ratified with an oath. So the people of Israel set out and came to the cities of the Gibeonites on the third day. That meant that the Gibeonites traveled three days or less to reach the camp of Israel in Gilgal. Now, forget about the worn clothes and shoes and old wineskins.

There is no need for a hasty decision.

We will end our journey with Joshua and start another journey with Paul and the Holy Spirit in Acts of the Apostles. We will turn our compass to the missionary journeys of Paul.

AUGUST DAY 1

[18] But the Israelites did not attack them, because the leaders of the assembly had sworn an oath to them by the LORD, the God of Israel. The whole assembly grumbled against the leaders, [19] but all the leaders answered, "We have given them our oath by the LORD, the God of Israel, and we cannot touch them now. Joshua: 9:18-19

"Let your yes be yes and your no be no. "The people of Israel understood what it meant to give a promise. They had made a treaty that has been ratified with an oath in the name of the Lord God of Israel. Although they did not consult the Lord when the oath was taken, yet they knew that they were bound by the oath. The word of the people of God has to be taken seriously. This is more so, when a promise had been made in the name of the Lord.

Now the whole plan for possessing the Promised Land had to be adjusted because of a hasty decision to enter into a treaty with a deceptive group of people. So the Israelites did not attack the Gibeonites who happened to be their neighbors. The question was: How was Israel going to treat a group of people who had tricked them into signing a peace treaty?

I find it interesting that the whole assembly of Israel grumbled against their leaders. This was not the first time that the assembly of Israel had grumbled against their leaders. Moses received his share of such murmurings. The only difference is that this time, the leaders knew that they had made a blunder. That does not mean that the people of Israel were blameless in this whole disaster. We never heard any of them speak out against the treaty. Moreover, none of them requested at the time that it might be helpful to seek the Lord in the matter. But hindsight is always twenty/twenty. So the assembly of Israel knew that their leaders had made a mistake.

All that the leaders could do was to keep their oath with the Gibeonites. They did not want to make things worse by breaking the oath they had made in the name of the Lord. Sometimes all we can do is to accept that we have made a mistake or we have sinned and ask for forgiveness.

AUGUST DAY 2

[20] This is what we will do to them: We will let them live, so that wrath will not fall on us for breaking the oath we swore to them." [21] They continued, "Let them live, but let them be woodcutters and water carriers for the entire community." So the leaders' promise to them was kept. Joshua 9:20-21

The people of Israel were angry with their leaders because they made a premature peace treaty with the Gibeonites. The Israelites were prepared to go ahead and fight with the Gibeonites and destroy them because they had lied and deceived them into making a treaty. Joshua and leaders knew that what the people were saying was right but they also understood the gravity of the oath they had made in the name of the Lord.

Joshua and the leaders had to come up with a compromise that would be acceptable to the agitators. Joshua seized on a statement that the Gibeonites made in verse eight when they were pleading for a peace treaty: "We are your servants!" The leadership exploited this statement to the full and allowed the Gibeonites to live but in exchange they were going to make them woodcutters and water carriers for the entire community of Israel. This way the leaders would keep the promise they made to the Gibeonites and also appease the common people who were agitating for revenge against the deception of their neighbors.

We always have to compromise when we fail to heed the Lord's instruction in the first place. The truth is that compromise would lead us down a slippery road that takes us farther from the Lord.

Let us be wary of compromises that do not involve the blessing of the Lord.

AUGUST DAY 3

²² Then Joshua summoned the Gibeonites and said, "Why did you deceive us by saying, 'We live a long way from you,' while actually you live near us? ²³ You are now under a curse: You will never cease to serve as woodcutters and water carriers for the house of my God." Joshua 9:22-23

Now, Joshua did what most people do when they have made a terrible mistake. He tried to shift the whole blame unto the Gibeonites. He summoned the people together and asked them why they decided to use deception to trick the leadership of Israel. The answer was obvious to Joshua even as he was posing the question.

Honestly, Joshua and his leadership were the ones who failed to exercise patience and to trust the God of Israel to guide them in this matter. They showed that apart from the Lord they were gullible like any other human being. It would have been more honorable if Joshua had admitted his fault in the whole manner. Unfortunately, people in positions of authority, be they Christians or not, find it difficult to admit that they are wrong.

This is sobering and requires soul searching on the part of all of us. As we try to push the blame on others. It is important for us to allow the Lord to search our hearts and reveal the role we have played in causing a particular blunder to take place. The fault is not completely on the part of the other person. We have a living God and the Holy Spirit and we could have come to a better conclusion with the help of the Lord.

Joshua communicated the verdict to the Gibeonites. And it was a sad one. The people were going to be slaves to the community of Israel and the house of God. How ironic? How can a people who have been liberated from slavery by the mighty hand of God force others into slavery? Someone would say that the people pleaded in verse eight to be slaves of Israel as part of the treaty. But that does not change the reality.

All this happened because someone failed to seek direction from the Lord.

AUGUST DAY 4

[24] They answered Joshua, "Your servants were clearly told how the LORD your God had commanded his servant Moses to give you the whole land and to wipe out all its inhabitants from before you. So we feared for our lives because of you, and that is why we did this. [25] We are now in your hands. Do to us whatever seems good and right to you [26] So Joshua saved them from the Israelites, and they did not kill them. [27] That day he made the Gibeonites woodcutters and water carriers for the community and for the altar of the LORD at the place the LORD would choose. And that is what they are to this day. Joshua 9: 24-27

Joshua wanted to know why the Gibeonites resorted to deception in asking for a peace treaty. Their answer was revealing as well as truthful. Apparently they heard about what the Lord, the God of Israel, had done to all those who stood in the way of Israel. In essence the Gibeonites confessed that they have been deceptive. What was their excuse? It was simply that they were afraid of the God Israel because of the track record of God.

Is fear of God a good reason to be deceptive and to lie? For the people of the world the end result justifies the means. That would not do for the people of God. The Gibeonites were ready to throw themselves at the mercy of Joshua and the God of Israel. They were counting on the fact that the people of God would be faithful to their treaty and to the oath that they made.

Of course Joshua was faithful to the oath that had been made. He spared the life of the Gibeonites but they agreed to be woodcutters and water carriers for Israel. From the perspective of the Gibeonites that was the best of the options available to them in the light of what God had done to other people who stood in the way of God's destiny for Israel.

Sometimes unbelievers show respect and reverence for the God of Israel than those who are supposed to be in covenant relationship.

AUGUST DAY 5

¹ Now Adoni-Zedek king of Jerusalem heard that Joshua had taken Ai and totally destroyed it, doing to Ai and its king as he had done to Jericho and its king, and that the people of Gibeon had made a treaty of peace with Israel and were living near them. ² He and his people were very much alarmed at this, because Gibeon was an important city, like one of the royal cities; it was larger than Ai, and all its men were good fighters. ³ So Adoni-Zedek king of Jerusalem appealed to Hoham king of Hebron, Piram king of Jarmuth, Japhia king of Lachish and Debir king of Eglon. ⁴ "Come up and help me attack Gibeon," he said, "because it has made peace with Joshua and the Israelites." Joshua 10:1-4

It is amazing how news traveled around very fast, even in those days, without a lot of our modern conveniences. One would have thought that the peace treaty with the people of Gibeon was a private matter since it did not involve any fighting or displacement of people. But the news was all over the place.

The King of Jerusalem and the surrounding nations had thought about the possibility of banding together as a group to fight the people of Israel. It was true that they have heard about all the exploits of Joshua and his fighting men under the direction of God. All the reports including exaggerated words indicated that the army of Israel was invincible. It was for that reason that the king of Jerusalem attempted to gather the nations west of the Jordan to band together and present a united front.

Now the report reaching that coalition was that the people of Gibeon have gone ahead and signed a peace treaty with Israel. The nations that were part of the coalition felt betrayed and angry at the action of Gibeon, because Gibeon was an important city in their coalition. Moreover, Gibeon had excellent troops who would be needed in the fight with Israel. The king of Jerusalem decided to punish Gibeon. He asked the other nations to join him in crushing Gibeon.

One is not surprised that those who seek peace are often confronted with unsolicited war. Blessed are the peacemakers even if that means suffering for that action.

AUGUST DAY 6

⁵ Then the five kings of the Amorites—the kings of Jerusalem, Hebron, Jarmuth, Lachish and Eglon—joined forces. They moved up with all their troops and took up positions against Gibeon and attacked it. ⁶ The Gibeonites then sent word to Joshua in the camp at Gilgal: "Do not abandon your servants. Come up to us quickly and save us! Help us, because all the Amorite kings from the hill country have joined forces against us." Joshua: 10:5-6

So five kings of the Amorites (kings of Jerusalem) joined forces and positioned themselves ready to attack the people of Gibeon. The only crime of the Gibeonites was that they had signed a peace treaty with Israel and it seemed to be working. The action of this combined force proved that the Gibeonites made a good move by not aligning themselves with these supposed friends.

Have you noticed that many people who call themselves friends are friends only when you do what they want you to do or you agree with them on every proposal they put forward? As soon as you break ranks on an issue they forget everything and begin to demonize you. That was the way the Amorite kings treated the people of Gibeon.

The people of Gibeon sent an emergency message to Joshua and the leaders of Israel at Gilgal. This time there was no deception or sugar coating the message. They appealed for help from Israel against the combined forces of the kings of the Amorites. The message was urgent and desperate because Gibeon could see the forces that had been put in place against them. The message went this way: "Do not abandon your servants. Come up to us quickly and save us!" They appealed to Israel on the basis of their new situation as servants of Israel. The fact that they humbled themselves went a long way to show that they had accepted their role in the community. They were also reminding Israel of the terms of the treaty.

Knowing how to ask for help is part of the covenant relationship we have with God. Sometimes all we have to do is to turn to God and ask for help.

AUGUST DAY 7

⁷ So Joshua marched up from Gilgal with his entire army, including all the best fighting men. ⁸ The LORD said to Joshua, "Do not be afraid of them; I have given them into your hand. Not one of them will be able to withstand you." Joshua 10:7-8

Joshua responded positively to the distress call from the Gibeonites. The latter had appealed to the leaders of Israel because the Amorites had come together to punish the Gibeonites for their decision to form a peace treaty with Israel. Joshua decided to honor the terms of the treaty and stand with the Gibeonites in their hour of distress.

The Lord does the same for all those who enter into a covenant relationship with God. Christians have access to God and they could expect the protection of the Lord because of the grace that has been offered in Jesus Christ. Anyone who attacks a child of God should know that they are fighting a losing battle because the Lord promises to stand by His own.

Joshua had the forces ready for battle. He took the best of his fighting men. But the word of God was the determining factor. It does not matter what preparations that we have made, it is advisable to wait for the "word of the Lord". When the Lord spoke it was clear and definitive. "Do not be afraid of them; I have given them into your hand. Not one of them will be able to withstand you." Joshua and the people of Israel needed to hear those words.

Now, they had something more substantive to hang their hat on if they were going to face the Amorites in battle. It was not just because they were coerced into a treaty and felt obligated to fulfill a promise. It was because the Lord had spoken and given them assurance of victory.

Joshua needed to be reminded of the promise the Lord had given when he took over as commander of the army of Israel. The same words come to us today. "Do not be afraid".

"Not one of them will be able to withstand you".

AUGUST DAY 8

⁹ After an all-night march from Gilgal, Joshua took them by surprise. ¹⁰ The LORD threw them into confusion before Israel, who defeated them in a great victory at Gibeon. Israel pursued them along the road going up to Beth Horon and cut them down all the way to Azekah and Makkedah. ¹¹ As they fled before Israel on the road down from Beth Horon to Azekah, the LORD hurled large hailstones down on them from the sky, and more of them died from the hailstones than were killed by the swords of the Israelites. Joshua 10:9-11

One thing that I have come to appreciate in walking with the Lord is that God does not have one method of doing things. So none of us can predict how God is going to come through for us at any particular time. All we can count is that the Lord would be there and in the final analysis God would win the victory.

That did not preclude an all-night march with a bunch of fighting men from Gilgal to the place where the Amorites had camped against the Gibeonites. The Lord used the element of surprise this time. The armies of the Amorite kings were thrown into confusion and started to run for their lives. All it took was to throw the elite army of the Amorites into confusion and the battle was over.

God is able to throw all the people who are fighting against you and all the situations into confusion. They will not know what to do and what they are up against until victory is won. Oh by the way the Lord has other weapons that we may not have counted on. These are the forces of nature.

I like it when I read that the forces of nature (hailstones) were part of God's strategy. And that the hailstones did more damage than what the fighting men were able to do. When the Lord decides to fight alongside the covenant people, everyday occurrences could be used to the glory of God.

Just open your eyes and behold that God is using all the circumstances around you today to the glory of the Lord. There is nothing too hard for the Lord. I would hate to be fighting against the Lord who has the whole world in His hands.

August Day 9

12 On the day the LORD gave the Amorites over to Israel, Joshua said to the LORD in the presence of Israel: "O sun, stand still over Gibeon, O moon, over the Valley of Aijalon." 13 So the sun stood still, and the moon stopped, till the nation avenged itself on its enemies, as it is written in the Book of Jashar. The sun stopped in the middle of the sky and delayed going down about a full day. 14 There has never been a day like it before or since, a day when the LORD listened to a man. Surely the LORD was fighting for Israel! 15 Then Joshua returned with all Israel to the camp at Gilgal. Joshua 10:12-15

It is not often that we hear people of faith exercise their God given potential by speaking to the forces of nature and expect God to honor the word that was spoken in faith. Joshua dared to speak to the sun and the moon in the fight against the Amorite kings. What is impressive is that Joshua did this in the presence of all Israel. It was a prayer that was directed to the Lord because Joshua knew that this miracle could only be accomplished by the hand of God.

We are told that the sun stopped in the middle of the sky and delayed going down for a full day. Some people were wondering what was happening and others were busy reading astrology to explain what was happening. In the meantime, Joshua was busy finishing the mission of the Lord in defeating the Amorites. There was a task to be accomplished and in God's wisdom this miracle happened in answer to the prayer of a man just like any of us.

Elijah was a man of like nature and he prayed that it might not rain and the rains were stopped for three and half years. Some people would look at these events as co incidences but Christians know that things happen when the people of God pray. These are God's incidences in response to prayer and for a purpose. It is time for us to ask that God's work on earth would be accomplished in any way that God chooses.

Leave the skepticism and debate to those who enjoy doing that. But as for you, go forward to speak the word of faith so that the mountains would move.

Dr. Seth Asare

AUGUST DAY 10

In the church at Antioch there were prophets and teachers: Barnabas, Simeon called Niger, Lucius of Cyrene, Manaen (who had been brought up with Herod the tetrarch) and Saul. Acts 13:1

"In the church at Antioch there were prophets and teachers". That is a remarkable statement. There is a need for prophets and teachers in every Church. These are the persons who foretell of God's mighty acts in the future and at the same time proclaim what God is doing in each and every generation. The teachers, on the other hand, are those who have dedicated themselves to instructing the people in the ways of the Lord. Thus completing the cycle of proclamation, instruction, and foretelling the purposes of God revealed in Christ Jesus.

The persecution that arose after the stoning of Stephen led to the scattering of women and men in the young Christian Church. Some of the people went as far as Antioch proclaiming the message of the resurrected Christ to the Jews who would listen. In Acts 11:20 we are told: *"Some of them, however, men from Cyprus and Cyrene, went to Antioch and began to speak to Greeks also, telling them the good news about the Lord Jesus. The Lord's hand was with them, and a great number of people believed and turned to the Lord."*

Here we have an early record of the gospel being proclaimed to non-Jews. The Greeks in Antioch believed and were converted to Christianity.

When news of Gentiles coming into the fold of Christianity reached Jerusalem, Barnabas was the logical ambassador sent to teach and encourage the newly established church in Antioch. Barnabas was described as a man full of the Holy Spirit and of faith, and he instructed the church at Antioch to be faithful in their walk with the Lord Jesus Christ. The ministry of this good man yielded much fruit and many were brought to the Lord.

Barnabas made an important decision with the guidance of the Holy Spirit that was going to shape the history of Christianity. He went to Tarsus to fetch that individual who once persecuted the Christian Church. He brought Saul of Tarsus to Antioch to help with the work that the Lord had started there. Acts 11:24 say: *"So for a whole year Barnabas and Saul met with the church and taught great numbers of people. The disciples were called Christians first at Antioch.* It is indeed amazing that this Gentile church in Antioch earned the name Christian because they were followers of Jesus Christ.

In this Church, we read that there were prophets and teachers. But the most interesting thing was that Saul was not listed as one of these prophets and teachers. He was an appendix (if I may use that word) to the prophets and teachers at Antioch. But in the workings of God, the people who seem to be an addition could turn out to be mighty instruments in the hands of God.

You and I are miracles waiting to happen in the hands of God.

AUGUST DAY 11

In the church at Antioch there were prophets and teachers: Barnabas, Simeon called Niger, Lucius of Cyrene, Manaen (who had been brought up with Herod the tetrarch) and Saul. While they were worshiping the Lord and fasting, the Holy Spirit said, "Set apart for me Barnabas and Saul for the work to which I have called them." So after they had fasted and prayed, they placed their hands on them and sent them off. Acts 13:1-3

Prophets and teachers at Antioch were worshipping the Lord. Saul happened to be there in that worship, and of course Barnabas was also there. But the latter would be numbered among the prophets and teachers. The most interesting thing in this worship was that the Lord spoke to them and they heard it. Sometimes I wonder if the Church of Jesus Christ is ready to hear their Lord speak in their worship services. The truth is that God still speaks when two or three are gathered in the name of the Lord.

The Holy Spirit wanted Barnabas and Saul to be set apart for the work which they were being called to do. People would not be surprised by the choice of Barnabas, but the call of Saul to be in this special group would cause a few eyebrows to be raised. After all, Saul was the one who a few months earlier was persecuting the Christians. On the other hand, the early Church had learned not to question the leading of the Holy Spirit. So they continued to do what they were doing before that word of prophecy came. They were worshiping the Lord and fasting, and the urgency was heightened by the new revelation of the Holy Spirit.

It is important that we position ourselves in places where we can hear and discern the voice of God. Fasting and prayer are important spiritual disciplines that enable us to discern the voice of God. These are not disciplines that can be started only when God wants to speak to us. These spiritual activities have to be part of the normal Christian life so that God can speak to us all the time.

When God speaks, then we must obey. In obedience, the church at Antioch placed their hands on the two individuals and sent them off to carry out the task that the Lord had called them to. It is important to note that the church commissioned those whom the Lord had already called. It cannot be the other way around.

When we are told that the church sent them off, that implies the Church was behind them spiritually and materially. The Church in Antioch accepted these two men as their missionaries and supported the mission of Barnabas and Saul to the full extent. Barnabas knew that they were accountable to the Lord first, but also to the Church at Antioch.

Could it be that the Lord is asking that we should be set apart for a work that God has for us in this area and in our Church? "Set apart for me Seth and…" Those who are set apart have to prepare themselves for God's task.

Dr. Seth Asare

AUGUST DAY 12

The two of them, sent on their way by the Holy Spirit, went down to Seleucia and sailed from there to Cyprus. When they arrived at Salamis, they proclaimed the word of God in the Jewish synagogues. John was with them as their helper. Acts 13:4-5

The first missionary journey of Barnabas and Saul began on a quiet note from a small town called Antioch. This mission work was born out of prayer and fasting. That is the appropriate starting place for God's mission. When Christians gather to fast and pray, things happen to the glory of God. In this case two men were sent forth by the Holy Spirit to do God's work.

The two men took with them John as their helper. John was a relative of Barnabas. John was eager to get his feet wet in the mission of God and he was invited to come along. They went down to the nearest port and sailed from Seleucia to the island of Cyprus. There was no laid down schedule on this particular mission trip. The missioners did not know how long they were to spend in a particular town and where they were to stay. They were assured of one thing and that was the presence of the Holy Spirit who sent them.

The missionaries arrived in Salamis and proclaimed the word of God there. The logical place they could minister was in the synagogue. After all they were all Jews and their master was also a Jew. They shared in the faith tradition of Abraham and in addition they proclaimed God's revelation to humanity in the person of Jesus Christ.

The uniqueness of their message was the fact that the Messiah had come in the person of Jesus Christ and he had risen from the dead and moreover Jesus had sent the Holy Spirit to live with God's people forever. They emphasized the universality of God's revelation. This Jewish Messiah was revealed for the whole world and those who believed in him would be transformed by the power of the Holy Spirit.

This was the word of God that was proclaimed by Barnabas and Saul in Salamis. Thank God that the same good news is available to all today.

AUGUST DAY 13

They traveled through the whole island until they came to Paphos. There they met a Jewish sorcerer and false prophet named Bar-Jesus, who was an attendant of the proconsul, Sergius Paulus. The proconsul, an intelligent man, sent for Barnabas and Saul because he wanted to hear the word of God. But Elymas the sorcerer (for that is what his name means) opposed them and tried to turn the proconsul from the faith. Acts 13:6-8

The missionaries were on the island of Cyprus and traveled through the whole island. I would like to believe that they were preaching the good news through the whole island, but I do not want to be presumptuous. It is possible that the Holy Spirit took them through the length and breadth of the island for another reason. We are not specifically told that Barnabas and Saul were preaching the word of God wherever they went on the island.

At Paphos, they encountered a false prophet who was an attendant to the proconsul. The latter wanted to hear the word of God. It is not very often that one hears of people in high places wanting to hear the good news of Jesus Christ. The name of the proconsul was Sergius Paulus and he is described as an intelligent man. He went out of his way to send for Paul and Barnabas. When the false prophet (Elymas) realized what was happening, he made up his mind to oppose the missionaries.

Elymas had a few reasons for attempting to prevent the proconsul from converting to Christianity. He realized that his own standing in the court of the proconsul would be jeopardized if the proconsul converted. He was also aware of how the proconsul's conversion would affect him materially. It was, therefore, beneficial for him to do everything possible to stop the interest that the proconsul was showing in the missionaries' message. Unfortunately, the same thing happens in our day when people become obstacles to others receiving the message of Christ.

Nothing will stop the good news of Christ from going forward. All attempts to hinder others from coming to the knowledge of the truth have not succeeded in times past, and will not succeed now.

August Day 14

Then Saul, who was also called Paul, filled with the Holy Spirit, looked straight at Elymas and said, "You are a child of the devil and an enemy of everything that is right! You are full of all kinds of deceit and trickery. Will you never stop perverting the right ways of the Lord? Now the hand of the Lord is against you. You are going to be blind, and for a time you will be unable to see the light of the sun."

Immediately mist and darkness came over him, and he groped about, seeking someone to lead him by the hand. When the proconsul saw what had happened, he believed, for he was amazed at the teaching about the Lord.

Acts 13:9-12

Saul decided to confront Elymas and his attempts to prevent the proconsul from receiving the good news. The words of Saul were direct and straight to the point. Saul, who is also called Paul, exhibited the gift of knowledge. He told Elymas exactly what was going to happen to him because he had resisted the gospel of Jesus Christ. Elymas was going to be blind for a time and would be unable to see the sun.

The words of Paul seemed harsh at the time that they were spoken. But when one considers the damage that would have been caused if this sorcerer were allowed to have his way in the court of the proconsul, then one can conclude that Saul did the right thing.

What made an impression on the proconsul and all those who had gathered was the effect of the words of Saul. "Immediately mist and darkness came over him, and he groped about, seeking someone to lead him by the hand." The result was swift and dramatic. No one was left in doubt as to what had caused Elymas to be blind. The proconsul experienced something that he had not witnessed before, and that was the power of the gospel of Jesus Christ. It was enough to make him take that step of faith in the direction of Jesus.

Not everyone will get the opportunity to witness the dramatic power of the gospel as the proconsul did, but everyone who believes will be able to experience a similar power in their own lives. The power to become new creations in Christ Jesus is offered to all those who would take a step of faith in the direction of Jesus.

I pray that you experience a measure of that power today

AUGUST DAY 15

From Paphos, Paul and his companions sailed to Perga in Pamphylia, where John left them to return to Jerusalem. From Perga they went on to Pisidian Antioch. Acts 13:13

After the conversion of the proconsul on the Island of Cyprus, Saul and his companions set sail from the island and went to the mainland in the region of Pamphylia. They settled in the town of Perga awhile. It was here that John decided that he had had enough of this mission trip, and decided to return home. We do not know all the circumstances surrounding the decision of this young would-be missionary and his return to Jerusalem. There have been many speculations ranging from his being homesick, to John realizing that this was not his calling at this time.

It will be enough to note that Barnabas and Saul were the two individuals who were set aside by the Holy Spirit through a word of prophecy for the mission task. Those who were commissioned continued on in their calling to the mission. Barnabas and Saul did not have the luxury of making a decision to turn around unless that was the leading of the Holy Spirit. There is a sense in which all those who have been called to follow Jesus Christ are bondservants of the Lord to do a particular task. Other people can decide to turn around, but that should not be the case for you and me.

I am reminded of the chorus we sang at youth camps: "I have decided to follow Jesus, and there is no turning back." That does not mean there will not be the temptation to do just that. We are praying that the one who has begun a good work in each one of us will provide all the resources needed to sustain us.

To be fair to John (Mark), it is important to note that he returned to Jerusalem and not to Antioch (in Syria) where the mission began. There was still much work to be done in Jerusalem for the cause of Jesus Christ. After all, that was the center of the persecution directed against the Christians. So John (Mark) was not leaving the mission field, he was in principle returning to another area of mission work.

The harvest is truly plentiful and we should be open to the calling of the Holy Spirit on others to serve in other areas. Barnabas and Saul, on the other hand, continued their mission work as they headed to Antioch in Pisidia.

We may be called to a particular task while others are called to move on. This is not the time to ask why, but to trust the leading of the Holy Spirit.

AUGUST DAY 16

From Perga they went on to Pisidian Antioch. On the Sabbath they entered the synagogue and sat down. After the reading from the Law and the Prophets, the synagogue rulers sent word to them, saying, "Brothers, if you have a message of encouragement for the people, please speak." Acts 13:14-15

After the departure of John from the missionary team, Barnabas and Saul wasted no time at Perga. They moved on to the region of Pisidia where there was another town named Antioch. This should not be confused with Antioch in Syria where the missionary journey started.

They went to the Synagogue on the Sabbath day and sat down to worship like any member of the Jewish faith would do. That is indicative of the fact that these missioners did not see themselves as starting a new faith or religion. They were happy and comfortable with their faith as Jews and did not see any contradiction in proclaiming that the expected Jewish Messiah had been revealed in the person of Jesus Christ who was crucified and had now risen from the dead.

What made the synagogue rulers send word to Saul and Barnabas to bring a word of encouragement? Most likely, news of their arrival had preceded them into the synagogue. It may also be that there was something that distinguished these traveling evangelists from all other visitors. It may be their way of dressing or the way they carried themselves.

I am impressed that they were asked to bring a word of encouragement to the gathered community of faith. The same word is needed today when the people of God gather. There is so much discouragement and bad news around that it is refreshing to hear some good news of encouragement. One may also call that a message of Hope.

The good news about the death and resurrection of Jesus Christ is a message of hope for the whole world. In it we are made to understand that God's word for the universe is abundant life. God's love has been revealed to all humanity so that we can all have a relationship with God through Jesus Christ. That is good news indeed!

AUGUST DAY 17

Standing up, Paul motioned with his hand and said: "Men of Israel and you Gentiles who worship God, listen to me! The God of the people of Israel chose our fathers; he made the people prosper during their stay in Egypt, with mighty power he led them out of that country, he endured their conduct for about forty years in the desert, he overthrew seven nations in Canaan and gave their land to his people as their inheritance. All this took about 450 years. Acts 13:16-20

Paul took advantage of the opportunity given to him to bring a word of encouragement. He stood up and with a motion of his hand he began to address the gathering in the Synagogue at Antioch in Pisidia. He addressed a wide variety of people in the congregation. To be specific, he described his audience as men of Israel and Gentiles who worship God. One would have expected the congregation to be comprised mainly of Jews. But it seems that was not the case there. There would be no doubt that the seating arrangements were configured to accommodate each group in their appropriate place in the Synagogue.

One could speculate that perhaps some prominent dignitaries had come to the Synagogue expecting that Paul and Barnabas would be given an opportunity to speak. But it is not far-fetched to expect to find Gentiles worshipping in the assembly of the Jews at this time.

Paul began by emphasizing the prevenient grace of God as well as the election of God. There is no reason given for the fact that God chose Israel. The same could be said for God's act of mercy to all peoples by offering a means of grace and salvation through Jesus Christ. No one questions God about the gracious acts of the Almighty. The deliverance of the people of Israel from slavery was captured in Paul's message as a demonstration of the mighty power of God. Paul also spoke of the disobedience of God's people in the wilderness.

The patience of God with the people of Israel reminds all of us that we would be nowhere had it not been for the patience of God. Paul emphasized the God who provided for the people all that they needed, even when they did not deserve the grace of God. Indeed, Paul was recounting the human story in this sermon at Antioch. We can all identify with the grace of God that is showered upon us when we are so much aware of our unworthiness.

AUGUST DAY 18

"After this, God gave them judges until the time of Samuel the prophet. Then the people asked for a king, and he gave them Saul son of Kish, of the tribe of Benjamin, who ruled forty years. After removing Saul, he made David their king. He testified concerning him: 'I have found David son of Jesse a man after my own heart; he will do everything I want him to do.'

"From this man's descendants God has brought to Israel the Savior Jesus, as he promised. Before the coming of Jesus, John preached repentance and baptism to all the people of Israel. As John was completing his work, he said: 'who do you think I am? I am not that one. No, but he is coming after me, whose sandals I am not worthy to untie.' Acts 13:20-25

Paul recounted the history of Israel from the time of the Judges through the request of the people for a king to be like the other nations around them. The reign of David was connected with the revelation of the Messiah. Thus, the introduction of Paul's message in the synagogue at Antioch sought to root the good news squarely in the history of Israel.

"From this man's descendants God has brought to Israel the Savior Jesus, as he promised." The person being talked about was no one other than the favorite King David of Israel who was described as a "man after God's own heart". There is a direct link from the Davidic Kingdom to the new Kingdom established by Jesus Christ.

Moreover, the reference to "the Savior" being brought to Israel was pointing to the much-awaited Messiah in Israel. Note that Paul did not just talk about a Savior, but rather "God has brought to Israel the Savior". Nothing was left in doubt that the preacher was referring to Christ. The promised Messiah had been revealed in the person of Jesus.

Paul went on in his sermon to show that John the Baptist came to bear witness and to prepare the way for the coming of Christ. John bore testimony to the coming of Christ, and there was no ambiguity in the testimony of John concerning who he was and the role he came to play. 'Who do you think I am? I am not that one. No, but he is coming after me, whose sandals I am not worthy to untie."

Everything in the message given by Paul pointed to Christ. And that is the way it should be with all that we do.

AUGUST DAY 19

Brothers, children of Abraham, and you God-fearing Gentiles, it is to us that this message of salvation has been sent. The people of Jerusalem and their rulers did not recognize Jesus, yet in condemning him they fulfilled the words of the prophets that are read every Sabbath. Though they found no proper ground for a death sentence, they asked Pilate to have him executed. When they had carried out all that was written about him, they took him down from the tree and laid him in a tomb. But God raised him from the dead, and for many days he was seen by those who had traveled with him from Galilee to Jerusalem. They are now his witnesses to our people. Acts 13:26-31

Paul continues his sermon at Antioch in Pisidia by placing his audience at the center of the unfolding history that he has been narrating. It is important to note how he groups the children of Abraham with God-fearing Gentiles and calls them brothers. Then he went on to say that: "it is to us that this message of salvation has been sent". Note the groups that Paul included in the "us". These groups, as indicated earlier, were children of Abraham (Jews), and God-fearing Gentiles and himself.

Paul is careful to attribute the death of Jesus to two things. First, the people of God failed to recognize the Messiah. Second, it was the fulfillment of the words of prophecy read every Sabbath. According to Paul, there was no reason to condemn Jesus to death apart from people carrying out what was written in scripture without knowing it.

Now Paul moved to the heart of the Christian message and that was: "God raised Jesus up from the dead". This was not resuscitation by healers or anything like that. The resurrection was a demonstration of God's victory over death. Humans had no part in the resurrection of Jesus except to witness the fact that it had happened.

Many people saw the resurrected Christ for several days. This was not a hallucination because people talked with him and he showed them many proofs that he was the same Christ who had walked with them. All those who experienced the resurrected Christ became his witnesses. Things have not changed. Everyone who encounters this Christ becomes a witness for him.

August Day 20

"We tell you the good news: What God promised our fathers he has fulfilled for us, their children, by raising up Jesus. As it is written in the second Psalm: "You are my Son; today I have become your Father. The fact that God raised him from the dead, never to decay, is stated in these words: "'I will give you the holy and sure blessings promised to David.' So it is stated elsewhere: 'You will not let your Holy One see decay.' For when David had served God's purpose in his own generation, he fell asleep; he was buried with his fathers and his body decayed. But the one whom God raised from the dead did not see decay. Acts 13:32-37

"We tell you the good news". The whole sermon had been leading to this: "The telling of the good news". Indeed, that should be the focal point of all sermons in the Christian church. The Church has a message to proclaim and that message is about what God has done for humanity. God had a purpose and a plan since the foundation of the world to reconcile humanity to God.

Paul called this plan "what God promised our fathers". God's promise to Adam, Abraham, Jacob, and Moses was to call together a people who would walk in God's ways. A relationship with God was at the center of God's promises and his dealings with humanity. Paul is saying that this promise has been fulfilled in the raising of Jesus from the dead.

There had been claims of people being raised from the dead before. But Paul takes the trouble to explain that those individuals died again and their bodies decayed in the ground. The type of resurrection that took place in the case of Jesus Christ was different in the sense that he rose up never to die again. He is alive forevermore. In so doing, Christ was and is able to reconcile all of us to God.

Once and for all time God has fulfilled what God promised. That is the nature and character of God. This is good news indeed. We have come to know God as the one who fulfills what has been promised and, because of that we are able to trust and take giant and little steps of faith in the direction of God.

August Day 21

"Therefore, my brothers, I want you to know that through Jesus the forgiveness of sins is proclaimed to you. Through him everyone who believes is justified from everything you could not be justified from by the Law of Moses. Take care that what the prophets have said does not happen to you: "'Look, you scoffers, wonder and perish, for I am going to do something in your days that you would never believe, even if someone told you.'" Acts 13:38-41

The conclusion of the Sermon at Antioch drove home the main points that Paul had tried to make. "I want you to know that through Jesus the forgiveness of sins is proclaimed to you." That is the first clear point that Paul made. It had pleased God to provide forgiveness of sin through Jesus Christ as opposed to the slaughtering of animals in the Temple. That was, indeed, a radical shift from what had been accepted in the practice and worship of the Hebrew people.

Paul went on to elaborate on that point by saying that "through Christ everyone who believes is justified from everything that you could not be justified from by the Law of Moses". In these words, we find the fulfillment of the statement that Jesus made: "I came to fulfill the Law and not to abolish it". There was still the need for forgiveness of sin and, the price for sin still had to be paid with a sacrifice of blood. The only difference was that God had provided himself the needed sacrifice.

The Abrahamic understanding of justification was invoked here. "Abraham believed God and it was reckoned to him as righteousness." Now, we are told in this sermon that all those who believe in Jesus Christ are justified and forgiven all their sins. That is good news indeed.

Paul made another point and that was this, it was easy to miss out on what God was doing because it was not the normal way people had seen God operate in the past. It is the prerogative of God to do new things, and those who have got God figured out will struggle to accept the new things that God is doing.

Let us be open to the new thing that God seeks to do in our lives and in our day.

Dr. Seth Asare

AUGUST DAY 22

As Paul and Barnabas were leaving the synagogue, the people invited them to speak further about these things on the next Sabbath. When the congregation was dismissed, many of the Jews and devout converts to Judaism followed Paul and Barnabas, who talked with them and urged them to continue in the grace of God.

On the next Sabbath almost the whole city gathered to hear the word of the Lord. When the Jews saw the crowds, they were filled with jealousy and talked abusively against what Paul was saying. Acts 13:42-45

Paul and Barnabas were invited to return on the next Sabbath by the people who heard them. It is important to note that it was not the religious leaders who invited them to return on the next Sabbath. Very often when the Gospel is proclaimed with power, the people who are excited about the message are the average people. They relate to the message of God better than those who interpret the message in terms of power dynamics.

It is also important to observe that the evangelists were invited back not to give a word of encouragement or any particular teaching, but to "speak further about these things". They were referring specifically to the message about Jesus Christ and how it related to their understanding of God. One could surmise that there was a thirst in the heart of the audience for more of the good news.

Jews and Gentiles followed Paul and Barnabas after the worship experience in the synagogue. They "talked with them and encouraged them to continue in the grace of God". It seemed that people were already responding to the message proclaimed by Paul and Barnabas. The Gospel of Jesus has power to transform people who open themselves to it.

"On the next Sabbath almost the whole city gathered to hear the word of the Lord." When the Jews saw the crowd their attitude changed and they were filled with jealousy. They were no longer open to the message of the evangelists and they started talking abusively about them. The power structures are never pleased when they see the message of the Gospel triumph. The Gospel has a way of changing people and setting them free to be themselves in the sight of God. That type of freedom will always threaten some people.

You will know the truth and the truth will set you free.

AUGUST DAY 23

Then Paul and Barnabas answered them boldly: "We had to speak the word of God to you first. Since you reject it and do not consider yourselves worthy of eternal life, we now turn to the Gentiles. For this is what the Lord has commanded us:

"'I have made you a light for the Gentiles, that you may bring salvation to the ends of the earth.'" When the Gentiles heard this, they were glad and honored the word of the Lord; and all who were appointed for eternal life believed. Acts 13:46-48

We heard from yesterday's reading that jealousy set in when the Jews and the rulers of the Synagogue observed the response of those in the city of Antioch to the message of Paul and Barnabas. When one group or an individual begins to draw large crowds, then observers get worried. In this case, there was a definite attempt to curb their privileges in the Synagogue. They were not allowed to speak freely to the crowd as they had done on the previous Sabbath.

Paul and Barnabas caught on quickly to what was happening, so they responded boldly with these words: "We had to speak the word of God to you first." This was a declaration that they considered the Jewish faith as the natural home of the Christian message. After all, Jesus was a Jew and those carrying the Gospel from place to place at this time were all Jews. It was a matter of course that the first audience of the Gospel had to be Jews wherever it was preached during those times.

Now that the Jews in Antioch were indicating their rejection of the message of Paul and Barnabas, they were left with no alternative but to turn to the Gentiles who had responded favorably. In support of what was happening, Paul quoted scripture to indicate the plan of God for all ages. He noted that it had always been part of God's plan to bring salvation to both Jews and Gentiles. He also saw himself as an apostle to the Gentiles so that the light of God would shine to all people.

The universal availability of the salvation of God is emphasized here. The Gospel was never intended for any group or any culture. The light of God's salvation is able to take root in every place on earth. When the Gentiles heard these words, they were all the more glad because they sensed the liberating power of this Gospel to make all people first class citizens in the Kingdom of God. Many of the Gentiles believed the message and received eternal life. The availability of eternal life to all is something that must be proclaimed without reservation. Those who are willing to receive Jesus Christ as Lord become partakers of this eternal life.

August Day 24

The word of the Lord spread through the whole region. But the Jews incited the God-fearing women of high standing and the leading men of the city. They stirred up persecution against Paul and Barnabas, and expelled them from their region. So they shook the dust from their feet in protest against them and went to Iconium. And the disciples were filled with joy and with the Holy Spirit. Acts 13:49-52

Something was started at Antioch in Pisidia with the two weeks preaching and sharing of the good news. Those who believed were urged on to live out their newfound faith and to share it. That was exactly what they did and the result was fantastic. "The word of the Lord spread through the whole region". That is what happens when people are willing to live out the Gospel of Jesus Christ. The Holy Spirit does the drawing of others to the light of Christ. A whole region was affected by the word of the Lord.

There is always a push back when the word of the Lord starts to take root. In this particular instance, it started with the Jews inciting people of high standing in the city. What did they use to incite them? They used fear tactics. They made Paul and Barnabas seem like troublemakers who were going to bring division and confusion in the city. The people of Antioch believed these influential people and started to persecute the messengers of the Good News. Paul and Barnabas were expelled from the region because those who felt threatened by the message and the effect of the Gospel had their way.

The apostles shook the dust from their feet in protest to the action of the leaders of Antioch. They accepted the verdict and moved on to Iconium to spread the message of Jesus Christ. They were not discouraged by what happened at Antioch, but rather they were "filled with joy and with the Holy Spirit". They considered it a blessing to be instruments of the Good News.

All those who decide to be agents of the Good News are going to be led by the Holy Spirit. There will be times of persecution, but one thing will be certain. The joy of the Lord will be their strength.

The Holy Spirit will provide the joy and the strength you need for today.

AUGUST DAY 25

At Iconium Paul and Barnabas went as usual into the Jewish synagogue. There they spoke so effectively that a great number of Jews and Gentiles believed. But the Jews who refused to believe stirred up the Gentiles and poisoned their minds against the brothers. So Paul and Barnabas spent considerable time there, speaking boldly for the Lord, who confirmed the message of his grace by enabling them to do miraculous signs and wonders. Acts 14:1-3

Why did Paul and Barnabas go to the Synagogue at Iconium after the treatment they received from the Jews in Pisidia? It was because it was the right thing to do. The Gospel had to be preached first to the Jews because it was a progression of the Jewish faith and, the disciples had the need to worship with their countrymen. It had, therefore, become their habit to go to the synagogue in town to start their witness about the Jewish Messiah.

"They spoke so effectively that a great number of Jews and Gentiles believed." That is an achievement that would be attributed to the Holy Spirit. The disciples needed some encouragement after their experience in Antioch of Pisidia. It must have been a big boost to Paul and Barnabas to witness the response to their preaching. But whenever there is a victory for Jesus Christ, it seems the enemy has a way of inciting trouble.

We are told that "the Jews who refused to believe stirred up the Gentiles and poisoned their minds" against Paul and Barnabas. Since the region was mainly a Gentile region, the Jews had to stir up the Gentiles who were the people in power to rise up against Paul and Barnabas. So we hear that they poisoned the minds of the Gentiles; it means they had to say atrocious things about their fellow Jews and the message they were proclaiming. It had to be so bad that no one would want to listen to the message.

The apostles decided to continue to speak the word boldly and allow time to prove their detractors wrong. The most important thing was that God confirmed their message with miraculous signs and wonders. There is nothing more convincing than results. The apostles did not use miracles to convert the people, but rather it was God who confirmed the message of grace that was preached with signs and wonders.

God is still working in different ways to confirm the message that we preach. Every sign that God provides is an indication that the message we preach has power to change people. God is still at work in each one of us making possible the daily miracles of life. You can expect a miracle from God today. Look for it and it will happen.

AUGUST DAY 26

The people of the city were divided; some sided with the Jews, others with the apostles. There was a plot afoot among the Gentiles and Jews, together with their leaders, to mistreat them and stone them. But they found out about it and fled to the Lycaonian cities of Lystra and Derbe and to the surrounding country, where they continued to preach the good news. Acts 14:4-7

The ministry in Iconium was very successful to the degree that the religious leaders who were threatened incited the Gentiles against Paul and Barnabas. There were, however, many others who responded favorably to the message of the apostles. The result was a divided city with factions supporting Paul and another faction on the side of the Jews. The sad thing about this type of division is that some people make it personal and see the other faction as enemies who have to be eliminated.

There was a plot to stone Paul and Barnabas in Iconium. The people involved in the plot were both Jews and Gentiles. Things were slightly complicated by the composition of the people who were conspiring against the apostles. It was not a simple situation of Gentiles on one side and Jews on the other. Some influential people got in on the plot and that made things difficult for Paul and Barnabas. The plan was to mistreat the apostles and to stone them.

It is difficult to come to terms with the fact that these apostles who were doing such a good job weren't allowed to continue their ministry. People have wondered why God did not promise to protect and to deliver them. The truth is that God did protect them, but sometimes not in ways that we would like. Somehow the apostles found out about the plot and fled the city. That discovery was miraculous by itself. God's ways are not our ways. I know I would have been disappointed if my mission trip was cut short by attempts of a group to sabotage the preaching of the good news. But it was necessary for the apostles to move on to Lystra.

The question that arises is this: "are we ready to move when the Holy Spirit asks us to move?" We should learn not to blame all things on the enemy. God may be saying things to us to which we need to pay attention. The apostles had to leave in a hurry and there was no time to say goodbye to friends. On the other hand, the good news had to be preached in the surrounding towns.

The Lord has given us a message that must be shared with all those who are willing to hear and believe. There is a sense that we are all sharing this good news wherever we go.

AUGUST DAY 27

In Lystra there sat a man crippled in his feet, who was lame from birth and had never walked. He listened to Paul as he was speaking. Paul looked directly at him, saw that he had faith to be healed and called out, "Stand up on your feet!" At that, the man jumped up and began to walk. Acts 14:8-10

When Paul and Barnabas arrived in Lystra, there was a challenge awaiting them. There was a man crippled in his feet. He had been lame from birth and had never walked. This was not someone who had walked before and was recently disabled. It meant that everyone in town knew this crippled person who was in the habit of sitting by the roadside. People looked at those who had a physical challenge from birth differently. Most of the time, their situations were considered hopeless.

There was something unique about this crippled individual at Lystra. It was the eagerness with which he listened to the preaching of Paul. It was obvious that he was taking the message about Jesus Christ in. Paul could see from his face and his expressions that he believed all that was being said. One could describe this crippled person as an individual who met the Gospel with faith. He did not need a healing to believe, and he did not need the use of his legs to have faith in the Lord Jesus Christ.

How often do we hear people giving mountains of excuses why they could not believe the message that is preached about Jesus Christ? Here we have someone who has all the reason in the world to ask: "Why me?" And yet, he had faith in the person that Paul was talking about. That was all that was needed. So Paul looked directly at him and called out, "Stand up on your feet!" Paul spoke the word of faith to the crippled man and the crippled man responded to the word in faith. That was what it took to bring about the healing at Lystra.

Most of the time, those are the conditions necessary for the miracle of God to take place. It takes women and men speaking the word of God in faith. We should be saying: "Stand up on your feet!" Or we should be saying something similar to that. God empowers us to speak the word of faith when we do not even know what the result will be.

Similarly, God wants us to respond to the word in faith. Both aspects are crucial for the miracle of God to take place. But we are also aware that God can work God's miracles without us.

Be ready to speak the word in faith. And, be ready to respond to the word in faith.

August Day 28

Paul looked directly at him, saw that he had faith to be healed and called out, "Stand up on your feet!" At that, the man jumped up and began to walk.

When the crowd saw what Paul had done, they shouted in the Lycaonian language, "The gods have come down to us in human form!" Barnabas they called Zeus, and Paul they called Hermes because he was the chief speaker. The priest of Zeus, whose temple was just outside the city, brought bulls and wreaths to the city gates because he and the crowd wanted to offer sacrifices to them. Acts 14:9-13

Nothing excites a crowd more than observing instantaneous healing. They all heard and watched as Paul spoke those words of faith: "Stand up on your feet!" They did not know what to expect, but when the crippled from birth rose up and started walking; they knew something extraordinary had taken place. This was not a daily occurrence, so there had to be an explanation for the events they had just witnessed. First, there was the powerful preaching of the Gospel about Jesus Christ and then, there was the healing of the man who had been crippled from birth.

"When the crowd saw what Paul had done, they shouted in the Lycaonian language, 'The gods have come down to us in human form!'" What else could they attribute this miracle to? In their frame of reference, it was the "gods" who had come down in human form. It was common at that time for people to attribute anything they could not understand to the "gods". So Paul was thought to be Hermes because he was the spokesperson and Barnabas was called Zeus.

That was the best explanation that the people at Lystra could come up with in the face of a miracle. What about you and me? When we witness the power of God in an unusual way, how do we react? We can certainly give praise to the Lord because we have a relationship with this God. We live in a society in which such things are often called coincidences. But we know better because we do experience them over and over again.

Have you witnessed a miracle of God today?

August Day 29

The priest of Zeus, whose temple was just outside the city, brought bulls and wreaths to the city gates because he and the crowd wanted to offer sacrifices to them. But when the apostles Barnabas and Paul heard of this, they tore their clothes and rushed out into the crowd, shouting: "Men, why are you doing this? We too are only men, human like you. We are bringing you good news, telling you to turn from these worthless things to the living God, who made heaven and earth and sea and everything in them. In the past, he let all nations go their own way. Yet he has not left himself without testimony: He has shown kindness by giving you rain from heaven and crops in their seasons; he provides you with plenty of food and fills your hearts with joy." Even with these words, they had difficulty keeping the crowd from sacrificing to them. Acts 14:13-18

When people are used to worshiping idols, they are ready to turn anything mysterious into an idol. That was what happened in Lystra. The priest of the god Zeus brought the appropriate animals to offer to what they all thought were gods come down in the form of humans. The priest was doing what the crowd wanted. It was a majority decision to worship Paul and Barnabas because of the miracle that had occurred in Lystra. This is a great lesson for all. The fact that the majority or the crowd is leaning in one direction does not mean that the people of God should follow suit.

When the apostles heard what the priest and the crowd were about to do, they tore their clothes and rushed into the crowds. Paul and Barnabas had to do something dramatic to get the attention of the crowd before they carried out their sacrifices. They also used the occasion as a teaching moment. They emphasized that they were human just like anybody else in the crowd. That was an important point to make, and leaders of churches in our time can learn a lot from that. There is always the tendency to exalt humans to a higher status because of gifts that God has endowed on them. Such individuals should be quick to point out that they are humans just like everyone else.

The apostles went on to say that they were bearers of the Good News. They were inviting people to abandon this worthless idol worship and turn to the living God. They emphasized that the time of ignorance which led people to worship idols was now over. It was time to turn to the God who provided them with rain and crops in their season. In other words, the benevolent God that has been with them all along has now been revealed in the person of Jesus Christ. There was, therefore, no need for idol worship now that this God has been made known.

Dr. Seth Asare

AUGUST DAY 30

Then some Jews came from Antioch and Iconium and won the crowd over. They stoned Paul and dragged him outside the city, thinking he was dead. But after the disciples had gathered around him, he got up and went back into the city. The next day he and Barnabas left for Derbe. Acts 14:19-20

There are some enemies of the Gospel who are determined to make sure that it does not succeed anywhere. The news about what God was doing through Paul and Barnabas started to spread all over the region. Some of their opponents in Antioch and Iconium heard of the wonderful and miraculous things that were happening in Lystra and decided that they were going to stop it by whatever means necessary. Why would people from these two towns go to all lengths to stop the preaching of the Good News?

First of all, they understood what was happening as a spiritual battle. They did not want to see this new message of Jesus Christ spread through the region. Secondly, they believed they were defending their way of life and the religion that they had come to accept and live by. They saw a threat to their way of worship and to their faith. Thirdly, they wanted to stamp out what they perceived to be a heresy that was attracting more people. For these and other reasons the Jews from Antioch and Iconium banded together in a joint effort to destroy the message and the messengers.

They infiltrated the people at Lystra with their counter message by poisoning the minds of their hearers against what Paul and Barnabas stood for. They managed to get several people to lean in their direction, and then incited hatred to the degree that the people were willing to stone Paul. We are not told exactly what they said against this spokesperson for the Gospel. The person who was likened to a god, in one day had now become an enemy who deserved to be stoned.

Paul's body was dragged outside the city and left on the ground. They thought that he was dead. I am wondering why they dragged the body outside the city. That might suggest that only a few people were involved in this crime and were afraid that when those who had believed the message of Paul found out what had happened, things might turn ugly.

The disciples gathered around Paul and prayed; he was revived and returned to town with them. It was time to move on, so they continued the mission to the next town.

Adversities do not dampen the spirit of those who are called by God. Paul and Barnabas were certain of the mission they were on and nothing would stop them. I pray that we also find out what God has called us to do and press forward in that.

Dr. Seth Asare

AUGUST DAY 31

They preached the good news in that city and won a large number of disciples. Then they returned to Lystra, Iconium and Antioch, strengthening the disciples and encouraging them to remain true to the faith. "We must go through many hardships to enter the kingdom of God," they said. Acts 14:21-22

Paul had been stoned, dragged outside the city gates of Lystra, and then left for dead. Thanks to friends and disciples who prayed and helped Paul, he reentered that same city afterwards. The next day, Paul and Barnabas moved on to Derbe, the next town. One would have expected Paul and Barnabas to tone down their message a little bit after their experience at Lystra, but that was not the case. They boldly preached the message of the death and resurrection of Jesus Christ in Derbe just as they had done in all the towns they had visited. Several people believed the Gospel and became disciples.

A great opportunity would have been lost if the apostles had allowed fear to dictate how and where they preached the Gospel. To make disciples meant that they stayed and taught the people until they were ready to witness themselves. Paul and Barnabas understood that it was not enough to have people respond to the message of the Gospel. One had to go through the next step of making disciples. That was the command of Jesus in Matthew's Gospel. "Go and make disciples of all nations, baptizing them in the name of the Father and of the Son and of the Holy Spirit."

Now the apostles did an amazing thing by going back to all the towns where they had made disciples for Jesus Christ. I call it amazing because most of us would have found good reasons not to go back to Lystra or Iconium or Antioch. These were the very places where they had been mistreated by some of the inhabitants. For Paul and Barnabas, there was work to be done for Jesus and nothing would stop them. They went back with this one purpose, "strengthening and encouraging the disciples".

And how did the Apostles do that? They encouraged the disciples to remain true to the faith. They also used what had happened to them as a way of preparing the disciples for the suffering that must come to all Christians.

We have to remain true to the calling that has been extended to us by the Lord Jesus Christ.

September Day 1

Paul and Barnabas appointed elders for them in each church and, with prayer and fasting, committed them to the Lord, in whom they had put their trust. After going through Pisidia, they came into Pamphylia, and when they had preached the word in Perga, they went down to Attalia. From Attalia they sailed back to Antioch, where they had been committed to the grace of God for the work they had now completed. On arriving there, they gathered the church together and reported all that God had done through them and how he had opened the door of faith to the Gentiles. And they stayed there a long time with the disciples. Acts 14:23-28

Paul and Barnabas went through all the places where they had made disciples encouraging and strengthening them. They also accepted the reality that these young groups needed leaders to guide the activities of these congregations. The approach of the apostles in appointing leaders was marked by fasting and praying. People fast and pray to seek wisdom and direction from God. And that was precisely what the apostles did. They did not make these decisions lightly. They were laying foundations for the work of God that was going to spread to the entire world. They might not have known that, but they approached the task of appointing leaders with all the seriousness that it deserved.

The apostles committed the disciples and their leaders in each town to the Lord. They were aware that after all the fasting and prayers were over and the decisions had been made, the apostles would have to move on. The new Christians would have to be left in the care of the Lord. The truth is that at some point, we all have to fall on the grace of the Lord to sustain where human effort would be inadequate.

On their return journey, the apostles preached the word along the way and made more disciples. But, their destination was Antioch in Syria where their first missionary journey had begun. This was the home base where the Holy Spirit had set them apart for the work just completed. They had had no idea of the scope of the work they were called to, but the Spirit who sent them was very much aware. Now it was time to give thanks and report on the marvelous work that God had done through the apostles.

The exciting part of the report was the fact that God had opened a door of faith for the Gentiles also. The Gospel of Jesus Christ had been freed from its cultural roots and was now available to all.

That is enough for all of us to say "Praise the Lord!"

September Day 2

Some men came down from Judea to Antioch and were teaching the brothers: "Unless you are circumcised, according to the custom taught by Moses, you cannot be saved." This brought Paul and Barnabas into sharp dispute and debate with them. So Paul and Barnabas were appointed, along with some other believers, to go up to Jerusalem to see the apostles and elders about this question. Acts 15:1-2

Paul and Barnabas returned to Antioch in Syria where the missionary journey began. They reported the results of the mission with emphasis on how God had opened a door for the Gentiles to be part of the family of God. Paul and Barnabas stayed in Antioch for a long time taking advantage of the time to rest.

In the meantime, some people came from Judea to Antioch preaching the Good News with a nuance that Paul and Barnabas found offensive. They were teaching that Gentiles who believed in Jesus Christ had to be circumcised because one could not be saved unless they adhered to the circumcision requirements in the Law. There was much debate over this topic, and Paul and Barnabas disputed the teachings of these individuals from Judea.

The community of believers thought it would be wise to get some clarification from the church leaders in Jerusalem just to be sure that the same Good News was being preached everywhere. So Paul and Barnabas as well as some other believers were appointed for this trip to Jerusalem to seek clarification on this issue.

This was the first dispute to arise in this young Christian church. It was inevitable considering that all the first Christians were people of Jewish origin. This meant that Christianity could have become a sect within Judaism in which case all the cultural trappings of Judaism would apply. On the other hand, Christianity could break out of the mold of Judaism and embrace different cultures and still keep the central core of its identity. These were the issues at stake when a delegation from Antioch was sent to Jerusalem for consultation.

It was appropriate that other members of the Church at Antioch were sent along with Paul and Barnabas. Everyone knew the views of these two men on this subject, so it was wise to send others along with them.

It is good to seek Christian counsel on issues that people cannot agree on.

SEPTEMBER DAY 3

The church sent them on their way, and as they traveled through Phoenicia and Samaria, they told how the Gentiles had been converted. This news made all the brothers very glad. When they came to Jerusalem, they were welcomed by the church and the apostles and elders, to whom they reported everything God had done through them. Acts 15:3-4

Paul and Barnabas were sent to Jerusalem to consult with the apostles and elders on a subject that was threatening to divide the church. The issue needing to be addressed was how to treat Gentiles who converted to Christianity. This had not been an issue when Christianity was considered a sect within Judaism. When all those who were converted were Jews, there was no problem. Gentiles who converted to Judaism at this time knew their place and never considered themselves as being fully integrated into the Jewish worship.

At the center of this controversy was the issue of circumcision. Circumcision was a rite that was performed on all male descendants of Abraham. God had given the instruction to Abraham and the practice had been maintained faithfully by all the offspring of Abraham. It had become what distinguished the male Jew from all others who sought to worship the God of Abraham.

Now the issue on the table was simply this: "Was it necessary to require all the Gentiles who wanted to embrace the faith of Abraham to be circumcised?" The Christians who argued for this were saying that they welcomed the entry of Gentiles into the faith. Their only requirement was that the Gentile Christians ought to be circumcised. Paul and Barnabas, on the other hand, believed that the free grace of God should be extended to all with no conditions.

Paul and Barnabas and the group elected to go with them traveled through Phoenicia and Samaria telling their story of how Gentiles had responded happily to faith in the Lord Jesus Christ. This was welcome news for all those who heard.

In Jerusalem, the apostles and elders welcomed the group from Antioch and were pleased to hear of all that God had accomplished through them. So the stage was set for what would later be called the Council of Jerusalem to decide on the first test that faced this young Christian movement.

September Day 4

Then some of the believers who belonged to the party of the Pharisees stood up and said, "The Gentiles must be circumcised and required to obey the Law of Moses." The apostles and elders met to consider this question. After much discussion, Peter got up and addressed them: Acts 15:5-7

The Council of Jerusalem was in full session and witnesses were called forward to present their statements. All the people present were believers in the Lord Jesus Christ. This was not a situation of Jews versus Gentiles, neither was it partisan politics clothed in religiosity. All present were looking for the best way to advance this newfound faith in Jesus Christ.

Sometimes the wrong impression is given by the way the Pharisees are presented elsewhere. Here, at the Council in Jerusalem we are told that there were believers who were also Pharisees. They meant well with their arguments and presentation. They put forward their statement in these words: "The Gentiles must be circumcised and required to obey the Law of Moses."

Note that they did not argue against the Gentiles becoming Christians; they only required them to obey the Law of Moses. When one understands what they meant by the Law of Moses, then it becomes apparent that the Gentile Christians were being expected to observe the ordinances and live like Jews. It seems that this stance generated a lively debate with everyone weighing in with an opinion on the subject.

After much discussion, we are told that Peter got up to speak on the issue at hand. It is healthy to entertain diverse opinions in Christian discussion. What was discussed at the Council of Jerusalem in the first century is very much with us today. Someone will ask me how? The answer is that wherever and whenever we see signs of cultural Christianity raising its head, then we know that we are keeping alive the debates of the Council of Jerusalem.

Each time we add something to salvation by faith because that is the way we have thought or have done it in the past, we are reviving the discussion. Is it possible that people who do not worship like we do could be acceptable to God?

It is not about circumcision or un-circumcision; it is about the centerpiece of the Gospel message.

September Day 5

After much discussion, Peter got up and addressed them: "Brothers, you know that some time ago God made a choice among you that the Gentiles might hear from my lips the message of the gospel and believe. God, who knows the heart, showed that he accepted them by giving the Holy Spirit to them, just as he did to us. He made no distinction between them, and us for he purified their hearts by faith. Now then, why do you try to test God by putting on the necks of the disciples a yoke that neither our fathers nor we have been able to bear? No! We believe it is through the grace of our Lord Jesus that we are saved, just as they are." Acts 15:7-11

Now it was Peter's turn to speak. The room must have been hushed as Peter rose to his feet. After all, he was the first disciple to confess Jesus Christ as the Messiah. The confession that made Jesus Christ say: "upon this rock I will build my Church". Everyone wanted to hear what this particular disciple had to say.

Peter began weighing in on the topic at hand with a personal testimony. It is still true that nothing beats a personal witness. Peter took the assembly back to the day of Pentecost and also to the house of a Roman soldier who had been sent by God to invite Peter to his household. Peter described that encounter this way: *"Brothers, you know that some time ago God made a choice among you that the Gentiles might hear from my lips the message of the gospel and believe. God, who knows the heart, showed that he accepted them by giving the Holy Spirit to them, just as he did to us. He made no distinction between us and them,"*

Peter made the point that the election of the Gentiles to receive the good news was primarily the choice of God, and it happened that he was one of the first people to be used in this cross cultural propagation of the gospel. Peter also indicated that God accepted the Gentiles who believed the message of the Gospel by giving them the Holy Spirit just as had happened on the day of Pentecost. In the words of Peter: *"God made no distinctions between Gentile Christians and Jewish Christians."*

So if God accepts all people without showing favoritism, then the discussion at hand may be pointing to something different. The question which Peter asked is the appropriate one: *"Now then, why do you try to test God by putting on the necks of the disciples a yoke that neither we nor our fathers have been able to bear?"* If one thought about it, this was exactly what was being discussed at this first Jerusalem Council. "What else should be added as requirements for Gentiles who have come into the faith?"

The recommendation by Peter was "no additional requirement". He based his argument on the fact that salvation for all people was through the grace of the Lord Jesus Christ. If the ultimate goal of the Good News is salvation for all people, then there was no need to burden any group of people with other laws.

That was a bold and progressive Christian message that ought to be heard in our day.

SEPTEMBER DAY 6

"...No! We believe it is through the grace of our Lord Jesus that we are saved, just as they are." The whole assembly became silent as they listened to Barnabas and Paul telling about the miraculous signs and wonders God had done among the Gentiles through them. Acts 15:11-12

There are testimonies and then there are testimonies from the pillars of the Church. I would have given almost anything to be a fly on the wall in the First Council at Jerusalem just to hear the powerful testimony of Peter which ended with a "punch line" that would have moved everyone in the room. *"No! We believe it is through the grace of our Lord Jesus that we are saved just as they are."*

Someone would say that Peter's statement was very revolutionary! It could even be described as heresy. Why would Peter dare to put the Gentile on the same footing as a Jew? Is Peter saying that faith in Jesus Christ breaks down all barriers between Jews and Gentiles? Then what would be the seating arrangements at the place of worship? And what would happen at fellowship meals? Are Jews going to have table fellowship with Gentiles? Now, you see how some would consider the statement of Peter as having gone too far.

The hush that fell on the gathering after the words of Peter was indescribable. So when Paul and Barnabas started to share their own testimonies, one could probably hear a pin drop in the room. They told the gathering about the miraculous signs and wonders God had done among the Gentiles through them.

One of the outstanding things for me about the Council of Jerusalem is the sharing of testimonies by the leaders of the church. Others came to discuss the merits and demerits of circumcision for Gentiles. But Peter, Barnabas and Paul came to share testimony about their experiences of God at work among the Gentiles. Nothing beats the sharing of personal experience of what God has done. That was all that Peter, Paul and Barnabas had to do.

I wish to suggest that as a model for the defense of the Gospel. What has God done through us today? We can share that with others.

SEPTEMBER DAY 7

When they finished, James spoke up: "Brothers, listen to me. Simon has described to us how God at first showed his concern by taking from the Gentiles a people for himself. The words of the prophets are in agreement with this, as it is written: "'after this I will return and rebuild David's fallen tent. Its ruins I will rebuild, and I will restore it, that the remnant of men may seek the Lord, and all the Gentiles who bear my name, says the Lord, who does these things' that have been known for ages. "It is my judgment, therefore, that we should not make it difficult for the Gentiles who are turning to God." Acts 15:13-19

The powerful witnesses to God's work among the Gentiles had now been presented to all gathered at the first Jerusalem Council. Now it was time for summation and ruling by the presiding person. James happened to be this individual who had listened carefully to the proceedings, and everyone was waiting for his verdict.

James invited the audience to pay careful attention to what he had to say. He decided not to go into the specifics of the case before the Council. He did not make any reference to the presentation of the believers from the party of the Pharisees; neither did he refer to the witness offered by Paul and Barnabas. Instead, he made reference to Peter being the first to be used by God to communicate the Good News to the Gentiles.

Then James moved quickly and extensively to Old Testament Scripture. He quoted a passage that indicated that God had always had a plan to include the Gentiles in God's saving grace. That meant that the inclusion of the Gentiles in the saving grace of God was a fulfillment of Scripture that needed to be celebrated.

Unfortunately, the history of the Church has been such that each time God does something unique among God's people, it becomes a source of division and controversy. The same thing happened when God asked Moses to select seventy elders to be anointed with the Spirit of God. The day of Pentecost was also no exception.

James did the right thing by appealing to the primacy of Scripture. In so doing, he set peoples' minds at ease in knowing that the entry of the Gentiles into the family of God was scriptural. He also set an example for generations of Christians to come to look for the scriptural basis of their decisions and theology.

The verdict was straightforward and swift. *"It is my judgment, therefore, that we should not make it difficult for the Gentiles who are turning to God. "This* was in agreement with the witness of Peter that no additional burden should be placed on the Gentile Christians when it came to circumcision.

God calls us to make bold decisions after we have researched scripture and heard what other believers have to say. There is freedom in Christ, which ought to be enjoyed by all who put their trust in Him.

September Day 8

"It is my judgment, therefore, that we should not make it difficult for the Gentiles who are turning to God. Instead we should write to them, telling them to abstain from food polluted by idols, from sexual immorality, from the meat of strangled animals and from blood. For Moses has been preached in every city from the earliest times and is read in the synagogues on every Sabbath." Acts 15:19-21

Why would the church make things hard for people who are turning from the world to God? Sometimes it is because people forget how difficult it was for them to be outsiders in an ongoing group. People also forget that they did not do anything to merit acceptance into the family of God. Finally, it is part of human nature to place roadblocks in the paths of unsuspecting newcomers.

James gave a verdict that combined God's grace with human responsibility. He wanted the grace of God to be extended to all those who were turning to God. There should not even be a mention of circumcision. At the same time, he wanted these new Christians to be aware of their Christian responsibility as people who bear the name of Christ. The admonition to live lives worthy of their call was not a new requirement for Gentile Christians. It was something expected of all Christians.

Idol worship was prevalent in that day, and food offered to idols could be a stumbling block for those who were young in the faith. All those who turned to Jesus Christ must sincerely turn from idol worship. There was no need to still dabble in food offered to idols. New Christians were encouraged to make a clean and complete break from their former way of life.

Sexual immorality was another vice that characterized the first century society. It was sometimes closely entangled with idol worship and fertility cults. An unsuspecting Christian could be led astray by all the prostitutes parading on the grounds of these places of idol worship. Christians were to be a people set apart by God and for God. So whether they were Jews or Gentiles, they were expected to live by a higher code of morality.

The eating of the blood of animals that had been strangled was not only repulsive, but it also carried with it so many health hazards that the people of God were admonished not to eat it. The blood held a significant place in atoning sacrifice, and was therefore something that the people of God were instructed to stay away from.

In terms of the main issue at stake at the Council of Jerusalem, James' summation concluded that the Gentiles would not be required to undergo circumcision.

September Day 9

Then the apostles and elders, with the whole church, decided to choose some of their own men and send them to Antioch with Paul and Barnabas. They chose Judas (called Barsabbas) and Silas, two men who were leaders among the brothers. With them they sent the following letter: The apostles and elders, your brothers, To the Gentile believers in Antioch, Syria and Cilicia: Greetings. Acts 15:22-23

The decision of the Council of Jerusalem was unanimous. Now there was the need to communicate the decision throughout the whole Christian World. After all, this was as high as it could get in the hierarchy of first century Christianity. The same Holy Spirit who had guided the decision making process was still in control of how it should be communicated. One should bear in mind that this decision had the potential of bringing about schisms within the young church.

The Council of Jerusalem decided to select some of the participants to accompany Paul and Barnabas to communicate the decision of the gathering. Why would they not allow Paul and Barnabas to go ahead and disseminate the decision of the Council? It was because they were aware of the position of these two individuals on this matter before the Council. They were also aware of the fact that the decision of the Council was closely aligned to Paul and Barnabas' position, and it might be difficult for people who had opposing views to accept the words of the two men.

Judas (called Barsabbas) and Silas were chosen to accompany Paul and Barnabas and travel throughout the known Christian world to convey the decision of the First Jerusalem Council. These two men were selected because they were leaders among the brothers. They were individuals who were known to have proven leadership skills. This was important for all who heard them affirming the decision of the apostles and the Council.

The leaders at the meeting in Jerusalem decided to send a letter with their own stamp on it with the messengers. They made sure that no one could mistake or misinterpret the decision of the gathering. There were four witnesses of the proceedings and then there was a signed letter to confirm the words of these messengers.

There was no doubt that the Apostles attached great importance to the deliberations and the decision that came out of the gathering at Jerusalem. There are times that the Holy Spirit may invite us to participate in a watershed event that may have a far reaching effect. During those moments, we should be ready like Judas and Barsabbas to do whatever is asked of us.

SEPTEMBER DAY 10

We have heard that some went out from us without our authorization and disturbed you, troubling your minds by what they said. So we all agreed to choose some men and send them to you with our dear friends Barnabas and Paul—men who have risked their lives for the name of our Lord Jesus Christ. Therefore, we are sending Judas and Silas to confirm by word of mouth what we are writing. It seemed good to the Holy Spirit and to us not to burden you with anything beyond the following requirements: Acts 15:24-28

I enjoy reading letters that are brief and straight to the point. This was not a five-page document to be preserved for posterity. It simply brought greetings and identified who were writing and who were the recipients. Then it outlined in a sentence the reason for writing, and the messengers who were going to bring the letter. Finally, the main point of the letter was given in a few sentences.

The reason for sending Judas and Silas was made clear in the letter. They were to confirm by mouth what had been written in the letter. What they were saying was that, anybody could come to you with a piece of paper saying that the Apostles and elders in Jerusalem wrote this. Also, anyone could claim they were ambassadors of the Jerusalem Church, but having all the pieces in place would make the message and the word spoken credible. They had Paul and Barnabas, Judas and Silas, a letter written by the Apostles, and then the witness (word of mouth) of the bearers of the letter.

The credentials of Paul and Barnabas outlined in the letter were a testimony of the high regard that the Apostles had for the work and tribulations endured by these men during their first missionary journey. They had risked their lives for the name of our Lord Jesus Christ. That was something not to be taken lightly. There is a sense in which all Christians are invited to do the same in their profession of faith.

The gist of the message in the letter was that the Holy Spirit had directed the Council not to burden the Gentile Christians with the circumcision requirement. The Apostles seem to be in agreement with the leading of the Holy Spirit on this matter. This statement represents an important understanding of Apostolic decision making. It always began with the Holy Spirit and what the Holy Spirit wanted to do.

I pray that seeking the guidance of the Holy Spirit will not be lost in all that we do.

September Day 11

It seemed good to the Holy Spirit and to us not to burden you with anything beyond the following requirements: You are to abstain from food sacrificed to idols, from blood, from the meat of strangled animals and from sexual immorality. You will do well to avoid these things. Farewell. Acts 15:28-29

There has been some debate about the requirements or stipulations that were laid down after the Council of Jerusalem. There are those who wish to argue that the requirements suggested here are cultural in nature. In other words, the decision did not result in total freedom for the Gentile Christian. And there are those who argue that the main issue before the Council was the circumcision of Gentile Christians. That being the case, then the requirements in the letter were nothing compared with the issue of circumcision of all Gentile Christians.

Moreover, the requirements stated in the letter were issues that were threatening the viability of the Christian Church in the face of idol worship and temple sacrifices to the numerous idols in the Gentile world. The eating of blood and strangled animals was more of a health hazard for all, and could be considered to be a practical concern.

Sexual immorality was something that could not be compromised in any civilized society. The call to follow Christ was a call to commit both soul and body to the cause of Christ. The promiscuous sexual practices that were common in the known world were not to be tolerated among any of those who turned to God in Christ Jesus. That stricture applied to all persons irrespective of cultural background.

If anyone was in Jesus Christ, they became new creations that aspired to be controlled by the Holy Spirit. The message was simple and clear; there would be one requirement for all who turned from the world to Jesus Christ and that was becoming new creatures.

The same requirement is expected of all of us who call ourselves by that Name.

SEPTEMBER DAY 12

The men were sent off and went down to Antioch, where they gathered the church together and delivered the letter. The people read it and were glad for its encouraging message. Judas and Silas, who themselves were prophets, said much to encourage and strengthen the brothers. After spending some time there, they were sent off by the brothers with the blessing of peace to return to those who had sent them. But Paul and Barnabas remained in Antioch, where they and many others taught and preached the word of the Lord. Acts 15:30-36

The ambassadors from the Council of Jerusalem were sent off with a mission to all the places where there had been confusion over the matter of Gentiles becoming part of the body of Christ. Their first stop was Antioch in Syria, the place where the believers were first called Christians. The messengers did the most responsible thing by gathering the church together and presenting the letter from Jerusalem.

The letter could have first been presented to the leadership of the Church in Antioch, but the ambassadors found it necessary to present the letter in the assembly of all the believers. There might have been a few reasons that necessitated this approach. It could be that they were aware that some in the leadership at Antioch had sympathies for the strict enforcement of Mosaic laws on the Gentile believers. So it would not have been helpful for people to take fixed positions before the full letter was put before the whole church.

There is the possibility that the ambassadors from Jerusalem felt that to prevent misconceptions, and encourage a better discussion of the matters at hand, this was the wisest approach. It seemed that the response to the letter from Jerusalem was better than expected. The audience was encouraged when they heard the contents of the letter. It must have been a great relief to all that finally the acrimony had been put to rest.

The church was encouraged by the precedent that was being set when it came to the matter of settling disputes. There was a body that had assumed the responsibility of listening carefully to the issues involved and coming out with an acceptable ruling or compromise. One could see the seeds of an institutional church being put into place. The best part of all this was that all the parties involved had mutual respect for one another and accepted the decision of the Council at Jerusalem.

It is apparent that Judas and Silas used their God given gifts to exhort the church members. The believers in Antioch affirmed the ministry of Judas and Silas. And they were sent back to Jerusalem after completing their mission.

September Day 13

Sometime later Paul said to Barnabas, "Let us go back and visit the brothers in all the towns where we preached the word of the Lord and see how they are doing." Barnabas wanted to take John, also called Mark, with them, but Paul did not think it wise to take him, because he had deserted them in Pamphylia and had not continued with them in the work. Acts 15:36-38

Paul and Barnabas had enjoyed some time of rest and renewal at Antioch in Syria. Paul decided that it was time to go back and visit all the churches that had been started during their first missionary journey.

Follow-up is one of the needed ministries in the Christian Church. Very often new disciples are left on their own for too long, and the result is that they fall prey to wrong teaching and divisions from within the church. So the decision to do a follow-up was a wise one.

Paul approached Barnabas with his proposal and since it seemed like the right thing to do, the two men started to make preparations for the trip. Barnabas wanted to take John Mark with them.

Paul did not agree with the suggestion made by Barnabas because of what had happened on the first missionary journey. When the missionaries got to Pamphylia, John Mark had decided that it was time for him to return home. It is believed that the young man was home sick. At that time, there was no indication that Paul was not pleased with John's decision to return home. But this time when Barnabas suggested that they should take John Mark along, Paul showed strong opposition to the idea.

Sometimes good Christians like Paul and Barnabas can disagree. It was not a question of who was right and who was wrong. They simply were not able to see eye to eye on this point, and they decided to disagree.

It is important to remember that none of us is perfect.

September Day 14

but Paul did not think it wise to take him, because he had deserted them in Pamphylia and had not continued with them in the work. They had such a sharp disagreement that they parted company. Barnabas took Mark and sailed for Cyprus, but Paul chose Silas and left, commended by the brothers to the grace of the Lord. He went through Syria and Cilicia, strengthening the churches. Acts 15:38-41

Barnabas was known in the early church as the encourager. He was the individual who could take the back seat and encourage ministry to happen. Barnabas was the one who looked for Saul of Tarsus at a time when no Christian would like to associate with him. He took Saul under his wings and went around introducing him and testifying about the genuineness of the conversion of Saul.

Now the two ambassadors who had stood side by side to spread the Christian Gospel to a Gentile world were at a crossroad in their relationship. The issue simply was whether John Mark should be included in the missionary trip to encourage the believers. We are told that the disagreement was so sharp that the two men decided to part company.

One finds it difficult to comprehend how such a simple issue could not have been resolved another way. All that had been deduced from this amicable agreeing to disagree was the formation of two missionary teams instead of one. Now two groups are sent out to encourage the Church. Barnabas went out with John Mark one way and Paul went with Silas the other way.

Barnabas and John decided to retrace the path of the first missionary journey by going to Cyprus while Paul and Silas chose a different route going through Syria and Cilicia. The brothers in Antioch commended them to the grace of God before they set off.

The two teams had one goal in mind and that was to strengthen the churches, and that was what they did wherever they went.

September Day 15

He came to Derbe and then to Lystra, where a disciple named Timothy lived, whose mother was a Jewess and a believer, but whose father was a Greek. The brothers at Lystra and Iconium spoke well of him. Paul wanted to take him along on the journey, so he circumcised him because of the Jews who lived in that area, for they all knew that his father was a Greek. Acts 16:1-3

Paul and Silas began the second missionary journey at the end of the first missionary journey. That tells us a lot about what Barnabas and Paul did when they got to Derbe. They could have taken the shortcut to return home to Antioch in Syria, but they decided to retrace their steps and went back to all the towns they had preached in with the sole purpose of strengthening the churches and establishing leaders.

Now Paul and Silas came to Derbe. They all knew Paul and how he endured difficulties to bring the word to the church in Derbe. The believers must have been filled with joy at the sight of the founder of their congregation. Silas must have added a lot to the team with the knowledge that he was an ambassador from the Church leaders in Jerusalem.

The missionaries moved to Lystra where a believer named Timothy lived. He came from a cross-cultural marriage. His mother was Jewish and his father was Greek. Timothy's mother was a believer; nothing is said about his father. There were positive testimonies given about Timothy and his faith in the Lord Jesus Christ.

Paul wanted him to join his missionary team. He was aware of the problems that Timothy's presence would pose as well as the positive impact that it could have as they traveled from town to town. Timothy was uncircumcised although his mother was Jewish. So Paul decided that he should be circumcised. This becomes problematic when one considers Paul's views on the circumcision of Gentiles.

I guess Paul would argue that since Timothy's mother was a Jew, he should have been circumcised in the first place. Paul knew that the Jews in every town they went would be spying on Timothy to create problems for the team. Paul did not want this issue that had been sorted out at the Council of Jerusalem to continue to distract from the Gospel. In principle, Timothy was Jewish and could take his seat with other Jews and Gentiles in discussing the merits of the Gospel.

Dr. Seth Asare

Some people would have preferred Paul to accept Timothy on his team as an uncircumcised brother in the Lord Jesus Christ. Paul did what he had to do to advance the Gospel of Jesus Christ.

There comes a time when we all have to do what is expedient without compromising the Gospel of Jesus Christ.

September Day 16

As they traveled from town to town, they delivered the decisions reached by the apostles and elders in Jerusalem for the people to obey. So the churches were strengthened in the faith and grew daily in numbers. Acts 16:4-5

Now we have two mission teams from Antioch out in the field. One team is comprised of Barnabas and John Mark. This team tried to retrace the steps of the first missionary journey, so they sailed to the island of Cyprus. The second team was made up of Paul and Silas. They decided to start from where the first missionary journey ended, so they went on to Derbe. At Lystra, Paul and Silas invited Timothy to join their team. Timothy's mother was a Jew, but his father was Greek.

Both teams had the same game and purpose, and that was to communicate the decisions reached by the apostles and elders in Jerusalem. One team had the fortune of having an emissary from Jerusalem with them -- Silas. Silas was one of the two sent with the letter from Jerusalem for the Gentile Church. So he was able to communicate directly to the churches what happened at the Council in Jerusalem.

The team of Barnabas and John were not as fortunate because the other person who was sent with Silas had returned to Jerusalem after the letter and the instructions had been delivered in Antioch and the surrounding towns. Unfortunately, we do not have a written down account of what happened on the mission involving Barnabas and John Mark. But one thing is certain, and that is they went out and did exactly what they set out to do. That lack of written detail is a constant reminder that there were many more things that happened in the spread of Christianity in the early centuries than what scriptural records can give us.

The churches were strengthened in the faith. That was the goal of the mission and one could say the goal was accomplished. But beyond that, the churches grew in numbers. The two go together most of the time, but the primary goal was focused on the faith of the believers.

Dr. Seth Asare

SEPTEMBER DAY 17

Paul and his companions traveled throughout the region of Phrygia and Galatia, having been kept by the Holy Spirit from preaching the word in the province of Asia. When they came to the border of Mysia, they tried to enter Bithynia, but the Spirit of Jesus would not allow them to. Acts 16:6-7

We are informed that as Paul, Silas and Timothy went from town to town together, the churches were strengthened and the number of believers grew daily. They must have been doing a lot of preaching, or the believers were witnessing in a manner that drew others into the fold. The fact that the numbers were growing daily suggests an exponential growth that could be the result of witnessing communities of faith.

When believers live up to their God given potentials, the world around takes notice and they are drawn to the life-changing message of Christ. The missioners decided to travel though the whole region of Phrygia and Galatia bearing the same message and establishing new churches. Next, we are told that the apostles were prevented from going into Asia, and we understand that it was the Holy Spirit who prevented them from doing that.

It is obvious that the apostles' traveling was not just random movement from town to town, but rather they prayed about where to go next and how long to stay there. This total dependence on the Holy Spirit for what to do next could be foreign to our modern understanding of Christian mission where everything is plotted out. The flexibility that allows the Holy Spirit to intervene in human actions worked well for Paul and his companions. On two occasions, they were prevented from going where they would have preferred to go. They decided not to fight the leading of the Holy Spirit, but rather to respond to it. They did not seek to understand why, instead they trusted in the Holy Spirit who had commissioned them for this trip.

God is ready to guide all of us if we are ready to listen. It may be your turn to listen to the leading of the Holy Spirit today.

September Day 18

So they passed by Mysia and went down to Troas. During the night Paul had a vision of a man of Macedonia standing and begging him, "Come over to Macedonia and help us." After Paul had seen the vision, we got ready at once to leave for Macedonia, concluding that God had called us to preach the gospel to them. Acts 16:8-10

"So they passed by Mysia and went down to Troas." It must have been tempting to stop by Mysia for one open air preaching. There must have been one person in Mysia who was open to the gospel of Jesus Christ. But that was not the issue. There was a Divine plan to follow, and what was asked of the ambassadors of the gospel was that they follow the leading of the Holy Spirit. So they had to pass by Mysia and go to Troas. They had no idea what was waiting for them in Troas, but they were soon to find out.

In Troas there was a vision in the night. Could the vision not come to them in any other town apart from Troas? That was not a question for the apostles to explore. They were led to Troas and the vision appeared there. In the vision Paul saw a man from Macedonia "standing and begging him". There was much urgency in the gesture of the man from Macedonia. How did Paul know that the man in the vision was from Macedonia? Could it be the way he was dressed? Or did he come out and say that: "I am from Macedonia"? It could be that they assumed that since he was beckoning them to Macedonia he must be from there.

Paul knew what he saw was from the Lord and that it was connected to the leading of the Holy Spirit who had directed them to avoid certain towns. "After Paul had seen the vision, we got ready at once to leave for Macedonia, concluding that God had called us to preach the gospel to them." There was no doubt in the mind of Paul what to do after seeing the vision. They got ready and departed for Macedonia in response to the vision.

It is that level of obedience that God seeks in all his children. When God has said it, what else do we need to hear? How does God speak to us? And what are our responses when we believe it is God speaking to us?

SEPTEMBER DAY 19

From Troas we put out to sea and sailed straight for Samothrace, and the next day on to Neapolis. From there we traveled to Philippi, a Roman colony and the leading city of that district of Macedonia. And we stayed there several days. Acts 16:11-12

Troas was the place where Paul saw a vision in the night. Paul took the vision he saw seriously and believed that God had a message for him in it. God spoke to Paul in a vision, but God speaks to us in several different ways. When Paul was prevented from preaching the Gospel in Asia, we do not hear about a vision. Although that does not mean that there was no vision, it suggests that God might have spoken to Paul by another means.

God still speaks to us through visions and dreams. God also speaks through the revealed word of God, and sometimes God speaks through people and by words of prophecy. There is always a certain peace that we experience when we know that God is leading and speaking. It is the peace that passes understanding. It does not mean that all doubt is removed, but it suggests that we have learned through practice to discern the leading of the Holy Spirit and the voice of God.

The children of God learn the voice of Abba through constant waiting and listening. After repeated experiences one is ready to yield to that still small voice or the loud voice or the vision that beckons us to go over to Macedonia and help.

There was nothing special about Troas; the vision could have appeared to Paul in any town or any place. We have the tendency of building shrines in places of God's epiphany. The important thing was the message in the vision and Paul's response to the message. Because he was convinced of the leading of the Holy Spirit, they set sail immediately in the direction of Macedonia. The response was impressive, but they arrived there and for days they stayed in Philippi waiting for the direction of the Holy Spirit on what to do.

Philippi, we are told, was a Roman colony and a leading city in the district of Macedonia. It must have been full of people from all over the known world. This was the place where God had led Paul and his companions. Now they waited for the next step.

Waiting is also part of the leading of the Holy Spirit. Sometimes we are called to wait instead of being out doing things. May the Lord teach us the lesson of waiting when that is called for!

SEPTEMBER DAY 20

On the Sabbath we went outside the city gate to the river, where we expected to find a place of prayer. We sat down and began to speak to the women who had gathered there. One of those listening was a woman named Lydia, a dealer in purple cloth from the city of Thyatira, who was a worshiper of God. The Lord opened her heart to respond to Paul's message. When she and the members of her household were baptized, she invited us to her home. "If you consider me a believer in the Lord," she said, "come and stay at my house." And she persuaded us. Acts 16:13-15

"On the Sabbath we went outside the city gate to the river, where we expected to find a place of prayer." It was the custom of Paul and his companions to go to the synagogue on the Sabbath. But there was none in Philippi. That showed that the city did not have enough Jewish men to constitute a synagogue. The next best thing was the gathering of the people beside a river for prayer. Such gatherings would be made up of largely women. So Paul and his companions went to find a place of prayer by the river. They found a gathering of women there who were more than eager to hear the three men bring them the good news.

One of those listening was Lydia. She was a woman of means who dealt in purple clothes. She was a trader and the item of her trade was for rich folks. She brought her wares from the city of Thyatira. The best part was that Lydia was described as a worshiper of God. That meant that she was religious and open to the things of God. The Lord opened the heart of Lydia to respond to the message of the good news proclaimed by Paul.

It is true that the message of God has to be interpreted to the hearts of people by the Holy Spirit. Unless there is a conviction of the Holy Spirit the words of the Gospel do not take root in peoples' heart. Lydia is an example of someone who was open to the Word of God. Thank God for the work of the Holy Spirit in the hearts of believers. Lydia responded to the message positively and requested that she be baptized with her household. That means that her household also believed in the message and there was a mass baptism in the river that Sabbath.

Lydia invited the three men to come and stay in their home and conduct their ministry from there. It did not take much twisting of the arm to get the men to stay in a home where they would receive Christian hospitality. This was also an opportunity for Paul to provide the much-needed follow up to these new converts.

SEPTEMBER DAY 21

Once when we were going to the place of prayer, we were met by a slave girl who had a spirit by which she predicted the future. She earned a great deal of money for her owners by fortune telling. This girl followed Paul and the rest of us, shouting, "These men are servants of the Most High God, who are telling you the way to be saved." She kept this up for many days. Finally, Paul became so troubled that he turned around and said to the spirit, "In the name of Jesus Christ I command you to come out of her!" At that moment the spirit left her. Acts 16:16-18

The riverside open-air prayer chapel had now become a popular and regular place for Paul and his companions. Most likely several people did gather there expecting to hear Paul and his companions bring the word of God.

A slave girl who had a spirit by which she could tell the future followed the apostles. She would not follow them quietly, rather she kept shouting: "These men are servants of the Most High God, who are telling you the way to be saved." Her masters to make money were using the slave girl. People would come up to her and she would tell them their future in exchange for a fee. What the girl was saying about the apostles was true and she acted like an unsolicited advertisement for the ministry.

The only problem was that this went on for days to the point that it became a distraction to the ministry. After all, the Good News did not need publicity from a spirit of divination. This is a good example of the saying that, "the end does not justify the means". The fact that the pronouncement from the evil spirit was generally true does not mean that one should promote fortune telling.

Paul decided that enough was enough and decided to cast out the spirit in the slave girl. Paul turned around and said to the spirit, "In the name of Jesus Christ I command you to come out of her!" "At that moment the spirit left her." The power in the command of Paul was apparent to the whole gathering. When the spirit left the girl, she stopped shouting and her ability to see into the future ceased immediately.

The same power has been given to us!

September Day 22

When the owners of the slave girl realized that their hope of making money was gone, they seized Paul and Silas and dragged them into the marketplace to face the authorities. They brought them before the magistrates and said, "These men are Jews, and are throwing our city into an uproar by advocating customs unlawful for us Romans to accept or practice." Acts 16:19-21

The powerful words of God spoken to the slave girl were what it took to set her free from the spiritual bondage that had gripped her. She was free on one hand, but economically she was still a slave and she had owners. That must have been a sad state of affairs to observe -- an individual who was spiritually and economically in bondage.

The owners did not bother Paul and his companions when the girl was demonstrating her ability to know things that the ordinary person would not. It was to their advantage that the girl could display her ability to discern things that were spiritual. All the public display and being part of the crowd ended quickly, however, when Paul commanded the spirit to come out of the slave girl and it happened.

As soon as the pocketbook of the slave owners was affected, all their admiration for Paul ended. He and his friends became public enemies. These influential businessmen dragged the apostles into town and treated them like criminals. They brought them to the marketplace to face the crowds and the authorities.

What I find interesting is the charge that was leveled against Paul and his friends. Nothing was said about the slave girl and the spirit that was cast out of her. Nothing was said about how that had resulted in financial shortfalls in some quarters. *They brought them before the magistrates and said, "These men are Jews, and are throwing our city into an uproar by advocating customs unlawful for us Romans to accept or practice."*

The crime they were charged with was that they were Jews who were causing public disturbance by advocating customs that were unlawful for Romans to accept. These were fabricated lies designed to bring about a conviction.

SEPTEMBER DAY 23

The crowd joined in the attack against Paul and Silas, and the magistrates ordered them to be stripped and beaten. After they had been severely flogged, they were thrown into prison, and the jailer was commanded to guard them carefully. Upon receiving such orders, he put them in the inner cell and fastened their feet in the stocks. Acts 16:22-24

The crowd joined in the attack against Paul and Silas in the marketplace. The owners of the slave girl knew what they were doing when they dragged Paul and Silas there. They knew that it would be easy to instigate the people into attacking these missionaries by making up false charges against them. The magistrates did not inquire into the matter to find out the truth. They did not attempt to hear what Paul had to say on the charges.

The magistrates pronounced Paul and Silas guilty as charged. In other words, these men were Jews who were causing uproar in Philippi. They were asking people to practice customs that were not in line with Roman laws. Paul and Silas were stripped of their clothes and severely beaten, and then they were thrown into prison. The missionaries were treated like hardened criminals who were a threat to the city and Roman laws.

The owners of the slave girl must have been powerful individuals with a lot of clout in the city of Philippi. They knew exactly what to say to whip up the crowd and they seem to have had the magistrates in their pocket. They wanted Paul and Silas to pay heavily for causing them financial loss. The jailer was given strict instructions to guard these men carefully.

The jailer, for his part, obeyed the orders and put the ambassadors of the gospel into the inner cell and fastened their feet in the stocks. The jailer understood that the men were flight risks and he wanted to make sure that there was no way of escape for them.

The inner cell must have been dark and well protected with security locks. It would take the presence of the jailer himself to get these men out of this maximum-security prison. What did they do to deserve this treatment? They preached the gospel and cast out an evil spirit from a slave girl.

People have suffered all over the world for the gospel and for the name of Jesus Christ. Things have not changed in our day; those who stand up for the good news and challenge the principalities and powers of our time will find themselves in situations they have never anticipated.

SEPTEMBER DAY 24

About midnight Paul and Silas were praying and singing hymns to God, and the other prisoners were listening to them. Acts 16:25

What would I have done if I was thrown into the inner jail with chained hands and my feet were put in stocks? I do not know if I would have had the presence of mind to organize a prayer meeting there. I do not know if I would be in the mood to sing hymns. I would like to think that my faith would be strong enough to follow through with such activities. What impresses me most about this passage is that Paul and Silas were praying at midnight. It is tough enough to organize a prayer meeting at seven in the evening or five in the morning. But praying at midnight is when people mean business with the Lord.

Some will say desperate times call for desperate measures. The two evangelists could see beyond their personal situations; they knew that they had a captive audience in the prison. The only complaint that could have come from the other inmates would have been that they were disturbing them with their prayers and singing. But when one is abandoned to the inner cells of a prison, prayer would be a very welcome exercise. This would be the case, if those doing the praying are men like Paul and Silas.

We are told the other prisoners were listening attentively to Paul and Silas. This was a situation where they could not pray in their cells because they did not understand the art of praying. Also, the evangelists were praying to a God who was foreign to these prisoners. Definitely the hymns would have been unfamiliar. So all they could do was to be silent participants in this midnight prayer meeting.

The prisoners seemed to be in agreement with whatever Paul and Silas were doing. They could have tuned them out and gone to sleep. They could have also called the jailer to discipline these men who would not allow them to have a good night's rest. But they did none of that except to listen.

What would we have done if we happened to be one of the prisoners with Paul and Silas? There was no way anyone was going to stop these midnight prayers. It might be wise to join them.

SEPTEMBER DAY 25

Suddenly there was such a violent earthquake that the foundations of the prison were shaken. At once all the prison doors flew open, and everybody's chains came loose. The jailer woke up, and when he saw the prison doors open, he drew his sword and was about to kill himself because he thought the prisoners had escaped. But Paul shouted "Don't harm yourself! We are all here!" Acts 16:26-28

The midnight prayer meeting was still in progress when something miraculous happened. Suddenly, there was such a violent earthquake that the foundations of the prison were shaken. Some people would attribute what happened to coincidence, but for those praying and singing hymns this was no coincidence. I am sure for the other prisoners who had become active participants through listening there was a connection between the prayer meeting and the earthquake.

Paul and Silas knew that this was a God incidence. The location of the earthquake and its effect on the foundations of the prison and the fact that the people inside the prison cells were not hurt only go to affirm the conviction of Paul and Silas. How else should they explain the breaking of chains and bonds that shackled them and the opening of prison doors without any physical injury to anyone?

The first reaction of the prisoners was not to escape. It seemed they were waiting for further instructions or they were waiting for something more to happen. The jailer woke up and saw what had happened and concluded that all the prisoners had escaped. He was ready to kill himself because he did not want to face the consequences of allowing the prisoners to escape. The jailer remembered the instructions he had been given when Paul and Silas were handed over to him.

Fortunately, Paul saw the jailer pull his sword and knew what he was about to do, so he shouted to him: ""Don't harm yourself! We are all here!" Those were welcome words for the jailer. They were words of assurance that there was no need for suicide.

God had mercy on the jailer in just the same way that all of us have been shown mercy.

September Day 26

But Paul shouted, "Don't harm yourself! We are all here!" The jailer called for lights, rushed in and fell trembling before Paul and Silas. He then brought them out and asked, "Sirs, what must I do to be saved?" They replied, "Believe in the Lord Jesus, and you will be saved—you and your household." Acts 16:28-31

The shouting that came out of the prison cell must have startled the jailer. He was not expecting to see or hear anything that resembled a prisoner in a cell with open doors. The words from Paul were more than reassuring. They were comforting. The prisoner was trying to save the physical life of the jailer. "Don't harm yourself! We are all here!"

The fact that the jailer called for lights was a sign that the prison must have been thrown into pitch darkness by the huge earthquake. The jailer needed lights to make sure that all the prisoners were there and also that it was safe for him to venture into the prison cells. The jailer rushed in and fell before Paul and Silas trembling.

What a reversal in the state of affairs. A few hours before this incident, it was the jailer who was in a superior position and was in charge of Paul and Silas who had been falsely accused. It was the jailer who put them in chains and put their feet in stocks. Now the roles have been reversed. The prisoners are no longer in chains and are preventing the jailer from harming himself. Moreover, the jailer has prostrated himself before his prisoners.

The jailer decided to bring the prisoners out of the cells and then asked the most important question in his life: "Sirs, what must I do to be saved?" Just imagine the jailer calling his prisoners, "Sirs"! Under ordinary conditions, that would never happen. But here we have the jailer wanting to know how he could be saved. The jailer was sincere about his actions. He realized that Paul and Silas had something that he did not have. So he did the best thing anyone could do, and that was to ask for information about how he could be saved.

The same question has been asked by countless numbers of people all over the world. Interestingly, people find out that it is not so much what they do, but what Jesus has done. So the answer to the jailer was straightforward. "Believe in the Lord Jesus and you will be saved!"

Salvation is an act of God. It depends on the grace of God.

September Day 27

They replied, "Believe in the Lord Jesus, and you will be saved—you and your household." Then they spoke the word of the Lord to him and to all the others in his house. At that hour of the night the jailer took them and washed their wounds; then immediately he and all his family were baptized. Acts 16:31-33

When Paul said you and your household will be saved, he might have been thinking of what happened in the household of Lydia in the same city. Paul had witnessed the salvation and the baptism of the entire household. But Paul was also aware that faith comes by hearing the word of God. How could the jailer and his household believe in one of whom they have never heard?

So the task of the evangelist was to speak the word of God to them. They were taught about the way to life, and the teaching was directed to everyone in the household. People have made the mistake of thinking that mass conversions come about without teaching. There is always teaching before and after the conversion of people to the Christian faith.

The jailer demonstrated his understanding of the message of Christ by submitting to baptism and allowing his whole household to be part of his new faith. When one finds something precious, they ought to share it with those around them. He also demonstrated Christian hospitality when he took his prisoners and washed their wounds. That must have been a sight to observe. When a jailer washes the wounds that he has inflicted on his prisoners directly or indirectly, there can be no doubt that a transformation has taken place in the life and household of the jailer.

Just imagine that! They could not wait until the morning to receive the teaching and the baptism. The events of the night had created a deep hunger in the hearts of the people in the jailer's family. Paul and Silas, on the other hand, were more than ready to lead them to a place where they could confess Jesus as Lord for themselves.

September Day 28

The jailer brought them into his house and set a meal before them; he was filled with joy because he had come to believe in God—he and his whole family. When it was daylight, the magistrates sent their officers to the jailer with the order: "Release those men." The jailer told Paul, "The magistrates have ordered that you and Silas be released. Now you can leave. Go in peace." Acts 16:34-36

How did Paul and Silas go from a midnight prayer meeting to a dawn love feast? It took a miracle of God to accomplish that feat. We are not told the last time the two men had a decent meal. The last time they were in an environment that resembled normalcy was at a prayer meeting by the riverside with Lydia and other believers from Philippi.

Now we hear this: "The jailer brought them into his house and set a meal before them." That was truly a miracle. Who could have believed that the same men who were locked up in prison a few hours earlier would be seated at table with their jailer? They did not ask for the food before dawn. But the jailer knew when they last ate and knew that his new Christian brothers must be starving. Nobody ordered the jailer to feed Paul and Silas; he did it because he was a new person.

It is true that if anyone is in Jesus Christ, that person is a new creation. The old has passed away and the new has come. (2 Corinthians 5:17) We are told that the jailer was filled with joy because he had come to believe in God – he and his household. This inexplicable joy is at the heart of Christianity. It is something that the Holy Spirit does in the heart of the believer. It is a joy that is not based on the absence of problems. In the case of the jailer, he did not spend time thinking about how he was going to explain to the magistrates why the men were out of jail. Even more seriously, he seemed to be aiding the prisoners.

The new joy of the jailer was worth more than the answers to these problems. It seemed the news of the Divine jailbreak at midnight had traveled fast in the city of Philippi. The magistrates even heard details and exaggerations of what really happened. They even knew that Paul and Silas were in the home of the jailer. So the magistrates sent the order to the jailer to set Paul and Silas free. This was an unusual move. The men were supposed to bring the evangelists into court and charge them with an offense. Now charges were being dropped without a hearing.

God moves in mysterious ways.

Dr. Seth Asare

SEPTEMBER DAY 29

The jailer told Paul, "The magistrates have ordered that you and Silas be released. Now you can leave. Go in peace." But Paul said to the officers: "They beat us publicly without a trial, even though we are Roman citizens, and threw us into prison. And now do they want to get rid of us quietly? No! Let them come themselves and escort us out." Acts 16:36-37

The magistrates sent officers to order the release of Paul and Silas. The jailer communicated the news to them; he told them that they could leave in peace. He was assuring them that the case had been thrown out and they were not going to receive any trouble from their accusers. In other words, the owners of the slave girl were not going to hassle Paul and Silas any more. So what happened to them being dragged into the market place? It would all be forgotten and thrown under the carpet.

Paul and Silas refused to go without a hearing. They wanted the magistrates themselves to come out and make the pronouncement that they were free to go. After all, the magistrates were the ones who ordered that they should be sent to jail and kept securely there. Paul knew that the law had to be followed in these matters. You do not order people to be sent to jail awaiting trial and then secretly send officers to tell them that they are free to go.

So, *Paul said to the officers: "They beat us publicly without a trial, even though we are Roman citizens, and threw us into prison. And now do they want to get rid of us quietly? No! Let them come themselves and escort us out."* Paul was insisting on his right as a Roman citizen. He should not have been beaten in public without a trial. They should have found him guilty of an offense before punishing him. Now, the officers and the magistrates were the ones who were guilty of not following their own laws.

Paul demanded that the people who put them in jail should come out and set them free. The tables were turned and the pressure was now on the authorities. God was fighting the battle for Paul and Silas and the Lord had a way out for them. It might not be the way they had imagined, but God was with them.

September Day 30

And now do they want to get rid of us quietly? No! Let them come themselves and escort us out." The officers reported this to the magistrates, and when they heard that Paul and Silas were Roman citizens, they were alarmed. They came to appease them and escorted them from the prison, requesting them to leave the city. After Paul and Silas came out of the prison, they went to Lydia's house, where they met with the brothers and encouraged them. Then they left. Acts 16:37b-40

Paul and Silas decided not to leave the confines of the prison until the magistrates who put them in jail came and escorted them out. The stand of Paul and Silas was reported to the magistrates. They were also informed that the people they beat and put in jail were Roman citizens. Being a Roman citizen was accompanied by some privileges. It included fair and sometimes preferential treatment in all the Roman provinces. This was something that the magistrates overlooked because they assumed that these men were Jews. They were alarmed when they learned that the preachers were not ordinary Jews propagating a religious idea.

The magistrates were forced to come out themselves and appease Paul and Silas. They had no choice but to extend to Paul and Silas the dignity that befitted Roman citizens. That meant the magistrates provided the escort that was required to lead the men out of jail. In other words, they had to succumb to the demands of Paul and Silas on the matter of an escort.

We do not hear of a mob action similar to what occurred in the marketplace. This was because Paul and Silas had an official escort out of the jail. And the escort was mounted by no other than the very magistrates who put them in jail. In other words, the evangelists were not run out of town. They were given the red carpet treatment.

They were now free to go and visit with their friends, so they went to the home of Lydia where they had stayed before their arrest. The joy in that home could not be described. The Christians in Philippi had gathered there to welcome Paul and Silas.

Could it be that while the midnight prayer meeting was taking place in the prison cells, there was another prayer meeting in the home of Lydia? If that were to be the case, then that would explain how all the Christians could gather so quickly when the evangelists were released. And again, if that were the case, the joy of these believers would be indescribable.

Just imagine Paul and Silas recounting what happened in the cells. I am sure their emphasis would be on the opportunity to witness. We can be witnesses for Christ wherever we find ourselves.

Dr. Seth Asare

September Extra

When they had passed through Amphipolis and Apollonia, they came to Thessalonica, where there was a Jewish synagogue. As his custom was, Paul went into the synagogue, and on three Sabbath days he reasoned with them from the Scriptures, Acts 17:1- 2

When Paul and his companions left Philippi they went through several areas until they came to Thessalonica. What prompted them to settle in this town? The answer is simply the Holy Spirit. The whole missionary journey had been under the guidance of the Holy Spirit who directed them to this region of Macedonia. The team had learned how to be guided by the Holy Spirit regarding where to stay longer and where to just pass through.

In Thessalonica, there was a Jewish synagogue. That was an indication that there was a larger Jewish community in Thessalonica than in Philippi. There were enough adult males to constitute a place of worship – a synagogue. It was Paul's custom to begin his ministry in the local synagogue. He understood that the Christian faith had its roots in Judaism. There were several things that were basic to both faiths. One did not have to explain to a Jew the idea of monotheism and God's revelation or the covenant with Abraham.

So Paul went to the synagogue in Thessalonica, and for three Sabbaths he tried to reason with those who attended using the very scriptures that they were familiar with. He showed them how the Hebrew Bible pointed to the coming of the Messiah. This was an idea that was not foreign to the Jewish worshippers. They had been expecting the coming of the Messiah based on the Old Testament prophecies.

Paul began from where the people were in their faith concerning these prophecies and was determined to take them a step further. This was all part of the work of the Holy Spirit. It was not just a methodology to be learned and repeated; rather it was people allowing themselves to be used by the Holy Spirit in a particular context.

Be open to what the Holy Spirit wants to use to communicate the message of Christ to someone today.

We will continue our reflections with the missionary journey of Paul and his companions because there is so much to learn from the way God used these individuals to extend the Christian mission in its infancy. They were paving a trail for many who were to come after them.

OCTOBER DAY 1

As his custom was, Paul went into the synagogue, and on three Sabbath days he reasoned with them from the Scriptures, explaining and proving that the Christ had to suffer and rise from the dead. "This Jesus I am proclaiming to you is the Christ," he said. Some of the Jews were persuaded and joined Paul and Silas, as did a large number of God-fearing Greeks and not a few prominent women. Acts 17:2-4

In Thessalonica, Paul and his companions spent three weeks reasoning with worshippers about what the scriptures said concerning the coming Messiah. The concept of a suffering Messiah and a dying Messiah did not fit into the expectations of the Hebrew people. Their history had prepared them for a conquering Messiah who was coming to deliver them from the physical oppression of the powers that were enslaving them.

Although there were passages in the Hebrew Bible that pointed to a suffering Christ, that did not fit into the worldview of those who attended worship at Thessalonica and for that matter, any Jew who wanted to be true to his tradition. The experience of the Hebrew people conditioned them to expect a liberating Christ.

Paul had an uphill task of explaining to those in the Synagogue that the Christ promised in scripture had to suffer, die and rise from the dead. As anyone can imagine, only the Holy Spirit of God could accomplish the task of convincing people of this fact. The people may have heard of the events concerning the carpenter's son who was crucified. They may even have heard stories of his resurrection. Now Paul was proclaiming that this man from Nazareth was more than a historical figure. "This Jesus I am proclaiming to you is the Christ," That statement must have come across forcefully to the hearers of Paul. For some, it was a shocking assertion to make. For others, it may have bordered on blasphemy. But that was the thrust of the message of the gospel preached by Paul and the early church.

Some of the Jews believed and decided to follow Paul and Silas. Several Gentiles and prominent God-fearing people joined the group of believers. These were drawn by the Holy Spirit to follow Christ.

October Day 2

But the Jews were jealous; so they rounded up some bad characters from the marketplace, formed a mob and started a riot in the city. They rushed to Jason's house in search of Paul and Silas in order to bring them out to the crowd. But when they did not find them, they dragged Jason and some other brothers before the city officials. Acts 17: 5-6

The ministry of Paul and Silas was becoming fruitful in Thessalonica. Both Jews and Gentiles were responding to the gospel. The result was jealousy from other religious authorities who decided to stop these ambassadors of the gospel. They used the oldest trick in the book, and that was to round up some people with suspicious characters and incite them to cause trouble for Paul and Silas. These were people hanging around the marketplace with no productive business.

The religious leaders managed to get these young men in the marketplace to start a riot. Their goal was to start a commotion that would destabilize the city and then force the hand of the city authorities against Paul and Silas. The mob rushed to the house of Jason in search of Paul and Silas. Their hope was to bring them out to the crowd in the marketplace. They knew that such an attack was sure to end the ministry of these apostles in Thessalonica.

Jason was one of the individuals who had responded positively to the gospel message. It would seem that his home was being used as a gathering place for the Christians, so the rioters assumed that Paul and Silas were staying there. Interestingly, they did not find the evangelists there. But that did not deter the rioters. They decided to drag Jason and some of the brothers before the city officials.

The rioters had not heard the preaching and the teaching of these evangelists. They were mostly hired men, so they had to make up charges to bring to the city officials. All they could do was to shout at the top of their voices one thing after the other. It is sad to observe what hatred without a cause can do.

Jason and these new Christians were being introduced to what happened when people decided to follow Jesus. This was not what they expected when they decided to follow Jesus.

When the unexpected happens, let us be prepared to hold on to our faith.

OCTOBER DAY 3

But when they did not find them, they dragged Jason and some other brothers before the city officials, shouting: "These men who have caused trouble all over the world have now come here, and Jason has welcomed them into his house. They are all defying Caesar's decrees, saying that there is another king, one called Jesus." When they heard this, the crowd and the city officials were thrown into turmoil. Then they made Jason and the others post bond and let them go. Acts 17: 6-9

What happens when one is looking for something and cannot find it? They get frustrated and sometimes they start lashing out at everything in sight. The rioters in Thessalonica had expected to find Paul and Silas in the home of Jason. That was the information they had received. They went there and did not find the evangelists. So they decided to grab anyone they could find in Jason's home. They dragged out Jason and some of the brothers in the house and treated them as if they were Paul and Silas.

The rioters were shouting: "these men who have caused trouble all over the world have now come here, and Jason has welcomed them into his house." What was interesting was that the men they were parading before the city officials were all from Thessalonica. They had not been in the party of Paul and Silas and they had not traveled around the world preaching the gospel.

The rioters knew that these flimsy accusations would be dismissed as insufficient evidence for any legal action against the Christians. They had to come up with something that would cause a stir. So the crowd added this charge: "they are all defying the decrees of Caesar saying that there is another King called Jesus". Certainly that should get the attention of anyone who is dwelling in a Roman colony. The last thing the city officials needed was to be accused of not taking seriously any group that was charged with defying the rule of Caesar.

That accusation alone was enough to throw the city into an uproar. Now the impression was that these Christians had gone too far. The accusation amounted to a charge of treason. Unfortunately, there was no attempt to ascertain the truth of the charges. Jason and his fellow Christians were all from Thessalonica and the message that was preached by Paul was not an affront to Caesar.

Christians have often been accused of not being patriotic enough because they do not subscribe to civil religion. The kingdom of this world is certainly different from the Kingdom of God. But Christians are the first to follow their Lord in saying, "give to Caesar what belongs to Caesar ......"

The officials made Jason and his group post bond and then let them go. The officials did not find any credible evidence in the charges that were brought by the rioters.

OCTOBER DAY 4

As soon as it was night, the brothers sent Paul and Silas away to Berea. On arriving there, they went to the Jewish synagogue. Now the Bereans were of more noble character than the Thessalonians, for they received the message with great eagerness and examined the Scriptures every day to see if what Paul said was true. Acts 17:10-11a

The hired men of disreputable character in Thessalonica realized that they did not get their way. Jason, who was from their town, was let go after posting a bond. He had not committed any crime. The only thing they had against him was that he had housed these visitors who were supposed to be turning the world upside down in every town they visited. The believers in Thessalonica were smart in realizing that the hired men of questionable character were not going to rest until they could locate Paul and Silas. And so they did the best thing possible by keeping them underground until it was dark.

In the night, the believers in Thessalonica sent Paul and Silas to Berea. They literally escorted them there and protected them from those who were seeking to arrest them and bring them before the city officials. One would have thought the evangelists would take a few days of rest before resuming their preaching and teaching. But, no! That was not the case. They went straight to work. On arriving in Berea, they went to the Jewish synagogue there and started teaching and expounding on scripture to those gathered.

Berea seems to be a prominent town because enough Jews had settled there to build their own synagogue. We are told that the people of Berea were of more noble character than those at Thessalonica. Why was this distinction made? It was because of the approach that the people in Berea took to the teaching of Paul and Silas. They decided first to listen carefully, and then they decided to search the scriptures to ascertain that what was being said and taught was indeed scriptural.

The examination of scripture to find the truth for themselves made the Bereans a special example to wherever the gospel is preached. That is still a challenge to our present generation. The study of scripture ought to be a priority in every place where the gospel of Christ has taken root.

Read your Bible and study it with others under the guidance of the Holy Spirit.

Dr. Seth Asare

OCTOBER DAY 5

Now the Bereans were of more noble character than the Thessalonians, for they received the message with great eagerness and examined the Scriptures every day to see if what Paul said was true. Many of the Jews believed, as did also a number of prominent Greek women and many Greek men. Acts 17:11-12

We cannot say enough about the example set by the people of Berea in their response to the gospel. They received the message of the apostles with open minds and with eagerness; then they examined the scriptures every day. It was the daily examination of the scriptures that set the Bereans apart. It seems as if they were hungry for the word of God. One can also say that this was none other than the work of the Holy Spirit. There have been testimonies all over the world of men and women who have taken the Bible and prayed to God to reveal himself to them. In almost all such instances, these individuals have come to a saving knowledge of Jesus Christ.

I have heard testimonies of politicians who have been thrown into jail in Africa and the only reading material they were given was the Bible. These men came out of jail transformed by the power of the word of God. When the Bereans decided to do a daily study to find out if the message they were hearing was correct, they placed themselves in the path of transformation. They examined the Old Testament prophecies about the coming Messiah and they tried to understand the salvation history of God as it unfolded through the covenant people. The more they searched, the more they were convinced that Jesus was the Christ.

Now what they came to believe in did not rest on the words of Paul and Silas. Their new faith rested in the unchangeable word of God. It was no longer because Paul said it or a preacher said it. It was because God had spoken to them in the word of God.

The people in Berea had also learned the discipline of going into the well of God and quenching their thirst every day. They did not have to wait for a Sabbath day or a Sunday to receive the word of God. They had discovered the fountain that would never run dry.

One is not surprised by the response to the message in this town. Jews and Greeks alike turned to the Lord. The practice of examining the scriptures yielded dividends. And that has not changed.

OCTOBER DAY 6

When the Jews in Thessalonica learned that Paul was preaching the word of God at Berea, they went there too, agitating the crowds and stirring them up. The brothers immediately sent Paul to the coast, but Silas and Timothy stayed at Berea. Acts 17:13-14

A good word travels fast! The Jews in Thessalonica, who had been looking for Paul to harm him, heard that he was preaching the good news in Berea. They decided to pursue him there. So they went to Berea searching for Paul.

Why would these men leave their own town and go to another place to cause trouble? It was because the ministry of Paul was flourishing in these regions and Satan would not have it so. The whole thing was a spiritual battle for the souls of the people in the region of Macedonia.

Paul was invited to this region in a vision that was inspired by the Holy Spirit. There was no promise that it was going to be easy, but the apostles knew that the same Holy Spirit who sent them on the mission would be with them.

The men from Thessalonica came to Berea to agitate the crowds and to stir them up. The agitators were aware that their influence in a different town was limited, so all they could do was to stir things up. They did not have the authority to drag the evangelists before the city officials. They were hoping to get the locals to do their dirty job for them.

The believers in Berea saw what the men from Thessalonica were trying to do. They also realized that most of their anger was directed against Paul. The other evangelists who had not been so vocal seemed to be able to blend in. Timothy, for example, had been there all along without calling attention to himself. And so it was decided that Paul should be sent to the coast while Silas and Timothy stayed behind to do the work. This seemed like a good plan.

Sometimes the Holy Spirit worked through the advice of the brothers and sisters. We must be open to what the Spirit would do at different times.

Dr. Seth Asare

OCTOBER DAY 7

The brothers immediately sent Paul to the coast, but Silas and Timothy stayed at Berea. The men who escorted Paul brought him to Athens and then left with instructions for Silas and Timothy to join him as soon as possible. Acts 17:14-15

The decision to move Paul from Berea and send him to the coast was a tactical move that had to be done quickly. Paul could have gone to one of the nearby towns, but the action of the trouble causers from Thessalonica demanded a swift and strategic action. The believers in Berea were also aware that there was the need for more teaching in the town since they were all new in the faith. Therefore, it was necessary for Timothy and Silas to remain for some time so that they could consolidate the work that had been started.

"Follow up" was an important phase in spreading the good news. It was not enough to go out and preach the gospel. There had to be a plan on how to establish the believers so that they could be self-supporting and self-propagating. This principle has worked well in many Christian missions all over the world. The modern church would call this "nurture". The nurturing of people in congregations for the purpose of going out to make disciples is still at the heart of the Great Commission.

We are told that Paul was escorted to Athens. The question is why did he need an escort by more than one person? It might have been that Paul was not familiar with this territory and he needed people to guide him. Certainly the believers in Berea did not want Paul to travel alone. Silas and Timothy had stayed behind in Berea and it was important for Paul to have traveling companions on his way to the coast. The agitations by the rioters from Thessalonica made the escorts necessary.

Paul was grateful for the escorts and when he arrived at Athens, he gave them instructions to send Timothy and Silas to him as soon as possible. He understood the work they were doing at Berea, but he also knew that the harvest was plentiful and they had to press forward with the good news.

There is no doubt that Paul missed his fellow workers. Their ministry had always been teamwork. He valued the contributions of Silas and Timothy, although it might seem that he was always doing the talking. We are all called to be part of a team in the ministry of Christ. Each person's contribution is important in this kingdom work.

October Day 8

While Paul was waiting for them in Athens, he was greatly distressed to see that the city was full of idols. So he reasoned in the synagogue with the Jews and the God-fearing Greeks, as well as in the marketplace day by day with those who happened to be there. A group of Epicurean and Stoic philosophers began to dispute with him. Some of them asked, "What is this babbler trying to say?" Others remarked, "He seems to be advocating foreign gods." They said this because Paul was preaching the good news about Jesus and the resurrection. Acts 17:16-18

While Paul was waiting in Athens, he decided to walk around and observe what the city looked like. He was surprised to find that the city was full of idols. Everywhere he turned, he found people worshipping graven images of all kinds. Everyone seemed to have his own idol. That must have distressed Paul. He decided to go to the Synagogue and reason with anyone who would listen to him. He even decided to go to the marketplace day by day to reason with those he found there.

Paul was telling the people about the good news of Jesus Christ. He was anxious to get his message across to whoever would listen to him, but his message seemed strange to his hearers. A group of Epicurean and Stoic philosophers began to dispute with him. They assumed that Paul was expounding a new philosophy. They were more interested in disputing and arguing with Paul than listening to the message that Paul had to present.

There were those who wanted to know what Paul had to say. The message presented by the apostle seemed foreign to those in Athens who were listening to him. They believed that Paul was teaching them about foreign gods. To some it seemed like foolishness. Interestingly, that perception has not changed. "The message of the cross seems foolish to those who are perishing."

How else does one explain a dying Savior? Or how does one make sense of the message of the resurrection of Christ? In a city where people worshipped idols that they could see and touch, Paul had a difficult time explaining how the creator of the universe had come down to be human in order to save us.

It is the same message that we preach today!

OCTOBER DAY 9

A group of Epicurean and Stoic philosophers began to dispute with him. Some of them asked, "What is this babbler trying to say?" Others remarked, "He seems to be advocating foreign gods." They said this because Paul was preaching the good news about Jesus and the resurrection. Acts 17:18

So who are the Epicurean and the Stoic philosophers? The Epicureans believed that the supreme good is happiness. In other words, the goal of humans was to live a happy life. The original Epicurean thought distinguished the happiness in their teaching from pleasure. They understood that momentary pleasure or gratification could not be equated with happiness. The Epicurean philosophy degenerated to more sensual teaching. In fact, by Paul's time the human gratification aspect had crept into the teaching of the Epicureans.

The Stoic philosophy, on the other hand, taught that people should learn to live with nature and stop complaining about everything. People were supposed to recognize the self-sufficiency and the independence that they have. In so doing, it is possible to suppress desires and rise above many human inclinations. The unfortunate development in Stoicism is that people could be filled with pride in their accomplishments. The practitioners of Stoicism tend to look down on all others who have not attained their level of "achievement".

The Stoics are the ones who would call Paul a "babbler". This is because in their minds, he is picking up little pieces of learning from different places without seriously thinking through them. So the Stoics would ask the question, "What is this babbler trying to say?"

It was obvious that Paul was facing what could be described as some of the most learned philosophers of his day at Athens. They seemed to have no regard for him and his message. At best, they considered him a peddler of foreign gods or a babbler.

The good news of the resurrection of Jesus Christ was indeed foreign to the people of Athens. My prayer is that the same message would be received by all of us with an open heart.

OCTOBER DAY 10

Then they took him and brought him to a meeting of the Areopagus, where they said to him, "May we know what this new teaching is that you are presenting? You are bringing some strange ideas to our ears, and we want to know what they mean." (All the Athenians and the foreigners who lived there spent their time doing nothing but talking about and listening to the latest ideas.). Acts 17:19-21

"Then they took him and brought him to a meeting." So who are the people who took Paul and brought him to this meeting? It must have been the Epicurean and Stoic philosophers who had been sharing ideas with him. The Areopagus was a council that had authority over matters of religion and morals. They held court in the Royal Portico and they considered themselves to be the custodians of the teachings that introduced new religions and foreign gods.

The philosophers felt that Paul needed to come to this forum and be heard by this council who could approve the new ideas they were hearing. That showed that these philosophers did not totally dismiss the teachings of Paul although they called him a "babbler". They wanted the council and many more people to weigh in on what Paul was saying.

At the Areopagus they were polite to Paul and asked: "May we know what this new teaching is that you are presenting? You are bringing some strange ideas to our ears, and we want to know what they mean." The philosophers admitted that the teaching of Paul was a new one. It was not something they had heard before. They described the message about Jesus Christ as strange ideas to their ears. But what I find interesting is that they wanted to know the meaning of a teaching that claims the Creator of the universe had visited this planet in the person of Jesus Christ. They wanted to hear more about the death and the resurrection of the central figure in Paul's message.

We are informed that the Athenians loved to hear and discuss new ideas from foreign lands. It seemed this was a curious group of people who were open to new ideas. They were more interested in debating these new ideas and accommodating those that made sense to them.

But Paul had something more in mind than what they had bargained for. He wanted to present The Christ who makes demands on people. One cannot be neutral to the message of the resurrected Christ.

October Day 11

Paul then stood up in the meeting of the Areopagus and said: "Men of Athens! I see that in every way you are very religious. Acts 17:22

The philosophers at Athens brought Paul to the meeting of the Areopagus. They wanted to hear more about the teaching that Paul was propagating. After all, the Areopagus was the Council responsible for certifying new religions and foreign gods.

Paul was quick to seize the opportunity that had presented itself and decided to address the Council. He stood up in the Council as he would have done in a law court and began by referring to his observations as he walked around town. He decided to affirm the people of Athens with these words: "Men of Athens! I see that in every way you are very religious."

Paul was making a deliberate attempt to separate the Gospel that he was preaching from the many religions of his day. Why would he want to do that? Is Christianity not a religion? Paul would be the first to admit that all religions are attempting to reach God or to understand God. But Paul would also proclaim that in Christianity, we find God's revelation to humanity. In other words, the reverse is true for Christianity. God in Jesus Christ reached down in search of a lost people.

So one can understand why Paul would call the attempts at Athens to search for different gods very religious. It is a shame to observe how many wars have been fought in the name of religion and intolerance.

The God who searches for a lost world is big enough to fight for himself. Unfortunately, many think that they should fight for the god they worship. The God of our Lord Jesus Christ is working to include all those who believe in the saving work of our Lord Jesus Christ.

Christ stands above religion and we should be careful not to bring Christ down to the level of the thinking in the Areopagus of our day.

October Day 12

For as I walked around and looked carefully at your objects of worship, I even found an altar with this inscription: TO AN UNKNOWN GOD. Now what you worship as something unknown I am going to proclaim to you. Acts 17:23

Paul had taken the time in his leisure hours to walk through Athens and observe the way of life of the people. So when he was given the opportunity to address the Areopagus, he started with his observation on what the people knew as god. Paul started with where the people of Athens were in terms of their understanding of God.

That was and still is a good method for communicating the gospel. It is helpful to begin with where the audience and the hearers are. The audience is able to identify with the message when they believe the communicator is identifying with them.

Paul noted that in his casual walks round Athens, he could observe their objects of worship. Is it possible that our objects of worship are all around us even if we have not purposely identified them as such? Whatever we put in place of God in our lives becomes an object of worship. Some of these are clearly marked and others are not. Paul's opening statement to the Areopagus was revealing, "I even found an altar with this inscription: TO AN UNKNOWN GOD".

Who would go through the trouble of building an altar to an "unknown God"? Such an individual must have come to the conclusion that there is another God who is beyond the gods that have been identified by the worshippers at Athens. Things have not changed much in our day. There are many who are still worshipping an unknown God. They are not able to name the God they worship, and they are religiously searching for the God who is higher than them.

Paul decided to make the subject of the unknown God the starting point of his message to the Areopagus. He said: "Now what you worship as something unknown I am going to proclaim to you." That must have gotten the attention of his hearers.

It is important to know the God we worship!

OCTOBER DAY 13

The God who made the earth and everything in it is the Lord of heaven and earth and does not live in temples built by hands. And he is not served by human hands, as if he needed anything, because he himself gives all men life and breath and everything else. Acts 17:24-25

Paul equated the "unknown God" in Athens to the Judeo Christian God. He told his hearers that the God that they called "unknown" was going to be the subject of his speech. He went ahead and made a bold statement that this God whom he was talking about made both earth and heaven. That must have shocked the hearers. How could anyone claim in the midst of a plethora of deity that his God made heaven and earth?

Paul then went ahead to make a statement that many in our day will call exclusive. He said this creator of God was Lord of everything. The God that Paul preached was not limited by space and time. This God did not dwell in human Temples and did not need the service of human hands. Paul wanted to assert the superiority of the God of Jesus Christ by saying that this God was in a completely different league compared to what he had witnessed in Athens.

The God of the Christian Gospel is the one who gives life to all. And in so doing makes it plain that God does not need anything from humans. Sometimes we behave as if God needs us. But that is far from the truth. God has done without us and can do without us for many years to come. The question is often asked: "Is there anything that we have that did not come as a gift from God?" The answer is "nothing" considering that even human breath is a gift from God.

That is a good reason to worship this God to whom we owe our life and our very existence. The worship of God then becomes an act of gratitude to the one who created us and has been revealed to us in ways that we can know him. There is so much to be thankful for each day. We just have to look around ourselves and say with the hymn writer: "What shall I render to my God for all his mercies? I will take the gifts he has bestowed and humbly ask for more."

Paul's opening statement to the Areopagus pointed to God as the creator to whom we owe everything.

OCTOBER DAY 14

From one man he made every nation of men, that they should inhabit the whole earth; and he determined the times set for them and the exact places where they should live. God did this so that men would seek him and perhaps reach out for him and find him, though he is not far from each one of us. Acts 17:26-27

Paul's message to the Areopagus in Athens began with the creation story. He wanted to establish the origins of humanity and he traced it to the one person created by the God he was presenting. He wanted his hearers to be aware of the fact that the God of his Gospel was the universal creator. Beyond that, Paul wanted to indicate that all the nations of the world came from the one man created by this God.

This was certainly a different concept in the midst of a polytheist society. Here was Paul standing in the midst of the different gods in Athens and proclaiming the one God who rules the whole world. Not only that, Paul was proposing that the times and seasons were set by this God that he was preaching. In other words, the ordering of the universe was not a matter of chance, but a definite plan of God. He said: "and he determined the times set for them and the exact places where they should live."

Paul preached that God knows so much about humanity that where we live and what we do were all part of divine knowledge. He was simply establishing the fact that God is and was omniscient. This must have unsettled the philosophers of Paul's day as they listened to him. But even more revolutionary was he thought that God did this so that humans would seek God.

God had placed thirst in the hearts of humanity to seek after God. According to Paul, everything happening to us and around us is supposed to lead us to want to know God better. In other words, the grace of God has gone ahead of all of us and is wooing us into a relationship with God. It is the plan of God for all those who seek, to find and that for whoever knocks, the door will be opened.

OCTOBER DAY 15

God did this so that men would seek him and perhaps reach out for him and find him, though he is not far from each one of us. 'For in him we live and move and have our being.' As some of your own poets have said, 'We are his offspring.' Acts 17: 27-28

The one who created all people did structure things in such a way that there would be a hunger in humans for their creator. This was Paul's way of connecting with the people of Athens and their philosophers. Creation, according to Paul, is not a haphazard event. Rather, there is an order that points to God. In other words, the God of creation has made himself known in the things that have been created.

"You will seek me and find me when you seek me with all your heart". The God of the gospel is a God of revelation. Throughout scripture we find this God appearing in dreams, visions, and in person to people. Even creation itself tells of the handiwork of God. So Paul boldly proclaims that all that God had set in place was so that people would seek after God and perhaps find what they are seeking for. But Paul is also saying that God had taken the initiative in ordering things in such a way that it is possible to know God.

So people in every place of this world are able to find and know God. What can be known about God is plain in the things that God has made. We just have to look around and see all the ways in which God is beckoning us to know God better.

Paul indicated the nearness of God with this statement:" though he is not far from each one of us." God is close to all of us if we care to tune in to God. Paul made that clear to his audience and even quoted from the poets who were known to his audience in Athens. As some of your own poets have said, 'We are his offspring.'

We are all the offspring of God.

October Day 16

Therefore, since we are God's offspring, we should not think that the divine being is like gold or silver or stone—an image made by man's design and skill. In the past God overlooked such ignorance, but now he commands all people everywhere to repent. Acts 17:29-30

God expects those who consider themselves to be God's offspring to think differently. Paul had established in his message that God was the creator of everything in the world. And that God created humans to seek and find their Creator. Those who accept this premise should have a different worldview as to who God is and how God operates.

The confusion in the minds of worshippers in Athens was addressed directly when Paul indicated that God was not like gold, or silver or stone. These are all materials that could be used to construct an object of worship. An image will remain an image irrespective of the material used in constructing that particular image. Paul was saying that human skill and design could not be used to reproduce God.

Certainly attempts have been made to fashion all forms of idols to be worshipped but none of them come close to representing the God who is the creator of the universe. Just think about it. How can the creature design its creator? That is impossible! In the same way, humans do not have the capacity to create an object that could be the true God.

It is for that reason that we are not encouraged to try. We should have no other god period. Not an image or part of the created order. That did not mean that people have not tried. But Paul now calls all attempts to make gods out of our own image the result of ignorance. Those who are groping in darkness tend to latch on to anything that they do not understand.

Paul indicated that God has decided to overlook those times of ignorance. In the past, people could worship anything because of ignorance. But now the ignorance has been replaced with God's revelation of Jesus Christ. The incarnation of Jesus Christ is an attempt by God to make things plain for everyone. It has pleased God to take on human form and be one of us. So there is no need to try and use images to get an idea of God.

All that is expected of people is that they repent of their ignorance and turn to God's revelation in Jesus Christ. There is no place for ignorance when the truth about God could be known and seen in Jesus Christ!

OCTOBER DAY 17

"For he has set a day when he will judge the world with justice by the man he has appointed. He has given proof of this to all men by raising him from the dead."
Acts 17:31

Paul decided to close his message at Athens by driving home the significance of Jesus Christ in the plan of God for humanity. He made it plain that this message was not about creation and it was about the comparison of the Jewish God with the unknown God at Athens. Paul wanted his audience to respond to the God who is the ruler of all things.

The sovereignty of God could not be questioned. This God had set a day when the whole world will be judged. Who else has the authority to call all people into account? It must be the one who made us and to whom we all owe allegiance. Paul indicated that God intended to judge the world with justice. There may be a number of partial judges out there, but we can count on the justice of God. People will not be judged by what they do not know or of that which they are ignorant.

The desire for justice on the part of God resulted in the revelation of Jesus Christ. God would not be fair if people were judged by what they did not know or by that which they had had no opportunity to respond. Moreover, the weight of sin had caused a separation in the relationship between God and humanity. The history of the human race confirmed the fact all had sinned, and even our righteous deeds were like filthy rags before God. Something had to be done to pay for the price of sin.

How else can a Holy God overlook sin when the same God had pronounced that the wages of sin is death? The incarnation of Jesus Christ broke the deadlock. The justice of God was satisfied in that the price for sin was paid by the sacrificial death of Jesus on the cross. So there was no need for people to pay for the price of sin again, since the perfect Lamb of God had been given for the salvation of the world.

Jesus was the appointed man of God that Paul referred to in this verse. Jesus is a demonstration of the love of God for the world. God gave proof to that by raising Jesus Christ from the dead. The resurrection of Jesus Christ is a monument in the Christian story. It is a testimony to the fact that Jesus was God's answer to the human problem.

October Day 18

When they heard about the resurrection of the dead, some of them sneered, but others said, "We want to hear you again on this subject." Acts 17:32

The resurrection of Jesus Christ from the dead continues to be critical to the Christian story. What would have happened if Jesus had not risen from the dead? For starters, the discouraged disciples would not have come out to bear testimony on behalf of Jesus Christ. The disciples were given new hope in their witness. Moreover, the resurrection gave the believers the assurance that the promise that was given to them had come true. When they saw the risen Lord, the declaration that after three days he would rise from the dead, then made sense to them.

The followers of Jesus Christ believed that the resurrection of Jesus Christ signaled the first fruits of what was to come for all people. Because their Lord had risen from the dead, all those who put their trust in the Lord would also rise from the dead. The message of the resurrection was not a popular one because people could not wrap their minds around it.

Paul found that out as he finished his message in Athens before the Areopagus. When he decided to end on the theme of the resurrection, some of his hearers sneered and mocked at the thought of people rising from the dead. But the reassuring thing was that some people wanted to hear Paul another time. Not only did they want to hear Paul, but some in the audience also wanted to hear him on the subject of the resurrection. That was an indication that there was the possibility for Paul to make headway in Athens.

The power of the gospel rests in the work of the Holy Spirit. And the Spirit is able to use the message spoken to work miracles in people's hearts.

October Day 19

At that, Paul left the Council. A few men became followers of Paul and believed. Among them was Dionysius, a member of the Areopagus, also a woman named Damaris, and a number of others. Acts 17:33-34

At the conclusion of Paul's message, the reaction of his audience was mixed. Some sneered and others were politer. They promised to hear Paul again on the subject of the resurrection. On that note, Paul left the Council. He knew that he had faithfully presented the gospel and the rest was in the hands of the Holy Spirit. That is exactly what all of us are called to do. We are asked to faithfully represent Christ, and the Lord whom we serve will take our witness and use it for God's glory.

As Paul departed from the Council, we are told a few men became followers and believed the message of Jesus Christ. Paul must have been pleasantly surprised, or probably he was not because he had observed the same results over and over again. Paul had come to accept that the power of the gospel did not depend on the eloquence of the preacher. People respond to the message of Jesus Christ because the Holy Spirit convicts and convinces them of the veracity of the life, death and resurrection of Christ.

One of the people who responded to the gospel preached in Athens was Dionysius, a member of the Areopagus. That must have surprised the other members of the Council. After all, they were the people who were supposed to impartially listen to the proponents of new religions and give their approval. Now they had one of their members deciding to be a Christian. The decision of Dionysius would have given a great boost to the small group of Christians at Athens.

OCTOBER DAY 20

After this, Paul left Athens and went to Corinth. There he met a Jew named Aquila, a native of Pontus, who had recently come from Italy with his wife Priscilla, because Claudius had ordered all the Jews to leave Rome. Paul went to see them, and because he was a tentmaker as they were, he stayed and worked with them. Every Sabbath he reasoned in the synagogue, trying to persuade Jews and Greeks. Acts 18:1-4

Paul had left his companions in Thessalonica and had arrived in Athens alone. After his message before the Council at Athens, it was time to move on again. The new converts had been brought to a place that Paul felt he could leave them alone and move on to the city of Corinth. The decision to move from Athens to Corinth must have been prompted by the Holy Spirit. It seems a bit sudden, but as always Paul had learned to trust the leading of the Holy Spirit in these matters.

At Corinth, Paul met Aquila and his wife Priscilla. This Jewish couple had suffered from the persecution of Jews in the first century under the emperor Claudius. There was an order for all Jews to leave Rome. Aquila and Priscilla had to comply, and so they found themselves in the city of Corinth. What would make one group of people hate another group so much that they would rather not co-exist with them? Unfortunately, ethnic and racial tensions are deep and they go way back in human history. Most of the time, the underlying factor is fear. Fear of the unknown and of those who do not look like us.

The couple made tents for a living. It so happened, that Paul was also in that business or he knew how to make tents and enjoyed it so much that he connected with them. Paul decided to stay with them and work with them in his spare time. Paul needed the fellowship of other believers in the absence of Timothy and Silas. This is a lesson that we should never lose sight of. Sometimes one has to make the effort to connect with people who share common interests, especially when it comes to their faith.

Most of the time, it takes effort and prayer to connect with a Christian fellowship that may be right for us. But it is something that must be done, especially so when people move to a new environment. Many Christians have moved into new neighborhoods and failed to identify themselves as Christians or looked for a place where they can plug in.

Paul was aware of the mutual benefit that would accrue as he joined forces with Aquila and Priscilla. As they continued their tent making, they did not lose sight of their calling to be ambassadors of the good news. Paul made it his mission to witness to both Greeks and Jews in the synagogue at Corinth every Sabbath. We are called to be witnesses under all circumstances.

Let us be witnesses for Christ today.

OCTOBER DAY 21

When Silas and Timothy came from Macedonia, Paul devoted himself exclusively to preaching, testifying to the Jews that Jesus was the Christ. Acts 18:5

Silas and Timothy had stayed behind in Thessalonica when Paul departed that region for Athens. It became apparent to the evangelists and the Christian community in Thessalonica that the best course of action was to remove Paul from the scene. Silas and Timothy did the follow-up work needed in Thessalonica while Paul was witnessing in Athens and eventually in Corinth.

In Corinth, Paul had teamed up with Aquila and Priscilla in tent ministry and also in sharing the word every Sabbath in the Synagogue. The two evangelists, Silas and Timothy subsequently joined him in Corinth. Now we have a team of five who are sharing the gospel and supporting themselves. Paul decided that it was time to devote himself exclusively to preaching. He further decided to focus on the Jews in Corinth. He had one goal in mind, and that was to testify to the fact that Jesus was the Christ.

Paul understood this to be the key obstacle for Jews. They believed in the coming of the Messiah or "The Christ". The prophecies in the book of Isaiah concerning the anointed one were not debatable. They were still expecting the Messiah at a future date. So Paul saw that to be the place to concentrate his ministry at Corinth. This was an intentional effort to show that Jesus was the Christ. He was of the opinion that if and when the Jews became convinced of this fact, they would come to accept the good news.

Paul was coming at this from his own experience. As a Jew who was trained under one of the best teachers of his day, he knew that it was the revelation of Jesus as "the Christ" on the Damascus road that settled the case for him. He had come face to face with Christ in an unusual way. He found out the Jesus he was persecuting was also the anointed one. So persecuting Jesus amounted to fighting against God. Paul came to the conclusion that his central message for Jews should attempt to point them to the fact that the anointed one has already been revealed in Jesus Christ.

He is here with us if we care to look around us!

Dr. Seth Asare

OCTOBER DAY 22

But when the Jews opposed Paul and became abusive, he shook out his clothes in protest and said to them, "Your blood be on your own heads! I am clear of my responsibility. From now on I will go to the Gentiles." Then Paul left the synagogue and went next door to the house of Titius Justus, a worshiper of God. Acts 18:6-7

When the Jews in Corinth saw what Paul was up to, they did not like it a bit. They realized that he was turning Jews to the Christian faith. Paul was teaching that Jesus of Nazareth was the Messiah that the Jews had been awaiting. It seemed to be working for Paul, so the Jews had to do something. They mounted up a strong opposition.

The Jews did not only oppose Paul, but they also became abusive. The Jews did not understand why a Jew like Paul would want to preach a message that was in contradiction to the Judaism that he had grown in. Matters got so bad that Paul had to make a clean break with the Synagogue in Corinth. Paul had always accepted the challenge of bringing the Christian message to his own people as a responsibility.

Why would Paul have this feeling of being responsible for what happened to his own people? Most likely he considered his own earlier opposition to the Christian faith. He had been convinced then about what he was doing. At that time Paul believed that the Christians were heretics who were adulterating Judaism. Paul also, at that time, believed that he was doing the right thing in his opposition to these Christians. Now Paul found himself at the receiving end of the Jews' anger.

Paul came to the conclusion that the time had come to move on and preach to the Gentiles. He did not have to go far to find them. Next door to the synagogue a home of a Gentile was opened to Paul to do ministry. Titius was a worshiper of God. That seemed to suggest that he was either a proselyte to Judaism or on his way to becoming one.

When one door for ministry closes, there is usually another door that is open. Paul was aware of this and seized the opportunity.

OCTOBER DAY 23

Then Paul left the synagogue and went next door to the house of Titius Justus, a worshiper of God. Crispus, the synagogue ruler, and his entire household believed in the Lord; and many of the Corinthians who heard him believed and were baptized.
Acts 18:7-8

Paul did not have much choice about leaving the synagogue in Corinth. The tension had increased and the abusive language was unbearable, so Paul moved on and started a house church next door in the home of Titius Justus. This individual opened his home for the Christians to meet there. We are told that he was a worshiper of God. That suggests that he was open to the things of God, and he had heard enough of the good news to risk the anger of the Jews in the synagogue by opening his home for worship.

The home of Titius was strategic in terms of its proximity to the synagogue. Those who wished to listen to Paul could find the place easily, and those who were sitting on the fence could slide over to the next house without attracting much attention.

One of the people who went over to worship in the home of Titius was Crispus, the ruler of the synagogue. He came with his whole family to listen to the message preached by Paul. They believed and were baptized into the faith. That must have caused a big stir in the community at Corinth. How does one wrap their mind around the fact that the ruler of the synagogue has now become a Christian and is worshiping next door?

We are informed that several others came to believe in the Lord Jesus and were baptized. The success that had accompanied the ministry of Paul and his companions in Corinth was now evident and had become noticeable in the community. That meant that they were also creating more enemies in the community, especially among those who worshipped in the synagogue.

God was using the words of his messengers to accomplish the purposes of God. Nothing has changed! God does the same work today.

OCTOBER DAY 24

One night the Lord spoke to Paul in a vision: "Do not be afraid; keep on speaking, do not be silent. Acts 18:9

The ministry at Corinth was going well. That did not mean that the opposition had abated for Paul and his companions. They lived with the unknown. They were never sure what the opposition was going to do next. When one considers the experience of the missionaries in Macedonia, one wonders how they were able to continue propagating the gospel. Yes, it is true that they moved from place to place, but the risk from the Jews was the same because of the message these missionaries preached.

There are times when people need assurance from the Lord. Paul and his friends found themselves in one of those moments, so the Lord sent a vision one night. We are not told why that particular night was the one chosen by God to speak to Paul. But God did it in a vision and Paul was given these words: "Do not be afraid". Paul does not seem like the type of person who would be scared by outside threats. But when God says: "Do not be afraid", we cannot doubt the discernment of God as to the true feelings in our hearts. Paul may have looked strong and courageous on the outside, but God told him not to be afraid.

Paul was also admonished to: "keep on speaking, do not to be silent." The temptation to be silent remains with a number of us. This is because it is much easier to keep silent when we ought to speak out. It would have been easier for Paul and his companions to concentrate on tent making instead of spreading the good news of the Kingdom. These words that Paul received in a vision were meant to encourage the apostles in the midst of a difficult ministry in Corinth.

The truth is that the gospel of Jesus would never have been spread by people who allowed their fears to have an upper hand. Such individuals choose silence over speaking out for the name of Jesus. The message that God is giving me today is, "speak out!" I pray that you would join me in speaking out with boldness for Jesus Christ in "Corinth".

The vision was not only for Paul; it is for all of us who are witnessing for Jesus Christ in a hostile environment.

OCTOBER DAY 25

One night the Lord spoke to Paul in a vision: "Do not be afraid; keep on speaking, do not be silent. For I am with you, and no one is going to attack and harm you, because I have many people in this city." Acts 18:9-10

Paul had received the vision in the night instructing him not to be afraid to speak out for the Lord Jesus Christ. There was more to that message that Paul received. There was a promise of the presence of the Lord. That is the greatest assurance anyone can receive. It is an assurance that cannot be traded for anything that this world can offer.

Moses received that assurance in the wilderness when he was leading the people of Israel to the Promised Land. He was told that: "My presence will go with you". That was all that Moses needed to hear. Jacob received that assurance at Bethel. He was assured of the presence of God as he journeyed to the house of Laban. The disciples of Jesus received the same assurance of the presence when they were given the Great Commission. The words were: "I will be with you till the end of the world."

These words came to the people of God when there was a risky mission ahead. The assurance of the presence of God was needed as a reminder to the people of God that they were not on a solo mission wherever they found themselves. That does not mean there would not be the temptation to feel cut off from everything. God understood how much Paul needed the assurance found in those words.

Paul must have recollected what happened in Philippi and Thessalonica, and how he had to leave Berea in a hurry because of the opposition of the trouble causers. In each place, the problem began just when people were responding to the gospel of Jesus Christ. Now Paul found himself at a similar crossroad in Corinth. People were responding to the message preached by Paul among the Gentiles. Just at the point where Paul was expecting the other shoe to drop, God brought the words of assurance. "For I am with you, and no one is going to attack and harm you, because I have many people in this city."

Those words sounded like music to the ears of Paul. He had endured several personal attacks in other cities and now the word was clear. He was going to be safe in Corinth because God had many people in that city that God was seeking to reach. God has many people in every place where we find ourselves. Today, I want to claim the word of God to Paul for myself and pray for all the people in the town that God has placed me. I pray that you do the same as we seek to be faithful to what God is saying to us in our environments.

OCTOBER DAY 26

For I am with you, and no one is going to attack and harm you, because I have many people in this city." So Paul stayed for a year and a half, teaching them the word of God. Acts 18:10-11

Paul had experienced many attacks in different towns, but now he was assured in this vision that no one was going to attack him in Corinth. And no one was going to harm him. That must have been a great relief to the Apostle. That did not mean that God was not with Paul on the other occasions when he was attacked. We are not told the reason why God allowed the attacks to occur in the first place. But we know that God delivered Paul from all those attacks.

The presence of God with the people of God does not mean that they will be immune from attacks and harms, but it means that God will walk with God's people no matter what happens. The fact that there was much work to be done in Corinth played into the assurance given to Paul. It was necessary that the mission of God should be accomplished in Corinth before any move was contemplated.

Paul took the word of God to heart and stayed in Corinth for a year and a half. That did not mean that there was no opposition to the gospel during that period. But it meant that Paul and his companions were committed to making sure that the many people who needed to hear the word of God had the opportunity to do so.

The ambassadors for Christ had decided to obey the heavenly vision, so they stayed as long as it was necessary to accomplish the work of God. The agenda should not depend on us or on our comfort. It would always be God's.

October Day 27

While Gallio was proconsul of Achaia, the Jews made a united attack on Paul and brought him into court. "This man," they charged, "is persuading the people to worship God in ways contrary to the law." Acts 18:12-13

Achaia was the province that included Corinth. The proconsuls were the representatives of the seat of power in Rome. We get a fairly accurate view of the timing of any incident when we know who the governing authorities were when the particular incident took place. We are told that the Jews made a united attack on Paul.

Prior to this, there had been opposition from different factions. There were those who did not believe in the resurrection from the dead, and so could not see eye to eye with the message of a resurrected Christ. Then there were the Pharisees who believed in life after death, and some of them could make room for the message of Paul. There were also factions about how much the Gentiles could participate in the fellowship of Judaism. Now, the different groups within Judaism decided to put their differences aside and confront what they saw as a dangerous teaching.

The Jews realized that they had no chance of winning their case in a court of law so long as they were divided over the message that was being preached by Paul. They decided to take Paul to court under a united front. They had to come up with a charge. Their charge against Paul was straight to the point. He was accused of "persuading the people to worship God in ways contrary to the law".

Paul's accusers were right on one point, and that was he was persuading people to worship God. They did not accuse him of introducing foreign forms of worship or idols. They admitted that Paul was preaching about the one God that the Jews worshipped. Thus, Paul believed that what he was preaching had its roots firmly grounded in Judaism. That would explain the reason why the first place that Paul would go in any city was the synagogue.

The problem that Paul's accusers had was that he was persuading people to worship in ways that were contrary to the law of the Jews. One can only guess what the opposition was driving at. Some of them may have been concerned about the manner in which Paul associated with the Gentiles. Others may have been concerned about his preaching on the life, death and the resurrection of Jesus.

The opposition was of the opinion that Paul had crossed the line in the proclamation of the gospel, and it was time to bring him to the courts for justice to be served.

But as usual, God had other plans.

Dr. Seth Asare

OCTOBER DAY 28

Just as Paul was about to speak, Gallio said to the Jews, "If you Jews were making a complaint about some misdemeanor or serious crime, it would be reasonable for me to listen to you. But since it involves questions about words and names and your own law—settle the matter yourselves. I will not be a judge of such things." So he had them ejected from the court. Then they all turned on Sosthenes the synagogue ruler and beat him in front of the court. But Gallio showed no concern whatever. Acts 18:14-17

Paul was ready to make his defense in the court of Gallio. The Jews had accused him of teaching people to worship in a manner that was inconsistent with the Jewish law. But just as Paul was ready to speak, the proconsul interrupted with his verdict.

Gallio surmised that the charges hinged on details in the Jewish law on acceptable worship practices. He indicated that the charges did not rise to the level of an offense that should be tried in a Roman Court of Law. He decided that they should settle the matter themselves. Gallio decided to eject the people who had gathered to hear the case from his court.

The mob did not like the ruling of the court and decided to force the hand of the court to intervene by creating a riot. The mob directed their anger at Sosthenes (the synagogue ruler who had converted to Christianity). They beat him in front of the court. They were expecting Gallio to change his mind and hear their case. But the proconsul decided not to get involved.

The Jews and the mob must have been disappointed at the outcome. But Paul knew that God was in control all along.

OCTOBER DAY 29

Paul stayed on in Corinth for some time. Then he left the brothers and sailed for Syria, accompanied by Priscilla and Aquila. Before he sailed, he had his hair cut off at Cenchrea because of a vow he had taken. They arrived at Ephesus, where Paul left Priscilla and Aquila. He himself went into the synagogue and reasoned with the Jews. When they asked him to spend more time with them, he declined. Acts 18:18-20

The case against Paul was thrown out of court because it did not have any merit. Paul was a free man again and he stayed on in Corinth to finish the mission that God had given him there. After some time, Paul decided to move on and he took with him Priscilla and Aquila. This couple had become part of Paul's ministry in more than one way. They were tentmakers and since Paul shared in the same trade, they worked together in tent making as well as in preaching the gospel in Corinth.

Paul had taken a vow in Corinth. We are not told the details of what was involved in the vow. But Paul had promised not to cut his hair for a period of time for a specific reason. Before he sailed from Cenchrea, Paul had his hair cut off. This signified the end of the vow. They sailed to Ephesus and decided to remain there a while. Paul went off to argue with the Jews in the synagogue there as was his custom.

One would have thought that Paul would shy away from the synagogues after his experiences in the other towns, but that was not the case. In Ephesus, he went to the synagogues to share the good news with the Jews. They gave him a warm reception and invited him to come back. But for some reason, Paul declined the invitation to stay longer and argue in the synagogue.

Paul left Priscilla and Aquila in Ephesus, and he listened to the leading of the Holy Spirit to move on. We must always be in tune with what the Spirit wants us to do at all times. It is far better to be in the will of the Lord than to continue working outside the will of the Lord.

October Day 30

But as he left, he promised, "I will come back if it is God's will." Then he set sail from Ephesus. When he landed at Caesarea, he went up and greeted the church and then went down to Antioch. Acts 18:21-22

Paul had left Priscilla and Aquila in Ephesus. He had declined the invitation of the Jews in the synagogue at Ephesus to stay longer. Paul knew that his mission was not controlled by the wishes of humans, but by the will of God. So Paul set sail from Ephesus and landed at Caesarea. It is important that Christians learn to move and act under the direction of the Holy Spirit. There are several voices in the world trying to make a claim on our lives. Some of them purport to be Christian, but when their actions and mode of operation are tested against what scripture says they are found to be lacking in what the Lord would have for us. Paul decided at the insistence of the Holy Spirit to move on from Ephesus at this time.

Paul promised to come to Ephesus if it was the will of God. How would Paul know when it was the will of God? He had learned from small things to discern the will of God. This could happen through prayer, sometimes through visions, and sometimes through scripture. Paul never questioned the leading of the Lord because he had grown to trust when the Lord speaks.

In Caesarea, Paul went to look for the Christians there and greeted them. Then he continued to Antioch in Syria. This was the place where the missionary journeys started. So Paul ended the second missionary journey by returning to those who commissioned him for the work of God. This was a good time of resting and being encouraged by the fellowship of other Christians. It is important that as people serve in the ministry of the Lord they find time for rest and recuperation.

We all need to identify our Antioch. This is a place that we can call our spiritual base for refreshment. This may not be a physical place, but it could be a fellowship of believers to whom we return from time to time for spiritual nourishment. This may be another individual at the other end of the phone whom you know you can turn to for prayer and spiritual renewal. This should not replace our own Sabbath that we need from time to time. Paul returned to Antioch for encouragement and renewal and we should do the same.

OCTOBER DAY 31

After spending some time in Antioch, Paul set out from there and traveled from place to place throughout the region of Galatia and Phrygia, strengthening all the disciples.
Acts 18:23

I can just hear the conversation between Paul and the elders at Antioch church! "Paul, rest a while; you look like you can use a lot more rest". Paul, on the other hand, is preoccupied with the state of the churches in the regions. He is thinking of Silas and Timothy. These are his traveling companions who are out in the field. He is also wondering how Aquila and Priscilla are doing in Ephesus. He did not have time to settle them in Ephesus, but he could trust the grace of the Lord to keep them safe and effective in the ministry. Still, the brethren at Antioch definitely prevailed on Paul to spend some time resting and enjoying some home cooking!

There is nothing more encouraging than being among a people who you know love you and care about your welfare. The Church at Antioch had a special kinship with the ministry of Paul. After all, this was the place where the believers were first called Christians. It was also the place that the Holy Spirit set apart Paul and Barnabas for the first missionary journey. And it was the place where Paul started the second missionary journey with Silas. Antioch was the place where the missionary journeys started and concluded.

The next phase of the missionary journeys started again in Antioch, and we are told that Paul traveled from place to place throughout the region of Galatia and Phrygia. There was a definite strategy on Paul's part as he set out from Antioch. The goal was to strengthen the disciples who have come into the faith. It is important not to forget this aspect of the Christian ministry. It is the follow-up and the nurture that is so much needed. One can imagine the encouragement that the believers received when Paul arrived in these regions.

It is important to observe that Paul did not go to these areas to make more disciples, but to strengthen those who were there. Paul believed that these disciples were able to carry the gospel forward with the power of the Holy Spirit. Learning to trust the message of Jesus Christ to others knowing that the Spirit will use them to take the message to the next level is needed in our time. There was no need for Paul to micromanage because it was God's work.

We all have to learn to leave things in the hands of God after prayer. God is able to do far more abundantly than what we can think or ask.

November Day 1

Meanwhile a Jew named Apollos, a native of Alexandria, came to Ephesus. He was a learned man, with a thorough knowledge of the Scriptures. He had been instructed in the way of the Lord, and he spoke with great fervor and taught about Jesus accurately, though he knew only the baptism of John. Acts 18: 24-25

"Meanwhile a Jew named Apollos, a native of Alexandria, came to Ephesus." Apollos was an interesting character. Here he was, a Jew who was a native of Alexandria in Egypt. He had a tremendous knowledge of the Scriptures. One should not be surprised by the extent to which the Jewish Scriptures and culture had spread in the Roman world. Although his name may not sound Jewish, Apollos had been influenced by his culture and was opened to the influences of his time.

We are told that Apollos had been instructed in the way of the Lord. The suggestion was that he was convinced about Christ being the expected Messiah of the Jews. We find out that Apollos had not only been instructed in the way of the Lord but, "he spoke with great fervor and taught about Jesus accurately".

Apollos had moved from being another believer to being a disciple of Jesus Christ. There are several Christians who are content to have received the faith and remain believers. But the circle is never completed until those who receive the Christian faith begin to teach it to others and make disciples. We are all called to be disciples who make other disciples.

It is one thing to teach about Jesus, and it is another to teach accurately. Apollos was a faithful witness to what he had received. He understood how John the Baptist was a forerunner of Jesus Christ. He also understood that John was calling people into a baptism of repentance in preparation for the one who was to come. He also had a full understanding that the Messiah had come in the person of Jesus Christ.

What is admirable about Apollos was his eagerness to teach accurately about what he had received concerning Jesus Christ. All of us can take a page from the book of Apollos. We do not have to know everything to start teaching. We can begin with what the Lord has given us, and then the Holy Spirit will lead us into all truth. Apollos arrived in Ephesus armed with his experience and knowledge of Christ and he never wasted time. He went straight to work for Jesus Christ.

We can all do the same!

Dr. Seth Asare

NOVEMBER DAY 2

He began to speak boldly in the synagogue. When Priscilla and Aquila heard him, they invited him to their home and explained to him the way of God more adequately.
Acts 18:26

Apollos arrived in Ephesus with a clear understanding of Scriptures and Jesus Christ. We are told that Apollos knew of the Baptism of John. Apollos came to Ephesus and started to speak boldly about Christ in the synagogue. He followed the example of Paul by first going into the Synagogue. Probably that was the only place for all those who wanted to preach the gospel to start. He began in the place where he had the Jewish audience and spoke so eloquently that he caught the attention of Priscilla and Aquila when they heard him.

Priscilla and Aquila exhibited a unique Christian quality. They listened to Apollos carefully and admired his zeal and message. But they also realized that he could benefit from a fuller understanding of the message of the gospel. So they did the best thing by inviting Apollos to their home and discussing the way of God more adequately. Aquila and Priscilla brought Apollos home to a setting where he could listen to the suggestions being made. It seemed that Apollos was receptive to the teaching provided by Priscilla and Aquila.

We should all be opened to a fuller understanding of God and the work of Christ. The most dangerous place to be as a Christian is the place where we think we know everything. Some people even give the impression that they know the mind of God on specific issues beyond what is outlined in Scripture. God has much to teach us through the word, the Holy Spirit and other Christians. Apollos did avail himself of the experience and knowledge of Aquila and Priscilla. And we can all do the same.

The Holy Spirit has something new to teach us today.

NOVEMBER DAY 3

When Apollos wanted to go to Achaia, the brothers encouraged him and wrote to the disciples there to welcome him. On arriving, he was a great help to those who by grace had believed. For he vigorously refuted the Jews in public debate, proving from the Scriptures that Jesus was the Christ. Acts 18:27-28

We are not told why Apollos wanted to go to Achaia. But the thought pleased the Christians at Ephesus. Priscilla and Aquila could see the tremendous asset that Apollos could be to the brethren in that region, so they encouraged him. It is possible to see how Apollos could have been urged on to go to that region because of the need there. Priscilla and Aquila had worked in the mission field in Achaia with Paul before moving to their present location. I am sure that they surmised that Apollos would be needed more in those regions.

The brothers in Ephesus wrote letters of introduction for Apollos and encouraged the brothers in Achaia to welcome him. When he arrived, he went straight to work and proved the brothers in Ephesus right. He was a great help to the ministry in those regions. Those who had believed in the gospel, by grace found that Apollos was the right person for them in the absence of Paul and his co-workers.

Apollos had a talent for debating and making his points forcefully. I do not know that his cultural background had something to do with this. But the message of the gospel had a power of its own that could stand the test of time. It was the Holy Spirit who was behind the effectiveness of the gospel presentation. The messenger was only an instrument in the hands of God. After saying that, it is important to acknowledge the talents and gifts that different people bring to the task of proclamation and refuting the arguments of others.

There is no doubt that the abilities of Apollos were used mightily by the Holy Spirit in refuting the arguments of the Jews who spoke with him. The main point that Apollos sought to present to his hearers was that Jesus of Nazareth was the Christ. This he did effectively.

We have been given the same task in our postmodern world -- to present the One who died and rose from the dead as the Christ. I pray that we do it with all the energy and strength that God gives to us.

NOVEMBER DAY 4

While Apollos was at Corinth, Paul took the road through the interior and arrived at Ephesus. There he found some disciples and asked them, "Did you receive the Holy Spirit when you believed?" They answered, "No, we have not even heard that there is a Holy Spirit." Acts 19: 1-2

"While Apollos was at Corinth". What was the significance of this statement? Paul was definitely trying to make a point about the activities of Apollos in the region of Achaia. Apollos had been active in spreading the gospel in the region. Aquila and Priscilla had instructed Apollos on the baptism that came through Jesus. So Apollos was confidently traveling through the area making converts for Jesus Christ.

Paul decided to travel by road through the interior and arrived at Ephesus. There he found some disciples and asked them a strange question. "Did you receive the Holy Spirit when you believed?" The fact that Paul called them disciples underscored the point that there was no question about the faith of these disciples. They were disciples in the full sense of the word. So what prompted Paul to ask this question? Was it an observation he made in their worship? Did something stand out in the way they practiced their faith? We are not told what made Paul ask this question.

But the answer of the disciples at Ephesus was very revealing. They answered Paul's question in the negative. Not only that, they indicated that they had not even heard of the Holy Spirit. That answer shows that they had not received any teaching on the Holy Spirit. The subject of the Holy Spirit was a controversial topic then, as it is now. People prefer to shy away from the Holy Spirit either because they have not received a teaching on who the Third person of the Trinity is, or because of the controversy that often surrounds the manifestations of the Holy Spirit.

The fear that surrounds the manifestation of the Holy Spirit does not, however, mean that there should not be a teaching on the Holy Spirit. But more importantly, the absence of teaching on the Holy Spirit did not negate the faith of these early Christians who had placed their faith in the Lord Jesus Christ. God has a way of gently leading us into all truth.

God is patient with our ignorance!

NOVEMBER DAY 5

So Paul asked, "Then what baptism did you receive?" "John's baptism," they replied. Paul said, "John's baptism was a baptism of repentance. He told the people to believe in the one coming after him, that is, in Jesus." On hearing this, they were baptized into the name of the Lord Jesus. When Paul placed his hands on them, the Holy Spirit came on them, and they spoke in tongues and prophesied. There were about twelve men in all. Acts 19:3-7

Paul was a little bit surprised that these disciples at Ephesus had not heard of the Holy Spirit and had not received any teaching on the Holy Spirit. So Paul asked the obvious question: "Then what baptism did you receive?" Paul wanted to get to the source of the problem and the question that he posed did just that. The answer that came from the Christians at Ephesus revealed the source of the problem.

Paul indicated that John's baptism was a baptism of repentance. John was telling people to turn to the one who was coming after him. Yes, it was true that he was pointing people to Jesus Christ. He wanted people to put their faith in the Lord Jesus Christ and not him.

John accomplished his mission by baptizing people in the name of the Lord Jesus Christ. There was not much difference between what John the Baptist was teaching and the message of the gospel. Paul decided to place his hands on these disciples at Ephesus. The result was dramatic. The Holy Spirit came on these disciples and they spoke in tongues and prophesied as the Holy Spirit enabled them.

What happened was a teaching moment on the baptism of the Holy Spirit.

NOVEMBER DAY 6

Paul entered the synagogue and spoke boldly there for three months, arguing persuasively about the kingdom of God. But some of them became obstinate; they refused to believe and publicly maligned the Way. So Paul left them. He took the disciples with him and had discussions daily in the lecture hall of Tyrannus. Acts 19: 8-9

Twelve disciples in Ephesus were given teaching on the Holy Spirit. After that, Paul placed his hands on them and they received the baptism of the Holy Spirit. Paul continued his ministry in Ephesus by entering the synagogue and speaking boldly there for three months. He focused on the kingdom of God and how to enter the realm of God.

Paul argued that faith in Jesus Christ enabled people to enter the kingdom of God. Thus, the door was opened for all people to be part of the family God. Those who heard Paul in the synagogue were disturbed by the fact that Gentiles could have the same standing as Jews in the kingdom of God. One can understand how some of these folks would oppose Paul fiercely. The gospel message was seen to be a direct affront to the Jewish faith and with that view, there was no way that the message of Paul was going to find a favorable audience in the synagogue.

Those who opposed Paul decided to malign the message of Paul to the degree that it was impossible for him to continue his teachings in the synagogue. So he left the synagogue, took his disciples with him, and started teaching daily in the lecture hall of Tyrannus. Paul assessed the situation correctly and did the right thing by moving to an audience that was hungry for the good news. There is always an audience for the message of the gospel. We are challenged to move the message to areas where people are open to the message of Christ.

NOVEMBER DAY 7

This went on for two years, so that all the Jews and Greeks who lived in the province of Asia heard the word of the Lord. God did extraordinary miracles through Paul, so that even handkerchiefs and aprons that had touched him were taken to the sick, and their illnesses were cured and the evil spirits left them. Acts 19:10-12

Paul decided to take the converts to Christianity in Ephesus with him. They started daily meetings in the hall of Tyrannus. Those who came to these meetings were open to the message of the gospel. At these meetings both Jews and Greeks gathered to learn and to receive teaching on the Holy Spirit. From all indications, what was happening in Ephesus seemed to affect the whole province of Asia. People heard and were taught the full gospel of Jesus Christ for two years.

We are told that God did extraordinary miracles through Paul. I like the way that sentence is phrased. It was God who did the miracles. Paul just happened to be the agent of the work of God. Sometimes people give the impression that they are the miracle workers. Some even go as far as calling themselves Divine Healers. But that is not the suggestion that we get from this verse. It was God who worked the extraordinary miracles through Paul.

So what are some of these extraordinary miracles? Handkerchiefs and aprons that had touched Paul were taken to the sick. Just think about that. People who could not come to the meeting places received their prayer through items that had touched Paul or possibly had been prayed over by Paul. The scope of what was happening made it necessary to spell out the fact the miracles were done by God and not by Paul or the handkerchiefs or aprons. Unfortunately, there are people who are selling handkerchiefs today because they are convinced that these items possess healing powers. We should be deliberate and careful to point out that God is the healer.

God still cures miraculously and God is able to use any method to achieve that purpose. The problem is that people try to put God in a box. The idea that God should work only in a particular way should be avoided. God will continue to be God even if that does not fit our expectations.

Let us open ourselves to extraordinary miracles from God.

November Day 8

Some Jews who went around driving out evil spirits tried to invoke the name of the Lord Jesus over those who were demon-possessed. They would say, "In the name of Jesus, whom Paul preaches, I command you to come out." Seven sons of Sceva, a Jewish chief priest, were doing this. Acts 19: 13-14

News of the extraordinary miracles that God worked through Paul became common knowledge in the area. Some people thought that all that you had to do was to imitate the method that Paul and the apostles were using. These imitators assumed that all that one had to do was to invoke the name of Jesus and miracles would happen. Unfortunately, what these imposters did not know, neither did they understand that it was God who worked the miracles that they were observing.

The other thing that the imposters failed to appreciate was that there was a need for a relationship with God through Jesus Christ for one to be used by God. The power of the Holy Spirit was underscoring all the activities that were taking place.

Some Jews went around trying to invoke the name of Jesus Christ over people who were demon-possessed. One is not sure of the motivation for this action. Were they doing it for money? Or were they doing this to impress people and show that they could perform the same miracles that the Christians were performing?

But what was peculiar was that they were trying to use the name of Jesus Christ. Their words of invocation included these words: "In the name of Jesus, whom Paul preaches, I command you to come out." This demonstrated that these individuals did not believe that they had the authority or the power to perform the miracles on their own. So they resorted to invoking the name of Jesus whom Paul preached.

Why would Jews who did not believe in the name of Jesus use the same name to perform miracles? To make matters interesting, the children of a Jewish chief priest were responsible for these activities. They seemed to be making some progress with their diabolic plans, but imposters do not get far with activities like this.

November Day 9

Seven sons of Sceva, a Jewish chief priest, were doing this. (One day) the evil spirit answered them, "Jesus I know, and I know about Paul, but who are you?" Acts 19:14-15

I often refer to this passage as the ineffectiveness of "Third Party Christianity". Seven sons of Sceva, a Jewish chief priest, attempted to use the disguise of "Third Party Christianity" to work miracles. These seven boys had paid careful attention to the way Paul cast out evil spirits. They heard the words used and they believed that the power was in the words. So they memorized the words with little alteration.

They went out casting evil spirits in the name of the Jesus whom Paul preached. They had the right words. After all, they were working the miracles in the name of Jesus Christ. The only problem was that the boys did not have a first-hand experience of this Jesus Christ. One day these boys met their match as the spirit asked them the most pointed question, "Jesus I know, and I know about Paul, but who are you?"

Can you imagine the surprise and the fear that these boys experienced when the spirit spoke back directly to them? They had underestimated the seriousness of the game they were playing. There are those who take lightly the reality of the spiritual realm with which we have to deal. The seven sons of Sceva were shocked that the spirit recognized them and knew them to be frauds.

We cannot pretend to be what we are not. And we cannot use the name of Jesus Christ without understanding the power in that name. Those who have experienced that name are able to work miracles with the name of Jesus. Jesus said: "whatever you ask the Father in my name, I will do it" This is a promise for all those who have experienced the power of the Lord "first-hand".

NOVEMBER DAY 10

Then the man who had the evil spirit jumped on them and overpowered them all. He gave them such a beating that they ran out of the house naked and bleeding. Acts 19:16

People sometimes underestimate the power of evil that is in operation in the world. The forces that operate in the universe are principalities and powers that can do harm in our realm. The seven sons of Sceva did what people often do. They went out to experiment with spiritual matters that they did not understand and the results were not pleasant for them.

The man who had the evil spirit jumped on them. However, the boys believed in the power of numbers and thought the odds were in their favor. They went on this venture thinking that no one could overpower seven of them if they worked together. They were trusting in the physical strength of seven people against any individual they were going to encounter. They had not counted on another factor in the equation and that was the fact that they were now dabbling in spiritual things that were beyond their league. They were certainly surprised by the power the power that was unleashed against them by this one individual who was possessed by an evil spirit.

The seven young men were not only overpowered, they were given a sound beating. When seven young people are forced to run away naked, you know that they are in serious trouble. It was not only their pride that was hurt but they were physically wounded also.

It is important to know our limitations and to understand that the physical realm is very different from the spiritual one. When people come into a relation with Christ, they are transformed by the Holy Spirit and given the resources to put on the whole armor of God.

NOVEMBER DAY 11

When this became known to the Jews and Greeks living in Ephesus, they were all seized with fear, and the name of the Lord Jesus was held in high honor. Many of those who believed now came and openly confessed their evil deeds. Acts 19:17-18

It became known to all the people in Ephesus that the seven sons of Sceva tried to imitate Paul and the Christians. They learned that the evil spirits are able to distinguish between who is a Christian and who is not. There was no point trying to disguise oneself as a Christian because the spirits could tell the difference. This knowledge sparked fear among those who heard what happened to these young men.

We are told that: "the name of the Lord Jesus was held in high honor". Why would the name of the Lord Jesus be held in high honor when an evil spirit beat seven young imposters? It is because of what these guys were trying to do. They were trying to use the name of Jesus improperly. That indicated that there is absolute power in the name of Jesus Christ when one knows the Lord Jesus and has a relationship with him.

The name of the Lord Jesus is not something to be taken lightly or used in casual ways. It is a name that transforms and heals, and that name is never to be used lightly. As a result of this incident, many people believed. Something happens when the name of Jesus Christ is lifted up. Jesus said: "when I am lifted up I will draw all people to myself".

The result was that those who believed came out openly to confess their faith in the Lord Jesus. Not only that, but they confessed their sins and turned to the Lord. That is what it is all about. It is about bringing people to a saving relationship with Jesus Christ.

NOVEMBER DAY 12

A number who had practiced sorcery brought their scrolls together and burned them publicly. When they calculated the value of the scrolls, the total came to fifty thousand drachmas. In this way the word of the Lord spread widely and grew in power. Acts 19:19-20

It seemed sorcery was a huge enterprise in the region of Ephesus. That would make sense why the seven sons of Sceva were eager to get involved in casting out demons. The preaching of the good news and the response gave people the confidence to throw away their scrolls that they used in the practice of sorcery. These books were considered precious and they were not to be destroyed. But the leaders of the church of Jesus Christ were confident in the power of the gospel to the degree that they burned the scrolls publicly.

The public burning of these scrolls must have attracted several people who were curious to observe what would happen to the Christians. I remember a time in the small town where I grew up in Africa when I had to burn books and equipment that had been used in black magic. The spectators who had gathered for this spectacle were expecting something to happen to me in the process. That was an opportunity to bear witness to the power of the Gospel of Jesus Christ.

The value of the scrolls came to fifty thousand drachmas. Why would people give up these valuable scrolls? The only explanation would be that they have come to possess something that is far more valuable than these documents. More importantly, the owners of these documents had been liberated from the evil powers that held them bondage. The experience that comes with the freedom in Christ cannot be measured in monetary terms.

The word of the Lord grew widely because of the presence of the Lord to confirm the word of God with signs and wonders. God is ready to do the same in our day if we will respond with faith and authority. We are the people who have been given the permission to use the name of the Lord without fear.

NOVEMBER DAY 13

In this way the word of the Lord spread widely and grew in power. After all this had happened, Paul decided to go to Jerusalem, passing through Macedonia and Achaia. "After I have been there," he said, "I must visit Rome also." He sent two of his helpers, Timothy and Erastus, to Macedonia, while he stayed in the province of Asia a little longer. Acts 19: 20-22

The news of the miraculous work of the Lord spread through the region and people wanted to know more about this gospel of Jesus Christ. People came to know more about the saving work of Jesus Christ, but they also came to experience the power of the Holy Spirit. There was no doubt about the effectiveness of the message that Paul was preaching in this region. At this point, Paul decided that it was time to go to Jerusalem.

Why did Paul decide on this trip to Jerusalem? There is no indication that Paul received an invitation from the leaders of the church in Jerusalem. We are also not sure that Paul was trying to take offerings to the saints in Jerusalem. All we know is that he had not visited Jerusalem for a while. He had been preaching in the Gentile regions for some years now. Probably he reasoned that it was necessary for him to touch base with the pillars of the church.

Paul decided to plan his trip in such a way that he went through Macedonia and Achaia. One can understand Paul as he lays out his itinerary for the next few years. At the center of his plans was a trip to Jerusalem. Probably Paul was aware that the Jews in the Gentile regions had taken reports about what he was preaching and doing to Jerusalem. Some of these reports might have been exaggerated and might not have been flattering about his ministry. It was necessary for someone to go to Jerusalem and correct some of the news coming from the Gentile regions.

Paul also had plans to go to Rome after visiting Jerusalem. Rome was the seat of the Roman Empire. Paul knew how important it would be for the message of the gospel to take root in Rome. People visiting the seat of the Roman Empire could go away experiencing the authentic power of the gospel. So Paul was ready to carry out this wonderful itinerary.

In the meantime, Paul sent two of his disciples ahead of him to Macedonia while he stayed on in the Province of Asia because there was much work to be done there. Paul was sensitive to God's timing, and he would rather wait and finish the work at hand before moving on.

Let us wait for God's timing.

NOVEMBER DAY 14

About that time there arose a great disturbance about the Way. A silversmith named Demetrius, who made silver shrines of Artemis, brought in no little business for the craftsmen. Acts 19:23 -24

When Paul was at Ephesus there arose a great disturbance about the "Way". This was one of the names given to the Christian faith at this time. It was called the "Way" because it pointed the way to God through Jesus Christ. The Christian faith also provided a way of living that was different from the way people had known prior to the coming of Christianity. It was true that the faith had its roots in Judaism, yet it pointed to a new understanding of a covenant relationship with God. One in which people turned from their old way of living to a relationship with Christ.

The new relationship was supposed to be seen in the behavior of these new persons in Christ. Thus, Christianity was a completely new way of living that could be described in the words of Paul: "if anyone is in Christ, they are a new creation; the old has passed away and the new has come."

The disturbance in Ephesus was directed against this new way of living that was being propagated by these people called Christians or the "Way". The leader of this disturbance was a silversmith named Demetrius. His business was to make silver shrines of Artemis. The latter was a goddess who was worshipped by many people in that region. The silver carvings and replicas of this goddess were a good source of income for the craftsmen. It seemed that the teaching of the people who belonged to the "Way" was in conflict with the possession of these idols. The Christian message emphasizes that there is only one God, and these idols were not to be given any credence.

As more and more people got converted to Christianity, the business of these craftsmen began to suffer. So Demetrius decided that it was time to do something about this group that was adversely affecting their business. Any time people begin to feel the effects of the change that Christianity brings, they push back. Often the ways they go about expressing their displeasure with Christianity's success lead to them inciting violence. The situation was no different in Ephesus.

The word of the Lord has power to bring positive change in society, but we should not expect things to go smoothly when the change affects the powers that be.

NOVEMBER DAY 15

A silversmith named Demetrius, who made silver shrines of Artemis, brought in no little business for the craftsmen. He called them together, along with the workmen in related trades, and said: "Men, you know we receive a good income from this business. And you see and hear how this fellow Paul has convinced and led astray large numbers of people here in Ephesus and in practically the whole province of Asia. He says that man-made gods are no gods at all. Acts 19:24 -26

The business of Demetrius and other craftsmen had been prospering because these silversmiths made shrines of Artemis. However, Paul's preaching and the conversion of many in the region had now become a problem of dwindling income for these craftsmen. The invitation extended to the silversmiths and other craftsmen to come together and discuss the future of their trades was a welcome opportunity for these folks.

Demetrius tried to incite the crowd, more than reason with them. He began by addressing the loss of income issue. This was because he knew that would appeal to his audience. He stated as a matter of fact that they all received good income from the trade of making shrines of Artemis. People get into a mob mentality under such circumstances, and they do not reason through what is being said.

Demetrius touched a sensitive nerve in these craftsmen, so they listened for what he wanted them to do. They did not question the motive of this self-styled leader of the craftsmen. Demetrius went ahead and cast Paul in a negative light just to get his audience to hate Paul. Paul was portrayed as the one who was leading large numbers of people astray in Ephesus and also in the whole province of Asia.

Demetrius could not separate his search for material prosperity from Paul's desire to bring spiritual transformation to the whole region. It was true that the two quests were often opposing each other. But the fact that Paul had as much right to pursue his spiritual endeavors as he did, escaped Demetrius.

His summary of what Paul was preaching was straight to the point. Paul was teaching that "man-made gods are no gods at all." One can understand how Paul's assertion infuriated Demetrius and his companions. Paul was making a Theological statement as well as a spiritual one. The other folks were, on the other hand, watching the impact of Paul's success on their bank accounts.

Jesus said "where our treasure is, there would our hearts be also". We have to be careful to know where our treasure is. Otherwise, we will be led astray by people like Demetrius.

NOVEMBER DAY 16

When they heard this, they were furious and began shouting: "Great is Artemis of the Ephesians!" Soon the whole city was in an uproar. The people seized Gaius and Aristarchus, Paul's traveling companions from Macedonia, and rushed as one man into the theater. Paul wanted to appear before the crowd, but the disciples would not let him. Even some of the officials of the province, friends of Paul, sent him a message begging him not to venture into the theater. Acts 19: 28-31

The crowd was incited by the speech of the self-styled leader who had his own agenda. The crowd was now convinced that their trade was in jeopardy because the goddess Artemis had lost her divine majesty according to Demetrius. Now, the crowd had no other alternative but to express their anger against the outsiders who were preaching the superiority of the God who was preached by Paul.

The crowd was furious and began shouting: "Great is Artemis of the Ephesians!" Now these silversmiths were giving the people of Ephesus something to rally around and express their pride. "Soon the whole city was in an uproar." People went on a rampage looking for those who were associated with Paul or the "Way". They seized Gaius and Aristarchus and dragged them into the theater. These two men were traveling companions of Paul, so they were considered to be part of the problem.

When Paul saw his friends dragged into the theater, he decided to go inside and appear before the crowd and make his defense before them. Paul was convinced that he could talk some sense into the heads of these rioters. The other disciples felt otherwise, however, because they were convinced that under these circumstances, people would not be thinking or acting rationally. Thus, Paul was prevented from entering the theater. Some of the officials of the province even sided with the disciples and convinced him not to enter the crowd.

Thank God for the counsel of other brothers and sisters who can prevail upon us in times when our emotions want to get the upper hand. We are never alone. God sends angels in the form of human flesh to help us out.

NOVEMBER DAY 17

There is danger not only that our trade will lose its good name, but also that the temple of the great goddess Artemis will be discredited, and the goddess herself, who is worshiped throughout the province of Asia and the world, will be robbed of her divine majesty." Acts 19:27

Sometimes it is difficult to know why people do the things they do. What was the motivation of Demetrius in his effort to malign Paul and the other Christians who were having a successful ministry in Ephesus? Demetrius had gathered the craftsmen and made a strong case to them as to why they should run these foreigners out of town. The question was why was he doing all this?

He gets to that in his concluding remarks. His first reason was the threat posed to the trade of the silversmiths. Demetrius was not pleading for a bailout openly, but he was indicating that if no action were taken then there would not be a future for this reputable trade.

When one considers the argument of Demetrius, it is obvious that it lacks credibility because there was no reason why the silversmith trade should be tied to the making of idols to the exclusion of all the possibilities available to them. There is a wide array of objects that could be made with silver. The real reason for the anger of Demetrius was a spiritual one.

Most of the time one finds that spiritual struggles are masked. People may exhibit strong aversions to a particular situation when in fact the underlying issue is spiritual. In the case of Demetrius, he finally came to the point by showing that he was concerned about the temple of the great goddess Artemis being discredited. One can now ask Demetrius what was his real issue?

He might be concerned for the great goddess being robbed of her majesty more than the bread and butter of his fellow tradesmen. He did not appreciate the spread of the good news of the Lord Jesus in the region. His goal was to start a riot with these tradesmen as the nucleus of his mob. Demetrius was bent on giving them a reason to resist the Gospel of Jesus Christ without their being aware of it.

We should be wide awake to the attempts of others to get us onboard their human agendas which turn out to be a spiritual battle against the faith of our Lord Jesus Christ. They can come as wolves in sheep's clothing.

Dr. Seth Asare

NOVEMBER DAY 18

The assembly was in confusion: Some were shouting one thing, some another. Most of the people did not even know why they were there. The Jews pushed Alexander to the front, and some of the crowd shouted instructions to him. He motioned for silence in order to make a defense before the people. But when they realized he was a Jew, they all shouted in unison for about two hours: "Great is Artemis of the Ephesians!" Acts 19:32 -34

The situation in the theater at Ephesus was rowdy and everybody was confused about what was happening. Here we have silversmiths who, being manipulated by Demetrius, had pushed their way into the theater dragging two companions of Paul with them. No one could guess what these rioters were going to do next. They might have tried something drastic if Paul had ventured into the theater.

The crowd was out of control. Some people in the theater did not even know why they were there. Some were shouting one thing, and others were shouting another. That was a clear indication that things were spinning out of control.

Now some Jews in the theater pushed Alexander forward to the front of the crowd. Alexander may have been an official, and it seems they were ready to sacrifice him to the crowds. Possibly the Jews knew Alexander to be a Christian, and they were making a point that Jews had nothing to do with the activities of the Christians. It looks like these Jews were hoping to distance themselves from the anger of the Greeks who were accusing those who worshipped one God as being the cause of their problem.

Alexander motioned to the crowd for silence so that he could make a defense. But that did not seem to calm the crowd who learned that Alexander was a Jew. For the Ephesians, there was no difference between Jews and Christians. All they knew was that they were both worshippers of one God. So the rioters decided to show their displeasure by shouting: "Great is Artemis of the Ephesians!" and they did this for two hours.

The Greeks were protesting the diminishing status of their goddess. The God who created the world has been revealed to all those who seek Him with all their heart.

November Day 19

The city clerk quieted the crowd and said: "Men of Ephesus, doesn't all the world know that the city of Ephesus is the guardian of the temple of the great Artemis and of her image, which fell from heaven? Therefore, since these facts are undeniable, you ought to be quiet and not do anything rash. Acts 19:35-36

I like the clerk of the city for his diplomatic approach to a tense situation. The rioting crowd had dragged two men into the theater while the Jews pushed Alexander to the front. The question was what was going to happen to these persons who were being held captive by the mob? It is at this juncture that the city clerk comes forward with what I consider to be a diplomatic response to a situation that could have turned tragic.

The city clerk asked a question that affirmed what the people wanted to hear. He said: *"Men of Ephesus, doesn't all the world know that the city of Ephesus is the guardian of the temple of the great Artemis and of her image, which fell from heaven?"* The clerk was saying that the belief that Artemis was the goddess of Ephesus was common knowledge and was not in question. He even affirms the notion that the goddess Artemis fell directly from heaven to her present location.

The city clerk called these assertions facts that were undeniable, and it seemed to work with the crowd. People became quiet and listened to him attentively. That was what was needed in order to be able to reason with the crowd. When rioters are operating under the mob mentality, it is difficult to reason logically with them. But when one is able to get their attention to the point that the shouting and screaming have died down, then one can get across what it is needed to disperse the crowd.

We are not told whether the city clerk was one of the Christians, but he surely was given wisdom that was divine to deal with the angry mob. We all need that type of wisdom that allows us to speak the right word to people who are acting irrationally.

It takes prayer and the power of the Holy Spirit to speak to situations that are beyond our control.

Dr. Seth Asare

NOVEMBER DAY 20

You have brought these men here, though they have neither robbed temples nor blasphemed our goddess. If, then, Demetrius and his fellow craftsmen have a grievance against anybody, the courts are open and there are proconsuls. They can press charges.
Acts 19:37-38

The city clerk managed to quiet the crowd in the theater at Ephesus. He did it by announcing to the people what they already knew and approved about the goddess Artemis of Ephesus. Now it was time for the city clerk to reason with the people about the actions that had been set in motion by their rioting.

The city clerk addressed the problem of dragging innocent men into the theater by force. He indicated that the men who were being held hostage have neither robbed temples nor blasphemed the goddess of Ephesus. The point that the city clerk was making was that these hostages were not guilty of any crime by the legal standards of Ephesus. So it was time to separate the dissatisfaction of Demetrius and his craftsmen from the concerns of the general public at Ephesus.

The city clerk managed to sow seeds of doubt in the minds of the rioters. They started to ask themselves why they were involved in a fight that was not their own. They came to understand that they were being used by Demetrius to accomplish his own illegal goals. The important point that was made was that the courts were open and there were proconsuls who were ready and able to hear their grievance.

The question that one would ask is this: Why would Demetrius and the craftsmen prefer mob action instead of pressing charges in the courts against the Christians? It was because they knew they had no legal case against the Christians. There was nothing against people professing their faith or religion in the Roman Empire. So the Christians were within their rights in teaching that Jesus was the way to God.

We are free to preach the Lordship of Jesus Christ in our society. We should by all means take advantage of the freedom of worship to preach our faith without fear and compromise. May God give us the boldness to let the whole world know that Jesus is Lord.

NOVEMBER DAY 21

If there is anything further you want to bring up, it must be settled in a legal assembly. As it is, we are in danger of being charged with rioting because of today's events. In that case we would not be able to account for this commotion, since there is no reason for it." After he had said this, he dismissed the assembly. Acts 19:39-41

The city clerk concluded his message to the crowd that was poised to cause disturbances by pointing them to the proper way to address grievances. The legal assembly was still open to hear any complaints that people like Demetrius and his group of silversmiths had. There was nothing preventing the artisans from taking their grievance to the courts.

The city clerk made the crowd aware of an interesting point, and that was they could be legally charged with rioting as a result of the events on that day. The charges could include kidnapping by force and disturbing public peace. And there was no reason for the commotion that had taken place.

The city clerk dismissed the assembly after saying all those words to them. What is interesting is that the crowd understood the reasons given and were dismissed. The hostages were let go and although there might have been some in the crowd who were not happy about the turn of affairs, everyone left the theater.

When one considered the intensity of the anger of the rioting crowd, one could say there was Divine intervention in the actions of the city clerk. It was not common to get an angry crowd to listen to reason from an individual. More so when one considered that the anger was directed against the Christians. They happened to be a minority group who could easily be sacrificed as scapegoats.

I believe God used the city clerk that day to save the lives of the two men who were dragged into the theater, and also the life of Alexander who was pushed to the front of the theater by the Jews. God works in mysterious ways to avert the anger of those who hate Christians with a passion.

As indicated earlier, the real cause for the riot was a spiritual one. It was for that reason that a Divine intervention was appropriate. God understands what is happening in your situation and mine. Whenever a supernatural intervention becomes necessary, we can be sure that God would provide it.

November Day 22

When the uproar had ended, Paul sent for the disciples and, after encouraging them, said good-by and set out for Macedonia. He traveled through that area, speaking many words of encouragement to the people, and finally arrived in Greece. Acts 20:1-2

There is a time to speak and a time to remain silent. Paul had wanted to venture into the midst of the rioting crowd at Ephesus. The Christian disciples in town prevailed upon him not to do that. They decided that it would be better for all of them if Paul kept a low profile at the time when tempers were high. That was exactly what Paul did when the proceedings were taking place in the theater.

When the uproar ended and the crowd dispersed, Paul called together the disciples at Ephesus to make known to them his future plans after assessing the situation. He encouraged the disciples in the faith. He reminded them of the trials and sufferings that would accompany the decision that they had made to be followers of Jesus Christ.

Paul said good-bye to the disciples at Ephesus and informed them that he was going on to the region of Macedonia. This was an area where he had ministered previously and had been opposed by the Jews in the area. But as we can see, Paul was not the type who backed away from what he believed God wanted him to do.

So Paul went ahead through the area speaking words of encouragement from town to town to all who would listen. The world we live in stands in need of encouragement. People are looking for someone with a word of hope to lift their spirits up. That word has already been provided in the gospel of our Lord and Savior Jesus Christ. The coming of Jesus Christ into our world is a message of hope and encouragement. Whenever we proclaim God's love for the world, we are encouraging people to consider an alternative to the life that they have known.

Paul continued in this mission encouraging the saints and anyone who would listen and believe. He finally ended in Greece. Are there some people in your life who can use some encouragement from you? We have been entrusted with the message of reconciliation. That means we have a word of hope.

NOVEMBER DAY 23

He traveled through that area, speaking many words of encouragement to the people, and finally arrived in Greece, where he stayed three months. Because the Jews made a plot against him just as he was about to sail for Syria, he decided to go back through Macedonia. He was accompanied by Sopater son of Pyrrhus from Berea, Aristarchus and Secundus from Thessalonica, Gaius from Derbe, Timothy also, and Tychicus and Trophimus from the province of Asia. Acts 20: 2-4

Paul arrived in Greece and stayed there for three months. What was the determining factor for how long Paul stayed in any one place? First, it was the leading of the Holy Spirit as we have gathered in the other places. Then, it is how much effective ministry could be accomplished in that location. The final one is related to the second, and that is the climate in the location for doing ministry. Sometimes, Paul and his friends did not have much choice but to move on because their lives were in danger or they were not helping the new converts by remaining in the location.

In Greece, there was a plot against Paul just about the time when he had decided to move on to another region. Several people who were co-workers as well as disciples accompanied Paul. These individuals came from different towns, and Paul was led to pick these folks for a reason that we are not told. But when one considers the number of towns these men came from, it becomes obvious what Paul was doing.

The following towns and areas were represented: Berea, Thessalonica, Derbe, and the province of Asia. Paul was training leaders for the future of the church of Jesus Christ. It was important that these leaders come from a diverse background so that the gospel of Jesus did not become confined to one town or area. These were all men who had been converted in their particular locations and were known and supported by their home churches.

In this way, Paul kept contact with all the places where these individuals came from. Paul also wanted to give these men a "hands-on" training in spreading the gospel. They experienced the joy of receiving people into the faith, but they were also confronted with threats and opposition as they shared the good news of Jesus Christ.

Paul had a vision for the gospel taking root in the known world. That vision included having trained leaders who could sustain the growth that was to take place.

Could it be that we are part of what God is doing for the future of the gospel in our own towns?

November Day 24

These men went on ahead and waited for us at Troas. But we sailed from Philippi after the Feast of Unleavened Bread, and five days later joined the others at Troas, where we stayed seven days Acts 20:5-6

There has been the suggestion that some of the men listed, if not all of them, were really representatives from the various regions who were supposed to accompany the offering received for the saints in Jerusalem. Paul had been going around to the churches raising support as well as preaching the gospel. In the name of transparency, it was expedient that each region, or at least some of the towns, appoint emissaries to accompany Paul on the trip to Jerusalem.

It seemed that Luke joined Paul's party at this point. Luke is included in the narrative and becomes the writer of what was happening. Troas was their rendezvous point. An advance party was sent ahead from the ship's port to Troas. The reason for this might have been logistics. Space availability on the vessel may have limited the numbers who could be in the advance party. Luke stayed behind with Paul and the group that was to go later.

Paul and the group with him celebrated the Feast of Unleavened Bread together. The Feast began with Passover and lasted for a week. The journey to Troas took five days then, they finally joined the advance group. Troas was the place where Paul had seen a vision of a man from Macedonia begging him to "come over to Macedonia and help". It was a place where Paul had received a direct intervention by God in his plans.

Paul did not have any plans, at that time, of going into the region of Macedonia. In fact, he was prevented from going into the area that he would have headed under normal circumstances.

Although Paul was in a hurry to get to Jerusalem, he stayed in Troas for a week. This might have been because of a ship schedule. In those days, one had to wait for the time when the outbound ship was ready to set sail. It could also be because Paul wanted to spend more time with the believers in the neighboring towns. Paul did put his time to good use and was always ready to minister and serve.

There may be times when our plans get altered because of unforeseeable circumstances. The way we respond to a change in our plans says a lot about us and the testimony that we bear to our faith.

NOVEMBER DAY 25

On the first day of the week we came together to break bread. Paul spoke to the people and, because he intended to leave the next day, kept on talking until midnight. There were many lamps in the upstairs room where we were meeting. Seated in a window was a young man named Eutychus, who was sinking into a deep sleep as Paul talked on and on. When he was sound asleep, he fell to the ground from the third story and was picked up dead. Acts 20:7-9

"On the first day of the week." This was a clear reference to Sunday and supports the idea that the early church met on Sundays. It was a day set aside for these mostly Gentile Christians to meet and celebrate the Lord's Supper. They took the command of the Lord seriously. They were going to remember the body and the blood of Jesus Christ each week as they gathered. The institution of this sacrament enabled the Christians to hear the good news of the life, death and resurrection of Jesus Christ reenacted in their worship.

The celebration of the sacrament of the Lord's Supper provided an opportunity for the confession of sins and for focusing on the suffering of Jesus Christ for the sins of the participants. The Lord's Supper was a fresh opportunity to rededicate oneself to the Lord Jesus.

Paul had plans to leave Troas the next day, so the service became longer than usual. He did what several preachers are accused of doing, and that is to try to give the audience all that they need to know in one day. It seemed that there was information overload, and even the bright lights in the upper room did not prevent those who were tired from falling asleep.

One such individual was Eutychus who had, unfortunately, selected the window as his seat. He could not help himself when he was so overtaken by sleep that he fell to his death from the window on the upper floor. There was no doubt that the commotion that ensued was such that all those who were sleeping had to wake up and try to find out what was happening.

I do not think we can blame Eutychus for falling asleep or for sitting in the window. The young man could not have anticipated such an outcome from his actions. I am sure he arrived anxious to hear Paul's message, and with as much eagerness as anyone else in the room.

I guess the message is that we should keep awake at all times. That message is even more relevant when we have preachers who have a tendency to preach long sermons.

November Day 26

Seated in a window was a young man named Eutychus, who was sinking into a deep sleep as Paul talked on and on. When he was sound asleep, he fell to the ground from the third story and was picked up dead. Paul went down, threw himself on the young man and put his arms around him. "Don't be alarmed," he said. "He's alive!" Then he went upstairs again and broke bread and ate. After talking until daylight, he left. The people took the young man home alive and were greatly comforted. Acts 20: 9-12

Eutychus succumbed to tiredness. The only problem was that he had an open window seat and so he fell through the window. He fell from a third story building and that did not give him much chance for survival. The action of Paul at this point was a demonstration of faith and the power of the risen Christ.

Paul stopped the long sermon and went down to where Eutychus was lying dead. Paul threw himself on the young man and put his arms around him. Some have suggested that Paul did a "mouth to mouth" resuscitation. Although that was not indicated in the passage, it seemed plausible that it happened. It would be fair and consistent with the ministry of Paul to expect him to pray over this young man as he put his arms around him.

There must have been a sigh of relief as Paul made the statement they had all been hoping for. "Don't be alarmed, he is alive". True to the word of Paul, Eutychus was restored to life. This incident must have left a lasting impression on the gathering. The power of God was evident in the restoration of Eutychus to life.

Paul went back to the third floor after the miracle and continued the service as if nothing had happened. They broke bread and ate. That may be a reference to the Lord's Supper or to a love feast. Paul continued to exhort and teach the gathering till daybreak.

What I found interesting was that Eutychus stayed awake till daybreak after his little episode. There is indeed nothing too hard for the Lord. Several folks gathered around the young man after the service and were prepared to take him home to make sure that everything was all right with him.

When God begins something, God sees it through. Eutychus was completely healed from the fall and there was no reason for anyone to be afraid.

November Day 27

We went on ahead to the ship and sailed for Assos, where we were going to take Paul aboard. He had made this arrangement because he was going there on foot. When he met us at Assos, we took him aboard and went on to Mitylene. The next day we set sail from there and arrived off Kios. The day after that we crossed over to Samos, and on the following day arrived at Miletus. Paul had decided to sail past Ephesus to avoid spending time in the province of Asia, for he was in a hurry to reach Jerusalem, if possible, by the day of Pentecost. Acts 20:13 -16

Luke and the other missionaries decided to travel by ship to Assos while Paul and a few folks were doing the trip on foot. To accomplish this, arrangements had to be made for the ship to pick up Paul at Assos so that the whole team could travel together. Paul had some business to accomplish in the neighboring towns that were only accessible by foot. He understood that there was some work that could not wait until his next trip to the region, so he tried to put in as much ministry as time would allow him when he was in the area.

There is a work for Jesus that no one can accomplish but us. When we realize that, then we always seek opportunities to be witnesses for Christ. After Paul had finished the work that had to be done, he joined up with the party on the ship at Assos. The ship made several stops, and it is possible that Paul and his companions seized the opportunity to share the good news in every place that the ship stopped. Finally, they arrived at Miletus. They had decided to sail past the region of Asia for a particular reason and that was to save time.

Paul had decided not to stop at Ephesus because he knew that that would be time consuming and he may miss his schedule to reach Jerusalem by Pentecost. Paul was in a hurry to bring the offering of the saints in the regions to the believers in Jerusalem.

Paul knew how the saints in Jerusalem needed the support of the Gentile churches and what a witness that would conjure for partnership in ministry. The sharing of the ministry that God has given to us is a witness to the world. So much can be done when we pool our resources together.

Those who are strong need to bear with the weak as we share one another's burdens.

NOVEMBER DAY 28

From Miletus, Paul sent to Ephesus for the elders of the church. When they arrived, he said to them: "You know how I lived the whole time I was with you, from the first day I came into the province of Asia. I served the Lord with great humility and with tears, although I was severely tested by the plots of the Jews. Acts 20:17-19

When Paul arrived in Miletus he sent a message to the elders of the church at Ephesus to come over to Miletus. This was an unusual request because normally Paul was the one who traveled to the towns he was to preach in. But Paul was in a hurry to get to Jerusalem. Paul also remembered the circumstances under which he left Ephesus and he was not ready to give his opposition grounds to cause disturbance. So this hurriedly arranged meeting took place in Miletus. The elders of the church were more than happy to come and meet with Paul and his companions.

Paul had a message for those who had been called of God to lead the church of Jesus Christ forward in the city of Ephesus. Paul thought it was appropriate to remind the gathering of his time with them at Ephesus. He wanted the leaders to understand that being called to a leadership position was not an opportunity to Lord it over the people. He noted that the way of living of the overseer was supposed to be an open book that could be read by everyone.

Paul reminded them of the requirements of servant leadership. His emphasis was serving the Lord wherever people found themselves. The challenge for this type of leadership is that most of the time people fail to be consistent. The Christian walk is a long journey and people cannot be half-hearted in their servant leadership. This becomes particularly difficult when the faith has to be lived out each day in the midst of the people one has been called to serve.

The living out of the faith that Paul talked about had been done with humility and with tears. The humility part involved the dependence on God for each step that had to be taken. One is humbled by the fact that left to the individual Christian one would fail in their service. But the grace of God provides the strength that is needed to achieve the goals that God has set for us.

The grace of God does not mean that there will be no tears. It also does not mean that everything will go without a hitch. There would be the unexpected and false accusations while ministering under the leadership of the Holy Spirit. Paul reminded the overseers at Ephesus of how he went through some of these obstacles while he was with them. So what he was saying to them just brought memories of the realities they had observed in Paul's life.

Paul called what he went through at Ephesus "a severe test". The issue was not that the leaders would be tested; that was a given. What Paul wanted them to think about was how they would come through their period of testing.

I want you to do the same. Several Christians have lost their testimonies in the period of testing. Jesus Christ went through every temptation and trial so that he would be able to help all of us in our time of testing. You are a leader in the books of God. If you did not know that, then let me give you a gentle reminder.

November Day 29

I served the Lord with great humility and with tears, although I was severely tested by the plots of the Jews. You know that I have not hesitated to preach anything that would be helpful to you but have taught you publicly and from house to house. I have declared to both Jews and Greeks that they must turn to God in repentance and have faith in our Lord Jesus. Acts 20:19-21

I thank God for the opportunity to lift up the incarnation of Christ during the Christmas season in a special way. But I am reminded that the message of the gospel is not time sensitive. Paul does a good job at relating the challenges and availability of the message to all people.

Serving the Lord Jesus is not a picnic to be engaged in without thinking through the ramifications. Paul had called together the leaders of the church at Ephesus to explain to them the ministry that he was leaving to their charge. He was not asking them to do something that he had not experienced. Paul had served with great humility in the face of many obstacles. Some of the problems he faced in many towns were repeated at Ephesus. So, Paul was speaking to a group that was familiar with the challenges that all who preached the gospel of Jesus Christ were going to face.

Paul reminded the assembled leaders how he had not hesitated to preach anything that would be helpful to them. Paul did not hold back the truth of the gospel from these folks. Sometimes the truth hurts, but it is better for people to know the truth. Leadership roles in the church may not be materially rewarding, but that is where God needs faithful men and women. There will be false accusations and plots, but God is looking for people who are willing and able to preach the good news in season and out of season.

The example that Paul was laying in front of the leaders at Ephesus was one of public proclamation, as well as "house to house" exhortation of the faithful. This type of ministry follows the example of Jesus Christ. The gospel is taken to people where they are. Also, the good news becomes universally available to all. Jews and Gentiles have equal access to the good news. The opportunity to repent and turn to the Lord Jesus Christ is a timeless message that has to be embraced by all.

NOVEMBER DAY 30

"And now, compelled by the Spirit, I am going to Jerusalem, not knowing what will happen to me there. I only know that in every city the Holy Spirit warns me that prison and hardships are facing me." Acts 20:22-23

What happens when the Holy Spirit of the Lord is leading us in directions that we do not wish to go? Most of the time, we find ourselves resisting what the Spirit is saying. We may even try to justify the fact that we may not have heard the leading of the Spirit correctly. Those who have been attuned to the leading of the Holy Spirit know beyond any shadow of doubt when the Lord is speaking to them.

In the case of Paul, as he spoke to the elders from Ephesus, it was not just the Holy Spirit speaking. He described being compelled by the Spirit to go to Jerusalem. Yes, it was true that Paul had the offering for the saints at Jerusalem to deliver. Moreover, he had the representatives with him from three different towns that had made contributions. This was a trip that had been planned to bring the love offering of the Gentile churches to their brothers in Jerusalem. The message that this offering symbolized was far reaching. Paul was determined to carry it through with the help of the Holy Spirit.

Paul was not sure about the reception that he was going to receive at Jerusalem. This was because news about Paul's ministry among the Gentiles and Jews had reached Jerusalem. People there were aware of the reports of resistance from the Jewish community that had sometimes resulted in riots. Paul understood how such news travels from one place to another. Sometimes, the exaggerations might cause tempers to flare up. Paul knew that the reception that he might receive from some quarters would not be all that cordial.

In a number of cities that he had been, the Holy Spirit had warned Paul that hardship and imprisonment awaited him in Jerusalem. What is interesting is that in none of the warnings was Paul told not to go to Jerusalem. One would have expected some assurance that the suffering ahead could be avoided. But that was not the case. The presence of the Holy Spirit on this trip was all that Paul needed.

Those who heard Paul outline the state of affairs must have been challenged by what it meant to be a follower of Jesus Christ. It was not an easy road, but the promise of the Lord's leading made all the difference.

Dr. Seth Asare

NOVEMBER EXTRA

However, I consider my life worth nothing to me, if only I may finish the race and complete the task the Lord Jesus has given me—the task of testifying to the gospel of God's grace. Acts 20:24

Paul had come to terms with the prophecies and the testimonies that he had been receiving concerning his trip to Jerusalem. They were not the most encouraging that he could have received. All that the Holy Spirit was indicating was that hardship and imprisonment awaited him.

Paul made a profound statement that should be the hallmark of all Christians: "I consider my life worth nothing to me". He did not say that his life was worth nothing, but in terms of personal gain or self-preservation Paul had abandoned everything for the sake of Christ. He indicated in his letter to the Philippians that he considered everything as loss because of the surpassing worth of knowing Christ Jesus.

Paul fully understood what it meant to be crucified with Christ. This is something that is sometimes easier said than done. Paul did indicate that the process of one being crucified with Christ culminated in living a life in the flesh that is by faith in the One who died for them. It was this understanding of a relationship with Jesus Christ that motivated Paul to press forward and finish the race that was set before him.

As we begin a new year, we know that God has set a task for each one of us to complete. The first challenge is to know what that task is and then the second would be to work to accomplish not just any task, but what the Lord Jesus has given to us. There are many tasks that we could all be involved in, but Paul identified the task of testifying to the gospel of God's grace as his preoccupation.

The urgency of the gospel of Jesus Christ is still with us today and we will do well to listen to what God wants us to make the main thing.

December Day 1

"Now I know that none of you among whom I have gone about preaching the kingdom will ever see me again. Therefore, I declare to you today that I am innocent of the blood of all men. For I have not hesitated to proclaim to you the whole will of God. Acts 20:25-27

Paul made a strange statement here in verse 25. He was certain that he was not going to see any of the people he had preached to again. That showed how seriously he took the words of prophecy that he was receiving from the Holy Spirit. There was no room for a maybe in his statement.

That thought made Paul do a serious reflection on his ministry to all these folks. When one is sure that they will not have another opportunity to present the gospel, one may begin to wonder if they have done all that they could to make the gospel plain. Paul was sure that he had done that and that gave him the peace of knowing that he had done his best.

That is certainly a challenge to all preachers and all of us who have been called to be witnesses to the gospel. There are some people who come into our lives for a season so that we can be the gospel to them. We pray that we do not miss those opportunities to present Jesus Christ as fully as we are able.

Paul was confident that he had discharged his duties to the best of his abilities so he said: "Therefore, I declare to you today that I am innocent of the blood of all men." That is indeed profound! The prophet Ezekiel indicated that God had made us watchmen over the souls of those around us and we are to warn them about what God says and requires and if we do not, then we will be responsible for their lack of repentance.

Paul stood in that tradition and stated that he had not hesitated to proclaim the whole "will" of God to his hearers. Whenever he had the opportunity, he presented the full gospel. That is a challenge to me and to you as we seek to be faithful to the gospel.

DECEMBER DAY 2

Keep watch over yourselves and all the flock of which the Holy Spirit has made you overseers. Be shepherds of the church of God which he bought with his own blood. I know that after I leave, savage wolves will come in among you and will not spare the flock. Acts 20:28-29

"Keep watch over yourselves". Those who aspire to be overseers must first learn how to keep watch over themselves. In other words, they must be spiritually connected to the source of all power and that is Jesus Christ. In the spiritual realm, one has to be in tune with the great Shepherd of the sheep in order to be of use to the Master.

When we have understood the need to watch over ourselves, then we are given the directive to watch over the flock. The responsibility for doing this is a charge entrusted to spiritual leaders by the Holy Spirit. We are all humbled by the fact that it has pleased the Holy Spirit to set us apart for this responsibility. The leaders of the church in Ephesus were made aware that they had been called to be shepherds of the Church of God.

People are called to be leaders in many areas in the normal walk of life. But in this particular case, the people are entrusted with something that is unique and at the same time fragile. It is the Church of God. Paul could envisage all the attempts that would be made to destroy this new entity called the Church of Jesus Christ. So he emphasized the preciousness of this body of Christ by stating that God bought the church with his own blood. The deity of Jesus Christ was implied in this verse. Paul interchanged the sacrificial work of Jesus Christ with God purchasing the Church.

Paul did not want these leaders to underestimate what was going to happen when he was gone. He indicated that savage wolves would come and they would attempt to destroy what God was doing. Things have not changed much since that time. We still have savage wolves with us who are attempting to destroy the work of Jesus Christ.

DECEMBER DAY 3

Even from your own number men will arise and distort the truth in order to draw away disciples after them. So be on your guard! Remember that for three years I never stopped warning each of you night and day with tears. Acts 20:30-31

The most difficult enemy to fight is the one within. Paul was aware of that and warned his audience about that. Paul indicated that people will arise from their midst with a particular agenda. These folks would seek to distort the truth. What does this mean? The truth of the gospel is that Jesus Christ is God's response to human sin among Jews and Gentiles. God's love for all humanity could not be compromised by favoritism.

That truth was meeting resistance from those who wished to exclude the Gentiles from the grace of God. These folks did not see themselves as having the same worship of God in Judaism. They were always suggesting a two-tier system with one group taking a lower position in the household of God. This was a situation that these Christians thought could appease those who were strongly opposed to bringing Gentiles into the faith.

Paul was vehemently opposed to any gospel that did not offer free grace to all people. So any compromise that might attract more votes was not what Paul wished to preach. Changing the gospel to draw disciples was a way of distorting the good news of Jesus Christ. So Paul warned the leaders he was addressing to be on their guard. He wanted them to pay attention to folks who will claim to be Christians and yet distort the gospel to draw more disciples.

Paul reminded his hearers of what happened in the three years that he spent in Ephesus preaching the gospel. He never stopped warning them of what was to happen after he had left them. He believed that the Christian life was a spiritual battle that had to be fought day and night with the power of the Holy Spirit.

Those who are looking for an easy road with no resistance are not ready to be called soldiers of Christ.

DECEMBER DAY 4

"Now I commit you to God and to the word of his grace, which can build you up and give you an inheritance among all those who are sanctified. I have not coveted anyone's silver or gold or clothing. Acts 20:32-33

Paul concluded his message by committing the leaders of the church to God. All of us need the assurance of God's protection. The one who fights for us does so not because we deserve it, but because of grace, and that is our hope.

The word of God's grace is what has sustained all the saints of old. The Word of God is there to build all those who submit themselves to it. The Word of God will either change us or we will stay away from it. Paul knew that the secret weapon of the Christian was the Word of God and all those who submit themselves to the Word are built up to become the mature people that God intended.

Paul wanted the leaders he was addressing to know that the power of the Word of God was something promised to all those who have been sanctified and gained an inheritance in the kingdom of God. This was not something reserved just for the Ephesians. It is the birthright of all the saints of God.

Paul moved on in his speech to a time of sober reflection. He said: "I have not coveted anyone's silver or gold or clothing". The statement seems out of place in the midst of all the spiritual considerations being discussed. But Paul wanted to make sure that he had set the record straight. He did not want anyone to accuse him of using the ministry for personal gain.

Transparency is important in the work of the Lord. Our witness depends on that.

December Day 5

You yourselves know that these hands of mine have supplied my own needs and the needs of my companions. In everything I did, I showed you that by this kind of hard work we must help the weak, remembering the words the Lord Jesus himself said: 'It is more blessed to give than to receive.' Acts 20:34-35

Paul had indicated to the audience that he had not coveted any material goods of theirs. He lived among them for three years without being a burden to anyone. How could that happen considering the large group that traveled along with Paul? He explained that his hands had supplied for the needs of his companions and himself. This was a known fact to his audience and they could not dispute it.

Paul was a tentmaker by trade and everywhere he went he applied his skill that was in demand. He had to make only a few tents to provide for his needs and those of his companions. Paul did not just work to meet his living expenses; he used that to teach the Christians a lesson. "In everything I did, I showed you that by this kind of hard work we must help the weak". Paul wanted to be an example and a model of Christian behavior.

The weak among the community needed help and what was the best way to help them? Paul believed that all the believers including the leadership should be involved in providing for the needs of the weak. This can be done through hard work.

Paul quoted the words of the Lord Jesus to encourage his hearers. People should not always be at the receiving end of things. There should be a mutual giving and receiving, but it is more blessed to give than to receive. We have all been given a lot by our Lord and Savior and we have something to give to others. In the big scheme of things, we have more to give.

Let us give as unto the Lord knowing that we have received so much from God.

December Day 6

When he had said this, he knelt down with all of them and prayed. They all wept as they embraced him and kissed him. What grieved them most was his statement that they would never see his face again. Then they accompanied him to the ship. Acts 20:36-38

Paul was blunt about what was going to happen to him in Jerusalem and also about the issue of his ministry in Ephesus. He told them he had worked with his hands to supply for his needs and those of his companions. No one disputed his assertions about not taking advantage of the people to whom he ministered.

Then Paul knelt down and prayed with the leaders of the church at Ephesus. That must have been a wonderful sight watching Paul and the leaders kneeling and praying after the admonitions and reflection that had taken place. Prayer was important to Paul and to the Christian community. It was a time to commune with God and commit what was ahead to the care of the almighty God.

There comes a time that we have to trust God for the many things over which we have little or no control. In fact, we have to do the same when we think that we have control over what is happening around us. Prayer for the Christian is an affirmation that we fully rely on God in all matters. Paul set the example for the leaders who had gathered. He knelt down as a sign of submission and reverence to God.

Those gathered wept as they embraced Paul and kissed him. This showing of emotion and affection was not typical of encounters between Paul and his congregations. This was a unique situation because Paul had said that those who had gathered would not see his face again. They took to heart the words of Paul and believed it to be a true prophecy. It must have been a strange feeling that the person they were talking to was going to be imprisoned or even killed. No doubt that they wept with such emotion.

Christian love is genuine and is expressed in different ways including tears when people get separated from one another.

DECEMBER DAY 7

After we had torn ourselves away from them, we put out to sea and sailed straight to Cos. The next day we went to Rhodes and from there to Patara. We found a ship crossing over to Phoenicia, went on board and set sail. After sighting Cyprus and passing to the south of it, we sailed on to Syria. We landed at Tyre, where our ship was to unload its cargo. Finding the disciples there, we stayed with them seven days. Through the Spirit they urged Paul not to go on to Jerusalem. Acts 21:1-4

The emotional farewell had to come to an end. It was not easy for Paul and his companions to leave the brothers and sisters they had ministered to for so long. The departure was described as a tearing away from them. They finally got on their ship and set sail.

There is a tie that binds Christians when they realize the bond of fellowship that they share in the Lord Jesus Christ. Some have found this bond of Christian fellowship to be stronger than anything they have known. In such cases, people do share their blessings and their sorrows and they become a support for one another.

Luke describes in some detail the voyage towards Jerusalem. It seems that there was no direct route; they had to change ships on the way and sometimes spend days in a city before continuing the trip. The ship was to unload cargo at Tyre. This unloading of cargo was a labor-intensive exercise that could stretch to days if not weeks.

Paul and his companions located Christians in the city and stayed with them for seven days. That was an opportunity for ministry. It is important to search for and find the body of believers in every place the Lord leads us. That is essential for Christian growth. Christians who have cut themselves off from other disciples tend to grow cold and find themselves in situations they may not have bargained for.

The disciples in Tyre urged Paul not to continue his trip to Jerusalem. It seems Paul took their suggestion under advisement. God had spoken to Paul and he was ready to follow through with his mission. It is important to know what God is saying to you otherwise, you could be swayed by good suggestions.

DECEMBER DAY 8

But when our time was up, we left and continued on our way. All the disciples and their wives and children accompanied us out of the city, and there on the beach we knelt to pray. Acts 21:5

Paul and his companions were proactive in locating Christian disciples when they arrived at Tyre. The fellowship was good, except that they received a message through the Spirit that they should not continue on the trip to Jerusalem. This was not the first time that they heard such discouraging news about the trip to Jerusalem.

When the seven days of layover was up, the ship was ready to set sail. All the disciples and their wives and children accompanied Paul and his companions out of the city to the beach where the ship awaited. There on the beach, they all knelt and prayed. This was a special outdoor prayer meeting that must have fascinated onlookers. Can you imagine a crowd of about fifty people kneeling on the beach when the ship in the background is ready to depart?

The testimony to the locals on the beach who may have come to see people off or who were unloading items from the ship must have been singular. Similarly, other passengers on the ship were forced to observe this group of men, women, and children in a spirit of prayer kneeling in the sand. This was not a planned meeting to witness or set the group apart as Christians. Instead, it was a spontaneous attempt to share Christian fellowship at a special moment in the lives of all who had gathered.

This was one of those God moments that one never forgets. Just hearing the voice of Paul say: "Let us pray" and then as if by design, all fall to their knees. No one cared who was watching or not watching. All that mattered was that the place on the beach had turned to Holy Ground. Do you realize that you might be standing on Holy Ground this very moment? All that you need to do is to fall on your knees and say: "Abba father, I know you are here."

DECEMBER DAY 9

After saying good-bye to each other, we went aboard the ship, and they returned home. We continued our voyage from Tyre and landed at Ptolemais, where we greeted the brothers and stayed with them for a day. Leaving the next day, we reached Caesarea and stayed at the house of Philip the evangelist, one of the Seven. He had four unmarried daughters who prophesied. Acts 21:6-9

The farewell celebrations of the Christians in Tyre were dramatic and elaborate. Paul and his companions were able to tear themselves from the group by going aboard the ship after saying good-bye to the gathered group. It was only then that the disciples from Tyre returned home. The love and affection of these Christians were commendable to say the least.

The ship set sail from Tyre and landed at Ptolemais. A welcoming party had also been assembled in this town to greet the missionaries. It was, however, more than a greeting party that met Paul; they were ready to accommodate him and his group for a day. This must have been a great encouragement to Paul and his companions to know that in every town there were disciples who were ready to extend Christian hospitality to them.

Traveling evangelists very much depended on the generosity of their hosts as they moved around with their message. Paul received more from the Christians in these towns. It would be needless to say that in every place where the missionaries landed, they provided the much needed teaching and exhortation that these disciples longed for.

The ship set sail from Ptolemais after a day and arrived at Caesarea. The missionaries "stayed at the house of Philip the evangelist, one of the seven". Philip was one of the seven deacons who were appointed by the leaders of the church in Jerusalem to serve the needs of the poor and the widows. He was a man full of the Holy Spirit. He had been used by the Spirit to minister to the Ethiopian Eunuch. One is not surprised that Paul and his companions stayed in the home of the prominent evangelist in the area.

We are also told that Philip had daughters who prophesied. Philip's home was a special place where the presence of the Lord was felt most of the time.

Be blessed as you sense the presence of the Lord in your home.

DECEMBER DAY 10

After we had been there a number of days, a prophet named Agabus came down from Judea. Coming over to us, he took Paul's belt, tied his own hands and feet with it and said, "The Holy Spirit says, 'In this way the Jews of Jerusalem will bind the owner of this belt and will hand him over to the Gentiles.' Acts 21:10-11

Paul and his companions stayed in the home of Philip at Caesarea. After some days, a prophet named Agabus came to Caesarea to visit. There were many in the early church who did exercise the gift of prophecy. We already encountered the daughters of Philip. They would often give prophetic utterances in the gatherings of the Christian community. Prophecy was understood as foretelling or forth telling the message of God. People expected these words of prophecy in church services.

Sometimes those with the gift of prophecy dramatized their message. This was not something new. The prophets of old were known to act out their messages in dramatic fashions. Prophets like Jeremiah and Ezekiel were known to bring the word of the Lord in this manner.

Prophet Agabus brought his word to the gathering by taking Paul's belt and using it to tie his own hands and feet. Then he said this was going to happen to the owner of this belt. He prophesied that Paul would be arrested and tied by the Jews in Jerusalem who would then hand him over to the Gentiles.

By referring to the Gentiles, Agabus was talking about the ruling authorities. In other words, Paul would be handed over to the Roman rulers who would judge him. Agabus stayed out of recommendations about what Paul should or should not do. He just stated the facts as they were revealed to him.

When God speaks, there is the temptation to try and interpret or extrapolate the message instead of allowing the word of God to stand on its own. Agabus brought the message of God and allowed others to worry about the implication.

December Day 11

When we heard this, we and the people there pleaded with Paul not to go up to Jerusalem. Then Paul answered, "Why are you weeping and breaking my heart? I am ready not only to be bound, but also to die in Jerusalem for the name of the Lord Jesus." When he would not be dissuaded, we gave up and said, "The Lord's will be done." Acts 21:12-14

The Prophet brought his message. It was not what anyone wanted to hear. It spelt out arrest and difficulty for Paul in Jerusalem. The message of the Prophet was consistent with earlier prophecies regarding the trip to Jerusalem. Those who had gathered in the home of Philip weighed the message of the Prophet carefully, and they were convinced that it was from the Lord. So they did what anyone of us would do under such circumstances. They pleaded with Paul not to go up to Jerusalem.

Paul had come very close to Jerusalem and now he was being advised by those in his inner circle not to finish the last leg of the trip. Yes, there were ways around Paul taking the risk of going to Jerusalem personally. The other missionaries could have delivered the Gentile offering for the brethren in Jerusalem and Philip could have gone with them.

Paul's response to the weeping and pleading of his friends in Caesarea was insightful. "Why are you weeping and breaking my heart?" he asked. They were behaving as if Paul was already dead. They did this out of their love for him and the ministry that God was accomplishing through him. Humanly speaking, they would rather have Paul with them than risk his arrest. But Paul was looking at the whole scenario differently. He saw a mission for God that had to be accomplished, and he knew that he was called to a ministry that included suffering for the name of Jesus Christ.

He made the ultimate pronouncement that showed that he had considered all options in the matter, and had come to his conclusion based on what the Lord had called him to do. He said: "I am ready not only to be bound, but to die in Jerusalem for the name of the Lord Jesus."

That is the type of witness that silences all attacks of the enemy. In our moments of doubt and seeking self-preservation, a firm confidence in the Lord sets us free.

DECEMBER DAY 12

When he would not be dissuaded, we gave up and said, "The Lord's will be done." After this, we got ready and went up to Jerusalem. Some of the disciples from Caesarea accompanied us and brought us to the home of Mnason, where we were to stay. He was a man from Cyprus and one of the early disciples. Acts 21:14-16

Luke was a member of the team that was trying to dissuade Paul from going on to Jerusalem. That means that it was not only the disciples in Caesarea, but his traveling companions were also of the opinion that Paul should not continue the trip to Jerusalem. But they all came to one conclusion, and that was the fact that Paul was convinced of the Lord's will for him. He was determined to press forward with the mission no matter what the consequences. And so they gave up. Sometimes we all need to recognize when it is futile fighting against the leading of the Lord.

After all, the prophecy of Agabus stated what would happen to the person who owned the belt that Paul was wearing. The message was clear about what was to happen and it did not give any directions about averting what was in store for Paul. The question was whether the Christian community was going to accept the revealed will of God or were they going to try to fight it with their prayers, crying and human manipulation of events. Luke and his companions finally came to the conclusion that it was better to accept the will of the Lord.

So they prayed the prayer that they should have prayed all along, "The Lord's will be done". Jesus taught us that prayer in the Garden of Gethsemane. When he was presented the bitter cup of suffering, he prayed that, if possible, the cup be taken away, but if it be the Lord's will, then he was ready to accept it. In so doing, Jesus set for all of us an example when it comes to facing adversities that we do not welcome.

After that prayer, the whole group felt free to move forward to Jerusalem. They knew they had committed the situation to the care of the Lord and they were no longer trying to control what should or should not happen. Some of the Christians from Caesarea accompanied Paul and his group to Jerusalem. That was a wonderful showing of support and solidarity.

When we pray and leave things in the hands of the Lord, we should not look back. Rather, we should press on and trust in the leading of the Lord.

December Day 13

Some of the disciples from Caesarea accompanied us and brought us to the home of Mnason, where we were to stay. He was a man from Cyprus and one of the early disciples. When we arrived at Jerusalem, the brothers received us warmly. The next day Paul and the rest of us went to see James, and all the elders were present. Paul greeted them and reported in detail what God had done among the Gentiles through his ministry. Acts 21:16-19

One of the early Christian disciples called Mnason decided to host Paul and his party. He was originally from Cyprus. It seems that he had enough rooms in his home to accommodate a few people, and that was where Paul and his group were led to stay.

The Christian brothers in Jerusalem received Paul and his party warmly. The hospitality that had characterized Christianity was extended to these missionaries. The next day the whole group was taken to James. He was the leader of the apostles at this time and all who belonged to the Christian community recognized his leadership. All the elders were present at this meeting. This means that all the original disciples of Jesus Christ who were still alive were present to hear the message that Paul and his group were bringing from their travels.

Paul brought greetings from all the Gentile churches that he had visited and reported in detail what God had done among the Gentiles in his ministry. Paul was first to recognize that God did all the work and the miracles that had taken place. So there was no room for boasting or taking the credit for what had happened.

The humility that accompanied Paul's report stood out. He gave credit to God, but he also showed respect to the apostles who had gone ahead of him in this ministry. He was very much aware of the fact that God was using him to continue in a vineyard that other workers had worked before him.

We are all parts of a puzzle in the hands of God. The master craftsman can use us where and when God chooses.

DECEMBER DAY 14

When they heard this, they praised God. Then they said to Paul: "You see, brother, how many thousands of Jews have believed, and all of them are zealous for the law. They have been informed that you teach all the Jews who live among the Gentiles to turn away from Moses, telling them not to circumcise their children or live according to our customs. Acts 21:20-21

When the Christians in Jerusalem heard the report of Paul, they rejoiced and praised God. They heard that the good news was advancing among the Gentiles and God was baptizing he Gentile world with the Holy Spirit in the same manner that God had done in Jerusalem.

There is always a reason to praise God when we hear testimonies of the advancement of the good news. Those who understand that the gospel has a universal appeal rejoice when the message is broadcasted abroad.

The Christians in Jerusalem however had a concern that they wanted to share with Paul and his group. Their desire to encourage the spread of the gospel did not allow them to gloss over some realities they were observing. The fact was that thousands of Jews had converted to Christianity. Most of these Jewish believers were very proud of their Jewish heritage and customs. The Jewish Christians were receiving disturbing reports about the ministry of Paul among the Gentiles.

The reports reaching Jerusalem was that Paul was teaching Jewish Christians to turn away from Moses and not to circumcise their children. And so one can imagine the hatred that some people had for Paul. The elders in Jerusalem did not believe the reports and after hearing Paul speak of his ministry among the Gentiles the Christians in Jerusalem had more reasons to support Paul. But the question was how to deal with the false allegations.

That was the challenge that faced Paul and the leaders of the Church in Jerusalem. It happens that misinformation create problems for ministry. But our assurance is that no matter what happens, God is in control.

DECEMBER DAY 15

What shall we do? They will certainly hear that you have come; [23] so do what we tell you. There are four men with us who have made a vow. Take these men, join in their purification rites and pay their expenses, so that they can have their heads shaved. Then everybody will know there is no truth in these reports about you, but that you yourself are living in obedience to the law. Acts 21:22-24

The leaders of the early church found themselves in a dilemma. On one hand, they had received a personal account of the ministry of Paul among the Gentiles. The leaders were in agreement with everything that Paul had recounted and they had joined Paul in praising God for the spread of the gospel. On the other hand, the rumors and misinformation about the ministry of Paul among the Gentiles were running like wild fire all over Jerusalem. People were going to hear that Paul was in Jerusalem and that he might have brought some Gentiles with him.

This was a time for a quick and wise action to counteract the notion that Paul was not faithful to the Jewish traditions. Paul was advised to accompany four Jewish men who had made a vow. This particular vow required a rite of purification. Paul was encouraged to join in the purification rites of these for men and go as far as paying for their expenses so that they can have their heads shaved.

The purpose of this elaborate plan was to disprove the reports that Paul did not observe Jewish rites and customs. There is no doubt that this was a time of desperation. One would not have expected Paul to go along with this plan just to please those who were falsely accusing him. But Paul saw the wisdom in the plan put forward by the leaders of the church in Jerusalem and decided to go along.

We are not sure at this point that Paul made the right decision. But he had a lot of respect for the leaders of the Church in Jerusalem and he did not see anything wrong with the proposal. After all, Paul was a Jew who happened to have been called to minister to Gentiles.

One cannot be sure of the right decision all the time. Sometimes all we can do is to trust ourselves to the Lord and move forward.

DECEMBER DAY 16

As for the Gentile believers, we have written to them our decision that they should abstain from food sacrificed to idols, from blood, from the meat of strangled animals and from sexual immorality 2⁶ The next day Paul took the men and purified himself along with them. Then he went to the temple to give notice of the date when the days of purification would end and the offering would be made for each of them. Acts 21:25-26

Knowing what we know about Paul, the decision to join in a purification rite with four men would be considered prayerfully. Paul would have sought the direction of the Lord in this matter. There is nothing to suggest that he did not. Often when we are confronted with major decisions, we turn to prayer without even thinking about it. Prayer should become the habit of every Christian.

In verse twenty-six, the leaders in Jerusalem affirmed their decision that was taken some time back concerning how to minister to and welcome Gentiles into the fold. It is interesting to observe that the issues stressed were tailored to a Jewish audience. There was no need to even mention circumcision.

The next day Paul decided to take the four men and purified himself along with them. As indicated earlier, this step must have been surrounded with prayer. Paul agreed with the agenda laid out by the leaders of the Church in Jerusalem. Paul went into the Temple to serve notice that they had begun the purification rite and it would end in a week. At the end of the purification, Paul would pay for the offering for these four men.

Paul had taken the steps to demonstrate his devotion to God and to his Jewish heritage. But Paul had a commitment first to God who had called him to bring the good news to Gentiles. We should never forget what God has called us to do.

DECEMBER DAY 17

When the seven days were nearly over, some Jews from the province of Asia saw Paul at the temple. They stirred up the whole crowd and seized him, ^{28} shouting, "Men of Israel, help us! This is the man who teaches all men everywhere against our people and our law and this place. And besides, he has brought Greeks into the temple area and defiled this holy place." ^{29}(They had previously seen Trophimus the Ephesian in the city with Paul and assumed that Paul had brought him into the temple area.) Acts 21:27-29

Part of the purification rite was regular visits to the Temple. Paul had been doing just that with the four Jewish men that he had joined himself to in the purification rite. It happened that some Jews from the province of Asia saw Paul in the Temple. These folks knew Paul personally and could positively identify him. The Jews from Asia had previously seen Paul in town. They saw him in the company of a Gentile from Ephesus.

When The Jews from Asia saw Paul in the Temple, they assumed that the Gentile they had seen with Paul earlier in town was one of the four men who were in the Temple with Paul. Assumptions! Assumptions and assumptions are at the center of this misunderstanding. The Jews from Asia made a wrong association and believed it strongly to the point that they started inciting other people in the Temple area. They stirred up the whole crowd and seized Paul.

The words of the men from Asia indicate that they were convinced of their accusations. They said: "Men of Israel, help us! This is the man who teaches all men everywhere against our people and our law and this place. And besides, he has brought Greeks into the temple area and defiled this holy place." As indicated earlier, the problem was a baseless assumption. Unfortunately, when the crowd was stirred up, there was no turning back or trying to find out about the truth.

The accusation of defiling the Temple was a serious one for every Jew. To think that Paul will deliberately bring Gentiles into the Temple in Jerusalem was unimaginable. But that was the charge that was leveled against Paul and it seemed the crowd bought into it.

A lot of harm can be caused by assumptions that might be false. It pays to be patient in analyzing situations before jumping to conclusions.

DECEMBER DAY 18

The whole city was aroused, and the people came running from all directions. Seizing Paul, they dragged him from the temple, and immediately the gates were shut. [31] While they were trying to kill him, news reached the commander of the Roman troops that the whole city of Jerusalem was in an uproar. [32] He at once took some officers and soldiers and ran down to the crowd. When the rioters saw the commander and his soldiers, they stopped beating Paul. Acts 21:30-32

Bad news travels fast. It did not take long for the whole city to be aroused. The news was that Paul had brought Gentiles into the Temple. People could not believe that any Jew would want to do such a terrible thing. People ran into the Temple courts from all directions. The crowd seized Paul and quickly dragged him from the Temple.

Why did they drag him from the Temple? It was because they did not want to defile the Temple by shedding human blood in the walls of the Temple. Their intention was very clear. They wanted to kill Paul and so they took the necessary precaution. They shut the gates of the Temple to make sure that nothing went wrong there.

The angry crowd was trying to kill Paul. The whole city was also in uproar over the events in the Temple area. News reached the commander of the Roman troops that the whole of Jerusalem was in uproar. The commander had to act quickly and so he did with officers and soldiers being dispatched to the Temple area to stop the riots. When the rioters saw the Roman detachment arriving they stopped beating Paul. But things were far from being over.

The whole situation had arisen because Paul wanted to convince the Jews that he had not departed from the religious rites of the Jews. He wanted to the right sacrifice in the Temple. Unfortunately, some people thought Paul was deliberately out to defile the Temple. Thanks to the Roman commander who saved the situation. No, this was not a coincidence; it was God intervening to save Paul.

DECEMBER DAY 19

The commander came up and arrested him and ordered him to be bound with two chains. Then he asked who he was and what he had done. ³⁴ Some in the crowd shouted one thing and some another, and since the commander could not get at the truth because of the uproar, he ordered that Paul be taken into the barracks. ³⁵ When Paul reached the steps; the violence of the mob was so great he had to be carried by the soldiers. ³⁶ The crowd that followed kept shouting, "Away with him!" Acts 21:33-36

The commander of the Roman detachment came and arrested Paul because he realized that Paul was the lightning rod for the riot. He ordered that Paul should be bound with two chains just to make sure that he does not get away. Paul was treated at this point like a dangerous criminal.

The commander of the Roman army wanted to find out from the crowd who Paul was and what he had done. The commander was surprised that the crowd did not have a straightforward answer. People were shouting and it seemed they did not know what Paul had done wrong. Some were shouting one thing and others were shouting another. The Roman commander came to the conclusion that there was no way he was going to get at the truth this way. So he decided that the interrogation should be done at a different location. He wanted to know the source of the riots and what Paul had done to anger so many people. So he ordered that Paul should be taken into the barracks.

The violence of the mob was so great that Paul could not be led down the steps. The soldiers had to Physically carry Paul down the steps. The crowd did not let up. They followed Paul and they kept shouting "Away with him". They wanted to have Paul killed.

What had caused this great anger? Some have heard about Paul defiling the Temple and others called him a friend of the Gentiles. But Paul was not a criminal who should be bound with chains.

DECEMBER DAY 20

As the soldiers were about to take Paul into the barracks, he asked the commander, "May I say something to you?" "Do you speak Greek?" he replied. [38] Aren't you the Egyptian who started a revolt and led four thousand terrorists out into the desert some time ago?" Acts 21:37-38

The soldiers were ready to take Paul into the barracks. Paul decided to seize the moment and ask for an opportunity to address the crowd. Paul took a courteous approach that seemed to win favor with the commander. He decided to speak to the commander in the official language of the Empire. It was the language of the cultured. The commander was impressed to hear Paul speak the Greek language.

The commander was surprised to hear Paul speak the Greek language and questioned him openly on that "Do you speak Greek?" what a question? It says a lot about the impressions that the commander had about Paul. The misconception that the Roman commander had was revealed in his question to Paul. He had all along assumed that Paul was an Egyptian and a leader in terrorism.

Paul did not allow the impressions of others to bother him. He rather used all the wisdom that God had given him to seize the opportunity at the right moment. It is important that Christians do not allow others to define who they are. God would have us step forward and shine for Jesus Christ at every opportune moment that comes to us.

The mind of people can change when they see what the Lord has done through us.

DECEMBER DAY 21

Paul answered, "I am a Jew, from Tarsus in Cilicia, a citizen of no ordinary city. Please let me speak to the people." [40] Having received the commander's permission; Paul stood on the steps and motioned to the crowd. When they were all silent, he said to them in Aramaic: Acts 21:39-40

The Roman commander realized that he had misjudged Paul. He had labeled Paul as a terrorist who had led an insurrection. He ordered two chains to be put on Paul because he assumed that he was a dangerous person who needed to be treated harshly. Now, Paul had demonstrated that he was a learned person who could speak the Greek language fluently. So the Roman commander openly confessed what he had thought of Paul. He showed his surprise and ignorance of the situation on the ground.

The comment of the Roman commander revealed that he had no understanding of the riot that he had come to bring under control. He also showed that he did not learn anything from the crowd about the cause of the riot. Paul's accusers had not made their case to the commander why they wanted to kill him. Now it was the turn of Paul to respond to respond to the commander.

Paul answered by telling the commander that he was first and foremost a Jew. That must have surprised the Roman commander since most of the shouting was pointing to Paul as a foreigner who was trying to defile the Jewish Holy place. Then Paul added that he came from Tarsus of Cilicia, and he was a citizen of no ordinary city. Paul had a reason for adding that information. He did not say it yet but he wanted the commander to know that he could be a Roman citizen.

Paul was given the permission that he requested from the commander and that was to address the crowd. He motioned to the crowd for silence and positioned himself on the steps so that everyone could hear him. Then he began his address.

What a change in affairs in such a short time. The one who was being beaten by the crowd has now calmed the crowd down and he is ready to speak to them. Only God can bring about such a change in fortunes.

December Day 22

"Brothers and fathers, listen now to my defense." When they heard him speak to them in Aramaic, they became very quiet. Then Paul said: ³ "I am a Jew, born in Tarsus of Cilicia, but brought up in this city. Under Gamaliel I was thoroughly trained in the law of our fathers and was just as zealous for God as any of you are today. Acts 22:1-3

Paul was given "the green light" to address the crowd by the commander. Paul who had earlier spoken in Greek to the commander decided to address the crowd in Aramaic. He began by respectfully pleading with the crowd to hear his side of the story. Most of the people in the crowd have not heard him speak. They were going on hearsay and the little they could gather through the rumor mill. Now they have the opportunity to hear the defense of Paul and make up their own minds.

Paul called them "Brothers and fathers". That might suggest that all of the people in the crowd were men. One would not expect any woman to dare into the rowdy crowd. Paul wanted to identify with the audience in his opening remark. It seemed to work at least at the beginning. The crowd became quiet and attentive.

Paul decided to introduce himself to the crowd and to the Roman commander in his opening remarks. He highlighted his Jewish credentials and also the fact that although he was born in Tarsus, he grew up in Jerusalem. He also indicated that his education was under the well-known Pharisee Gamaliel. Invoking the name of his teacher and mentor was supposed to quench any news that was going around about his lack of knowledge concerning the customs and practices of the Jewish people.

Paul noted that his training made him zealous for God, just like any of the people in the crowd. Paul wanted them to know that he understood the expression of rage and anger that was displayed by the crowd. He even attributed it to their zeal for God.

There is a zeal for God that could be misguided and lead to destruction. A zeal for God like that. Paul could see himself in his listeners. It is important to make sure that we are on the same page with God otherwise we will find ourselves fighting against God.

DECEMBER DAY 23

I persecuted the followers of this Way to their death, arresting both men and women and throwing them into prison, "s also the high priest and all the Council can testify. I even obtained letters from them to their brothers in Damascus, and went there to bring these people as prisoners to Jerusalem to be punished. Acts 22: 4-5

Paul tried to explain to the crowd what he meant when he said he had also been zealous for God in time past. He mentioned how he had persecuted the followers of "this way to their death". In other words, Paul was saying to the crowd that he was worse that the people in the crowd when it came to carrying out his zeal for the law and the Jewish traditions.

Paul said that he arrested both men and women and put them in prison. No wonder that the name of Saul was feared among the Christians in the early church. Paul indicated that the truth in what he was saying could be checked out with the high priest and the Jewish Council. These people were alive and could testify to the veracity of the exploits of Saul of Tarsus.

Paul received introduction letters from the Jewish leaders in Jerusalem to the powers that be in Damascus to permit him to come to their town and arrest Christians. He had by now decided to expand the scope of his persecution to Jerusalem.

The picture that Paul painted of his early life was not pretty at all. But that was his testimony and part of his story. He was not proud of his past but he could not run away from the truth of his convictions. Paul's testimony included his persecution of Christians. So he was never surprised when people hated with a passion the message that he preached.

Our life stories define who we are today. For Christians the thing that makes that story unique is the intersection of our journeys with Jesus Christ at some point.

Dr. Seth Asare

DECEMBER DAY 24

"About noon as I came near Damascus, suddenly a bright light from heaven flashed around me. [7] fell to the ground and heard a voice say to me, 'Saul! Saul! Why do you persecute me?' [8] 'Who are you, Lord?' I asked. "'I am Jesus of Nazareth, whom you are persecuting,' he replied. [9]My companions saw the light, but they did not understand the voice of him who was speaking to me. Acts 22: 6-9

Paul recounted his testimony to the crowd with the hope that they would get a better understanding of who he was. He started by telling them how he lived out his life as a strict Pharisee who had a zeal for God. He explained how that zeal made him persecute Christians. He narrated what happened on one of those zealous missions to Damascus to arrest and imprison the Christians there.

On the road to Damascus on that faithful day something happened that changed the course of his life and his faith. He said it was about noon that he was blinded by a light from heaven on the road to Damascus. Paul fell to the ground and heard a voice ask: "Saul! Saul! Why do you persecute me? "Saul was curious and wanted to know who was speaking. It was then that he was told: "I am Jesus of Nazareth, whom you are persecuting."

According to Paul, the whole experience seemed to happen just for him. It was his first direct encounter with the person he was persecuting. He had never seen himself as one who was fighting against God. He considered the Christians to be a heretic fringe group who were a nuisance to the Jewish faith. Now, the experience on Damascus road clearly forced him to rethink his view of these Christians.

There are some experiences that we cannot run away from. One of those is a personal encounter with the Lord Jesus Christ. When it happens one does not need any argument to convince him or her about the relationship that has been established. Others may view things differently. But those who have experienced the grace of the Lord Jesus know the one in him they have believed.

Our experiences may be different from that of Saul on the Damascus road, but one thing is sure, we have been saved by grace.

DECEMBER DAY 25

What shall I do, Lord?' I asked. "'Get up,' the Lord said, 'and go into Damascus. There you will be told all that you have been assigned to do.' [11] *My companions led me by the hand into Damascus, because the brilliance of the light had blinded me. Acts 22: 10-11*

Paul continued to share his testimony with the crowd that had sought to kill him a few hours earlier. He had told them about the blinding light from heaven that had thrown him to the ground. He learned there and then that he had been persecuting Jesus all along. So he asked the most important question that anyone would ask. "What shall I do Lord?"

That question showed that Saul of Tarsus was ready to submit to the one that he had been persecuting. The question was the beginning of the turnaround for Saul. It was a point of surrender when he realized that there was no point fighting a battle that one could not win. All of us have to know when to yield to God. We are sometimes knocked to the ground by circumstances beyond our control and we have to learn to ask the question "what shall I do Lord?"

God did answer Saul when he asked for direction. That is very reassuring for all of us. We know that when we sincerely seek the guidance of the Lord, we will get an answer. Saul was told to get up. He could not do anything just lying on the floor. He had to get up and go to Damascus and he would get further instructions on what to do. I cannot tell what went through the mind of Saul when he was told that he had to go to Damascus. He had to proceed to the very place where he was going to arrest Christians. Who were going to host Saul in Damascus? Could it be that one of the people he intended to arrest would be his host? It seemed that God had a sense of humor.

It was then that Saul realized that he could not see anything. The light on the road had blinded him and he was at the mercy of his companions. Saul decided to obey the instructions given to him by God. That was a wise decision.

On this Christmas day, let us remember missionaries who are under severe pressure as they share their faith. Have a Christ filled Christmas?

Dr. Seth Asare

DECEMBER DAY 26

"A man named Ananias came to see me. He was a devout observer of the law and highly respected by all the Jews living there. ¹³ He stood beside me and said, 'Brother Saul, receive your sight!' And at that very moment I was able to see him. Acts 22:12-13

Paul was now at the mercy of God and the Christians in Damascus. His name was Saul of Tarsus at that time. He continued his narration of events before the crowd. He told the audience that he was blinded on the Damascus road. Saul was told to go the city and wait for more instructions. The voice that had been communicating with Saul at this point identified himself as "the Jesus who you are persecuting".

It must have been frightening for Saul at this point. He was blind and being led by the hand into Damascus. Saul was taught a lesson in trusting God. That was all that he could do at this point apart from deciding to go home a blind man. Saul decided to listen to the directions of God, so he decided to go and wait in Damascus for whatever God had for him. My prayer is that we will be patient enough to wait for God under all circumstances.

God sent Ananias to do God's work. It is interesting how God would use one of the candidates who Saul might have arrested in Damascus to bring wholeness to Saul. Yes, Ananias might have had a few questions for God. But Saul did not know anything about that. Saul did not know Ananias, but the latter had heard a lot about Saul of Tarsus. It is not an exaggeration to say that all the Christians in Damascus lived in fear of Saul and his hatred for the Christians.

Ananias went to Saul and did exactly what God commanded him to do. He took a step of faith and said "Brother Saul, receive your sight!" At that moment Saul received his sight. Saul must have been surprised by the power of the spoken word from this respected Christian in Damascus.

There comes a time when we have to tell our story in sharing the gospel. You have a story to tell and I have one too. Let us be ready to do just that.

DECEMBER DAY 27

"Then he said: 'The God of our fathers has chosen you to know his will and to see the Righteous One and to hear words from his mouth. Acts 22:14

Saul was a recipient of a miracle of God. Ananias came and spoke the word of power and healing for the eyes of Saul to be opened. Immediately, there was an answer and Saul could see again.

Paul was narrating these events to his audience and they were listening patiently to get the gist of what the man was driving at. Then Saul reported what Ananias said after the healing. It was a message that transformed his ministry and set him on the course that he presently finds himself.

Ananias emphasized that Saul had been chosen for a particular purpose. Saul was chosen to know the will of God for all ages. He did not at this point elaborate on this will of God. Secondly Saul was chosen to see the Righteous One and to hear words from his mouth. In other words, the Damascus Road experience was a significant encounter where Paul Saw the Lord and heard words from the mouth of the Lord.

Later on, in his testimony and writings, Paul would return to this Damascus Road experience as the pivotal point in his conversion as he was doing in his message to the Jews who wanted to kill him in Jerusalem. Paul did personalize this encounter to mean that he received a direct calling like all the apostles. So Paul claimed his apostleship based on what happened and the message he received from the mouth of the Righteous One.

Ananias spoke about "knowing the will of God". This became a theme in the writings of Paul. The mystery to be revealed was that "In Christ" both Jews and Gentiles could be brought under one umbrella. There is no longer Jew or Gentile. God intends to bring all things under Christ.

December Day 28

"Then he said: 'The God of our fathers has chosen you to know his will and to see the Righteous One and to hear words from his mouth. ¹⁵ You will be his witness to all men of what you have seen and heard. ¹⁶ And now what are you waiting for? Get up, be baptized and wash your sins away, calling on his name.' Acts 22:14-16

Paul continued his defense before his attackers by announcing the message that he received from God through Ananias of Damascus. The man of God had impressed on Paul that he was chosen to know the will of God. In other words, the plan of God had been revealed to Paul. That plan was spelled out in these words: "You will be his witness to all men of what you have seen and heard"

What did it mean for Paul to be a witness to all men? The message of the gospel was now to be taken to all people meaning both Jews and Gentiles. Saul of Tarsus had an encounter with the person he was persecuting. He had also seen the power of forgiveness and love. Ananias had even called him "brother Saul". Why did the Christians in Damascus not take advantage of the blindness of the man who had sworn to arrest them?

Saul had indeed seen and heard a lot on the Damascus road and he was ordered to accept the offer of salvation. Saul had to respond by calling on the name of the Lord.

These words presented by Paul in his own defense give us a clue into what was expected of those who wanted to become members of the Christian community in the early church. There is the calling on the name of the Lord as it is written: "Everyone who calls on the name of the Lord will be saved". Then there is baptism for the washing away of sins. In all these, the individuals had to accept for themselves God's offer.

DECEMBER DAY 29

"When I returned to Jerusalem and was praying at the temple, I fell into a trance [18] and saw the Lord speaking. 'Quick!' he said to me. 'Leave Jerusalem immediately, because they will not accept your testimony about me.' Acts 22:17-18

Paul was telling his story to a crowd that did not understand him. They believed strongly that he did not observe Jewish customs and traditions. Some people had seen Paul walking with some Gentiles and when they saw Paul in the Temple area they had presumed that he had deliberately brought Gentiles into the Temple to defile it. This was what angered the crowd to the point that they tried to kill Paul. The intervention of the Roman commander was timely in preventing any bloodshed.

Paul was given permission to address the crowd. He did that by telling his story. The story was essentially his testimony of how he became a Christian and received a mission to the Gentiles from the same lord that he was persecuting. He now tells how he returned to Jerusalem after the Damascus Road experience. He went to the Temple to pray and fell into a trance. He heard and saw the Lord speaking to him clearly.

The message he heard was simple and straightforward: "Leave Jerusalem immediately." Paul was given a reason why he should depart from Jerusalem after his conversion. It was because the people there would not accept his testimony about the Lord Jesus Christ. The Lord who knows tomorrow from today gave Paul this urgent warning. We will never understand the way God works and for that reason the warnings of the Lord have to be taken seriously.

Paul learned that this was not the time to ask questions. When God speaks, all that we have to do is to follow. Most of the time the directives of the Lord may seem hurried or they may not make sense in our particular circumstance. But all disciples of the Lord Jesus must remember to first discern the voice of the Lord and then to follow wherever He leads us.

DECEMBER DAY 30

"'Lord,' I replied, 'these men know that I went from one synagogue to another to imprison and beat those who believe in you. [20] And when the blood of your martyr Stephen was shed, I stood there giving my approval and guarding the clothes of those who were killing him.' [21] Then the Lord said to me, 'Go; I will send you far away to the Gentiles.'" Acts 22:19-21

We continue the defense of Paul before a partisan crowd that had attempted to kill him earlier. He is telling them of the experiences that had led him to be a Christian. In the story, he had returned to Jerusalem after his experience on the Damascus road.

Paul was told by God in a vision to leave Jerusalem immediately. But Paul believed that there could be a scenario in which the Jews in Jerusalem would accept him. So he started giving reasons to God why he believed that way. He explained to God how the Jews in Jerusalem knew him as a zealot. He tried to lay out his past record as a persecutor of Christians.

Paul was doing what most of us do when God gives us instructions that we do not like. We try to convince God with our limited knowledge of the future. Just imagine Paul trying to inform the Lord about his exploits. He speaks about the death of Stephen as if God was not aware of all that. He claimed to be the master of ceremonies for the execution of Stephen.

Nothing happens to us that is outside the knowledge of God. After all, it was Jesus who confronted Paul about his persecution. All that Paul had to do was to agree to pack up and leave Jerusalem. According to Paul, the word finally came forcefully from God. "Go, I will send you far away to the Gentiles." Paul wanted his audience to know that the decision to move and work among the Gentiles was not something that he did without thinking through it.

Paul was given instructions to go and minister to the Gentiles and draw them into the family God. He was saying things that no Jew wanted to hear. He was saying that God had included Gentiles in the covenant.

God has a mission for each one of us. It will go well with us if we got on with the business of God.

DECEMBER DAY 31

The crowd listened to Paul until he said this. Then they raised their voices and shouted, "Rid the earth of him! He's not fit to live!" Acts 22:22

The crowd followed the narration of the testimony of Paul with much interest. They listened attentively as he talked about his zeal for God and how that caused him to persecute Christians. It was all right for the audience to hear Paul talk about his encounter with God and the people in Damascus. But then the testimony moved to Jerusalem where Paul saw and heard in a trance some directives from God

Paul was told by God in a vision to leave Jerusalem immediately. This instruction did not come across very well for the crowd. These people were Jews in Jerusalem who believed Jerusalem to be the Holy City of God. After all it was the place where the Temple was located. It was the most holy site for the Jewish People. Above all, Paul had been arrested in the Temple at Jerusalem because the men who were with him were falsely thought to be Gentiles.

How could Paul say to this Jerusalem crowd that God told him in a vision to "to arise and leave Jerusalem immediately?" Paul was just reporting what happened to his audience. But they read into those statement things that Paul had not intended. Paul did not mean to downplay the importance of Jerusalem to the Jewish people. Neither did he intend to suggest that there were better places to do ministry besides Jerusalem. He only wanted to report the series of events that took his ministry to the Gentiles.

We are often misquoted and misunderstood, and sometimes we can do very little about what people think and the conclusions they come to. All we can do is to pray that God protects us and keeps us safe. The crowd reacted violently on hearing Paul talk about leaving Jerusalem and taking the gospel to the Gentiles. They said "Rid the earth of this man, he is not fit to live"

That must have been a sober experience for Paul. When your audience brings such a verdict after sharing your testimony. That must be disappointing to say the least. People may not understand or appreciate our story. But we know that Jesus understands everything that has happened to us.

The only one who understands fully where we are coming from is our Lord and savior.